Mother of the Gods

Mother of the Gods

From Cybele to the Virgin Mary

Philippe Borgeaud
Translated by Lysa Hochroth

The Johns Hopkins University Press
Baltimore and London

Originally published as *La Mère des dieux: De Cybele à la Vierge Marie*
© 1996 Éditions du Seuil, Collection "La Librairie du XXᵉ siècle,"
directed by Maurice Olender
© 2004 The Johns Hopkins University Press

The Johns Hopkins University Press
2715 North Charles Street
Baltimore, Maryland 21218-4363
www.press.jhu.edu

Library of Congress Cataloging-in-Publication Data
Borgeaud, Philippe.
[Mère des dieux. English]
Mother of the gods : from Cybele to the Virgin Mary /
Philippe Borgeaud ; translated by Lysa Hochroth.
    p.   cm.
Includes bibliographical references and indexes.
ISBN 0-8018-7985-X (hardcover : alk. paper)
1. Cybele (Goddess) 2. Mary, Blessed Virgin, Saint — Devotion to.
3. Christianity and other religions — Roman. 4. Mother goddesses —
Rome. I. Title.
BL820.C8B6713 2004
202'.114 — dc22
2004004563

A catalog record for this book is available from the British Library.

For Isabelle

Contents

Translator's Preface

Translating Philippe Borgeaud's *Mother of the Gods* from French into English opens up a new chapter in the historical reappearances of this female divinity. From Cybele to the Virgin Mary, all of the intermediary metamorphoses of this figure, her many names, are introduced into a referenced repertory soon to reenter today's English-speaking world. In this context, belief and ritual dedicated to the Mother are strong marginal cults, faiths, and, indeed, religions that butt up against and sometimes intermingle with what is referred to as "serious academic scholarship." Not only traditional disciplines (history of religion, anthropology, archaeology, and classics) but also newly established interdisciplinary fields (such as women's studies, gender studies, ethnic studies, comparative literature) will provide a new forum in which to reexamine the Mother of the gods, especially in light of Borgeaud's comparative analysis of "interferences."

To act as a translator means that one plays a part in creating "interferences," assuming the technical role in diffusing ideas into new contexts and therefore in enabling different civilizations to adapt to, borrow from, and modify each other in the process. This assumes contact and communication between cultures and a certain delay between the original and its translation during which other contacts occur. Although this translation is a faithful rendering of the original, the very fact of having been interpreted into this language and published in this place at this time has changed it. The work exported is not necessarily the work imported. The reception of *Mother of the Gods* is likely to be exponentially multiplied like the Mother's many names: *Mētēr tōn theōn, Mētēr oreia, Agdistis, Inanna-Ishtar, Rhea, Deo-meter/Demeter, kubileia Matar, Cybébé, Kubéle, Cybele, Berecynthia, Tyché-Fortuna, Atargatis, Theotokos/Mētēr Theou. . . .*

Borgeaud's method is mirrored in his original style, which challenges the conscientious translator. His syntax and morphology are both perfectly French and yet impregnated with otherness: Hellenisms, Latinisms, a Swiss scholar's rhythms, and peripatetic phrasing such that the argumentation cannot be fragmented into parts, which, if broken up, do not equal the whole thought. Likewise, it is not as easy as it might be to link separate phrases to make a single sentence. Thus, we see the relevance of not interrupting the sinuous connections or attaching the broken lines of the Mother's "observable realities." We also see Borgeaud's strategy of not amalgamating singularities by specifically treating each of the divinity's appearances in terms of how they affect each other in a contentious context. In order to do so, Borgeaud slices a middle cut into the history of the Great Mother by selecting a segment of time, approximately 700 B.C.E.–600 C.E., when Greece, Gaul, and Rome came to dominate Asia Minor. He follows an itinerary from the anonymity of her image to various namings that constitute appearances, pinpointing specific relays in her multi-directional acculturation. If the author uses or attenuates etymologies to establish important connections (*Kuvav'* — *Kubeleia* — *Cybele*, *Gallu* — *galloi* — *galli*), he acts like a translator between two languages with the same alphabet and common roots, selecting the closest word(s) in light of the context but eliminating the less relevant connotations.

The believer, the historian, and the translator all actualize material from the past and in bringing it into the present move the virtual into the real. However, each retrieves and reiterates the Mother's names for different reasons. The believer ritualizes them to realize a faith, the historian excavates them to situate events, and the translator projects these names into a different future. In this case, Borgeaud reads the Mother's history in terms of how she is presented, made actual, differentiated, and therefore displaced from her past. The translator then re-presents this history, the work, sentence by sentence, rendering its stylized content into other words chosen from a different language. In this kind of repetition, the difference that emerges is a reorientation. By escorting the work, corroborating evidence through the plethora of proper names, the translator redirects its effects to a new potential public.

Although the reader, editor, critic, or scholar can take part in this redirection, their involvement with the work is selective. Only the faithful translator, like any mother, has the total responsibility for grappling with all the issues large and small. The translator's scope is none other than that of the work at hand.

I dedicate this translation of *Mother of the Gods* to the author of the work, Philippe Borgeaud, and to my children, Margot and Max, whose new lives have brightened the interval between its commencement and its completion.

Preface to the English-Language Edition

What is the provenance of this tenaciously stubborn idea seemingly resistant to all criticism: where does the modern myth of the Great Goddess come from? To attempt to answer this question, let us recall again that strange character from the Protestant city of nineteenth-century Basel, Johann Jacob Bachofen, author of *Mother Right (Mutterrecht)*, a bible of the matriarchate that appeared in 1861.[1] Bachofen believed that the different female figures in the Greek pantheon could ultimately be traced back to a single primordial goddess, the "Great Goddess." We note that this idea came to the mind of the Swiss scholar, my distant compatriot, after reading an article written by an archeologist friend specifically focusing on the goddess called "Mother of the gods" in the Athenian Agora. This goddess is indeed the subject of my own investigations in this book, which I am now pleased to present to anglophone readers thanks to Lysa Hochroth's translation.

In 1853, eight years before the publication of *Mother Right*, Bachofen had carefully read Eduard Gerhard's text on the *mētrōon*, the Athenian sanctuary of the Mother of the gods.[2] Gerhard interpreted the Mother of the gods of the Agora as a deity coming from elsewhere, a foreigner from Anatolia whose establishment during the age of Pericles had been made possible through a double amalgam. On one hand, this foreigner was to have been likened to the ancient goddess Gaïa (the Earth, model for a whole group of Greek female divinities linked to power and generation). On the other, since her cult was located in the *bouleuterion*, the Council room on the Agora, she was also assimilated to Athena, ancestor and protector of the city. Freely extrapolating Gerhard, Bachofen developed an entirely different idea in his notes, which are archived in the library of Basel. His idea was that the various multiple goddesses — and gods! — came from a single ancestor, a primordial female divinity. Gerhard considered that the Earth, this "Great Mother," was the supreme and even sole goddess of the most ancient inhabitants of Greece. Her cult would have preceded that of Demeter and those of the other deities. Whereas Gerhard reasoned in terms of diffusion, considering contacts and influences, and postulating an encounter followed by a synthesis between two religions that were foreign to each other, Bachofen situ-ated the evolution of the divine representations within the same single religion. He hypothesized an internal evolution in which a female-dominated ancient monotheism gave way to polytheism and the muliplication of the gods, both feminine and masculine, the male proceeding from the female. Here is an extract of the 1853 text where he first expressed the way in which he conceived of the origin of religion. According to Bachofen, the world of the gods developed and diversified from a very ancient and general unitary conception of the earth:

> It is she (the earth) that man scrutinizes, and not the Sky (masculine Ouranos). In a natural way, whilst man is still united to nature, he only perceives the closest princi-ple, that is, the earth, and not the most distant. People began to honor the earth, without attributing it a gender. . . . The distinction between the sexes only came later. Thus, this is how the masculine came from the feminine. First came the phallus and then its transformation into a person. This is how Zeus ended up becoming the principal entity. . . . *The gods are themselves engendered*, produced by the Earth, as are humans, and therefore are not primordial beings. Hence, God did not create the world, but the world (*die Welt*, a feminine word in German) created God. . . . The Olympians come from Gaia (the Earth).[3]

This idea of a great primordial goddess in Bachofen's (very patriarchal) philos-ophy is inseparable from that of "mother right," itself a derivative of the Greek concept of gynecocracy, or female rule. In *Mother Right*, the founding book on the matriarchal idea, the point of departure for Bachofen's reflection is this (an-cient) notion of gynecocracy, which is understood as a menace to civilization, capable of taking it back to a barbarian state.

The cult of the great goddess in today's world appears as a theme character-ized by a very widely shared system of representations evidenced in our book-stores by numerous vulgarizations of the subject of the Goddess (with a capital *G*). As in Bachofen, the setting is primeval. And the script tells a tale of treason or neglect. In the beginning (as in "once upon a time"), everywhere, the first reli-gion would have been that of the Great Mother, known through innumerable avatars passed down to us. Close to a philosophy of nature, the first universal belief was supposedly devoted to a female monotheistic figure, conceived of as unifying what ulterior polytheisms later distinguished as feminine and masculine principles, thus inventing the well-known pantheons that later became male-dominated in India, Greece, and elsewhere.

In the works of some feminist thinkers as well, this scenario increasingly appears as a bit of savant mythology, dependent on a mythical narrative.[4] What is fascinating is to observe how this mythology of the matriarchate (correlative of the modern Goddess cult) has reconstituted itself before our eyes. Indeed, this mythology (and perhaps even religion) has been emerging in our culture since the nineteenth century.

Given this type of phenomenon producing general universal theories on the evolution of religion, it is useful to return to the field to observe at close range the more ancient manifestations and metamorphoses of the divinity called "Mother of the gods." Here we seek to analyze this deity using her historical underpinnings as resources in the various contexts: Anatolian, Greek, and also Roman. This plunge into the diversity of lived experience in the field and in history aims at avoiding the monotonous repetitions of a prefabricated credo addressed to a synthetic image.

Since the publication of the French edition of this book, many important studies have enriched classical scholarship on the Mother of the gods without calling into question the construction of my own investigation. Among these, we should note Lynn E. Roller's *In Search of God the Mother*, which was written independently from my book. This is an excellent work that takes into account the historical and archeological evidence and follows an itinerary that I would consider complementary to my own.[5] More recently, Maria Grazia Lancellotti has published what now constitutes the reference work on the Goddess's mortal companion, the unfortunate Attis.[6] Her initial hypothesis is that a deep and archaic "nexus" indicates the royal and funerary aspect of this ancient Anatolian figure. Refuting the idea that Attis's divine nature would be for the most part an invention, or at least a re-working from the classical era, an idea that I continue to uphold even today, Maria Grazia Lancellotti bases her study on Phrygian culture. While I do recognize the interest in taking this approach, I personally opted to analyze not Phrygian culture (to which I feel I do not have direct access) but rather the image that the Greeks decided to construct of this Phrygia. This they did through their own conceptions aided by memorial elements drawn from their contacts with Lydia (and with Sardis in particular). Between the Greek imaginary world and Phrygian realities, I believe in the importance of the Lydian filter. In short, I am less a pre-historian than a historian of the imaginary, and I affirm the necessity and priority of accounting for accessible, observable realities.

The political role of the Mother of the gods in the Agora in Athens is one of these observable realities, as is her introduction into Rome's ancestral space in a highly ideological context.

At the end of this itinerary, the Mother of the gods comes upon Christianity in the Roman Empire. This experience is sometimes fraught with fantasies. Thus, the Christian poet Prudentius depicted the ritual of the taurobolia, a sacrifice to the goddess for the well-being of the Emperor, as a blood baptism and diabolical imitation of the Christian baptism in holy water. This description has generally been taken for granted by modern historians and my analysis, I have to say, encountered some resistance even if in fact no argument has seriously challenged it.[7] The interpretation of a fantasy is in itself an impassioned undertaking, and I for one will be satisfied if I have been able to shake up some of the evidence.

NOTES

1. See p. 133 n. 1 below.
2. Friedrich William Eduard Gerhard (1795–1867), "Metroon und Göttermutter," *Abhandlungen der Königlichen Akademie der Wissenschaften zu Berlin* (1849), 459–90.
3. The genesis of Bachofen's theory is detailed in Philippe Borgeaud, *La mythologie du matriarcat: l'atelier de Johann Jacob Bachofen* (Geneva, 1999). See also Borgeaud, "La mère des dieux et Bachofen en Grèce ancienne," *Metis* 9–10 (1994–95): 293–97.
4. Esp. Cynthia Eller, *The Myth of Matriarchal Prehistory: Why an Invented Past Won't Give Women a Future* (Boston, 2000).
5. *In Search of God the Mother: The Cult of Anatolian* (Berkeley: University of California Press, 1999). See also Eugene N. Lane, ed., *Cybele, Attis, and Related Cults: Essays in Memory of M. J. Vermaseren* (Leiden, 1996).
6. Maria Grazia Lancellotti, *Attis between Myth and History: King, Priest and God* (Leiden, 2002).
7. Two eminent specialists, Robert Schilling and Robert Turcan, were both a bit surprised by my approach. Compare, respectively, *Rivista di Filologia e di Istruzione Classica* 125 (1997): 319–23; *L'Antiquité classique* 67 (1998): 402–3.

Preface

The fate of the Mother, a captive of two scholarly myths that are as tenacious as they are ill-founded, is a surprising one. The first myth is that of the matriarchal stage and of its corollary, the cult of the Great Goddess. Designated as the Mother of the gods, Cybele becomes the exotic survivor in the classical pantheon of this ancestral, prehistoric, and universal figure, who ultimately metamorphoses into the multiple goddesses of polytheism. This myth originated in the nineteenth century and, in particular, from the evolutionary speculations of Johann Jakob Bachofen, a Swiss jurist and Hellenist. Bachofen's book *Das Mutterrecht* (*Maternal Right*), often cited, but rarely read, by Marxists, psychoanalysts, and feminists, appeared in 1861.[1] Given that Cybele owes her name and appearance to a Phrygian divinity from the high Anatolian plateaus, she was later hastily made out to be the immediate descendant of the goddess of the Neolithic site of Çatalhöyük. The effigy of this Neolithic goddess in the Museum of Anatolian Civilizations in Ankara shows her seated on a throne flanked by two leopards.[2] What was forgotten when this connection was made was that the two figures are separated by more than five millennia and several great civilizations. Nothing, aside from a few scholars' pipe dreams, leads us to recognize the divine sovereign of a matriarchal world in the Çatalhöyük goddess or her neighbors from Hacilar.

The second modern myth haunting the interpretations of Cybele portrays the Virgin Mary as the heiress of the ancient great goddesses. The suggestion is that there is a continuity, defined by the pure and simple transfer of symbols and functions, from paganism to Christianity, from the Mother of the gods to the Mother of God. Mary fills an empty space, so to speak, left vacant by the defeat and exile of the demonized divinities, especially the female divinities — Isis and Cybele, in particular. Michael P. Carroll advanced one of the most audacious versions of this scholarly fantasy in 1986. Observing that the goddess Cybele is surrounded by priests who have castrated themselves, the *galli*, this author constructed a veritable novel. The minor role of the paternal figure in working-class Roman family life, and particularly the father's lack of interest in his children's education, was supposed to have created a powerful, but severely repressed, desire in the son for his mother. This desire was then expressed in the cult of Cybele, characterized by acts of masochism on the part of its male constituents. When males from the Roman proletariat began to join the Christian Church during the fourth and fifth centuries, they ostensibly felt the need for a goddess like Cybele. This goddess was Mary, whose cult, under the control of a hierarchy dominated by the middle class, had lost the masochistic character that had led men of the old proletariat to value rites of bloody self-mutilation.[3] Although the premise of this reconstruction — that Cybele was a goddess of the people — is entirely erroneous, and ancient society and education are represented here in an entirely imaginary manner, this psychoanalytic-Marxist scenario nonetheless has the merit of inviting us to reconsider — on a new basis, and with due attention to the sources — the relationship of the Mother to her priests. Indeed, it is in terms of this relationship, but in its historical perspective, taking account of the real context pitting Christian apologists against the last worshipers of Cybele, that the documentation on the "interferences"* between the pagan goddess and the very human Virgin Mary should be evaluated. What results from this inquiry is not the idea of a direct inheritance but, on the contrary, that of a meeting, a debate, between two completely distinct figures. On one hand, as of the second century, the rites and myths of Cybele were transforming in terms of Christianity; on the other, Christian discourse on chastity was being determined using the *galli*'s practice as its yardstick.

These two modern myths obstructing the pathways to Cybele end up bearing the same message. Whether one returns to the most ancient past or interprets her in terms of her Christian future, the Mother of the gods serves as an argument for the fantasy of a feminine monotheism. From the Çatalhöyük goddess to the Virgin Mary, whether one escapes into origins or into the future, there is the same desire to economize on the diversity of cultural contexts and a careful historical course in space and time. Abundant, coherent documentation requires, however, that we be historically responsible. But who, then, in history, is the Mother of the gods? When and where do we encounter her?

Let us begin with a detour.

---

*The term *interférences*, translated here as "interferences," denotes a kind of multidirectional influence responsible for the appearance of certain cultural phenomena. Borgeaud points out the importance of cultural cross-pollination, or mutual influence, as opposed to one culture "inheriting" something from another, or unidirectional "influence." — Trans.

A magnificent silver disk with gold-leaf reliefs discovered during a 1969 archeological dig in Afghanistan depicts a goddess traveling in a chariot pulled by two lions. The summit of the mountain is designated as such by rocks covered with little engraved flowers in the foreground at the bottom. Between heaven and earth, near the sun, whose youthful, shining bust is accompanied by the crescent moon and a sixteen-pointed star, the goddess appears facing us, unlike the other characters, aside from the sun. Wearing a monumental headdress, called a *polos* in Greek, she is enveloped in a long robe, covered with a shawl. She sits upright, like an idol, in the carriage, driven by a winged Victory holding the reins and a long goad. On foot, behind the chariot, a priest wearing a conical hat holds the handle of an enormous parasol with both hands. A second priest, similar to the first, proceeds to fumigate the top of a stepped altar, toward which the procession is directed. The goddess's headdress, the chariot pulled by lions, and the mountainous scene give this goddess of the Hellenistic kingdoms of the East the familiar look of a Cybele, Mother of the gods, only one normal attribute of whom is missing — her big drum, the *tympanon*.[4] The name "Cybele" is, however, no more than a convention, encouraged by Greek iconography, for referring to well-known images. We do not know the precise name of the divinity presented here. Some of the features of this image from central Asia are undoubtedly borrowed from the Greek world: the goddess's headdress, the carriage pulled by lions, the golden winged Victory, the clothing of the female characters, the posture of the lions, and the shining bust of Helios. If one ignores the disheveled look of the cortège of the Phrygian goddess's eunuchs, who here seem to be engaged in a much more hieratic ceremony, this ritual is completely comparable to the Greek and Roman processions honoring the Mother of the gods. However, as archaeologists have discovered, "underneath the appearance of Hellenized art, there flows . . . profoundly and powerfully, a current of eastern inspiration." The structure of the chariot, the mountain, and the stepped altar have their most obvious parallels in Mesopotamia and Achaemenidian Iran, in Pasargad and Dura-Europus. The priests' costumes are typical of northern Syria and the upper Euphrates valley. Finally, the representation of the fumigation sacrifice and the procession itself with the parasol, a royal attribute, are obvious signs of this Orientalism.[5] This is the epiphany of an eastern goddess, iconographically likened to the Hellenic Mother of the gods. It is represented in the form of a procession for which the idol of the divinity was ritually taken out of the temple. Everything thus suggests that this disk from Bactria, on the fringe of the Seleucid empire, dating from the first half of the third century B.C.E., depicts a synthesis of the Hellenized Anatolian Cybele and the Syrian Atargatis, a goddess from Membij (ancient Hierapolis), whom the Romans called the Dea Syria. Other, more fragile hypotheses would attempt to identify the Mother of the gods with divinities from Iran and central Asia, such as Anaïtis, Nana from Nisa, and even Ardokhsho.

This procession, constituting a link between the Hellenized western world and ancient Syria, Mesopotamia, and Afghanistan, should logically lead us to India, where the fearsome Durga, the lion goddess, also presents many traits in common with Cybele. The problem is to determine in which direction the influence of iconography and perhaps ritual was felt. Was it from east to west, or rather, as the chronology seems to indicate, from the Hellenized world toward India? This question seems secondary to me, however. We should situate it within an even larger framework, including the countless images of a great and sovereign goddess, in ancient Egypt, in Mesopotamia, and deep into Asia, where she is seen from time immemorial, often cajoling or soothing wild animals, and sometimes as the Mother of other gods. What should we do with these scattered and repetitive symbols, as disparate as they may be, which some have interpreted as revelatory of a single archetype?[6]

Rather than remain prisoners of the choice between the diffusionist theory hypothesizing a prehistoric heritage and the dream of a religious structure common to all of humanity, it would be better to rely on history and specificity. I therefore opt to analyze only a part of this too obviously universal form. The name Cybele appears for the first time engraved on the façade of a Phrygian sanctuary. From the sixth century B.C.E. to the sixth century C.E., in a tight network of transit and exchange linking Phrygia and Asia Minor to Greece and Rome, this is a specifically identifiable divine figure, explicitly designated as "Mother," or "Mother of the gods." We are going to observe her emergence and establishment by exploring a domain where coherence is assured by the contiguity of time and place. This option is amply justified by the fact that this divine and maternal image, at the polytheistic dawn of our own civilization, ends up joining with, and for several centuries accompanying, the history of a living religion — the religion that has imposed the paradoxical figure of the Virgin Mary, mother of Jesus, sometimes called the "mother of God." From this point of view, it will be clear why we should completely reject facile comparative studies.

In drawing up a detailed itinerary for this expedition, there was much reflection and hesitation. Embarking on the traces left by the "companions of Cybele" — Attis, the Corybantes, the Dactyli, and the Cabiri — I found myself trapped in the labyrinth of literary, epigraphic, and archeological data, through which I wandered for a long time. Yet, as my students can attest, I never lost sight of the heart of the problem. The existence of a monumental old, but still useful, monograph by Henri Graillot and the documentation published by Friederike Naumann and Maarten Vermaseren enabled me to consult studies supporting the mass of material in my own files.[7] Its systematic presentation could not be accomplished without negatively affecting a coherent view of this subject. With the exception of Attis, Cybele's "companions" have been relegated to the background, since it became increasingly necessary to underscore, first and foremost, and in reaction to numerous mystifying interpretations, the central political and historical role in both Athens and Rome of a goddess joining together, in the different places where she emerged, the seemingly contradictory notions of exotic otherness and ancestral heritage.

I must thank the institutions and people who encouraged this adventure. The Fonds national suisse de la recherche scientifique made the first stages of this research possible long ago, on the campus of the University of Chicago from 1979 to 1980, as well as at the German Archaeological Institute in Athens and on the high Phrygian plateaus in Turkey in 1981. At the end of this meandering journey, the admirable hospitality and infallible resources of the Institute for Advanced Study in Princeton were offered to me from January to April 1995. I am indebted to the peaceful and stimulating atmosphere there, which finally allowed me to write the manuscript [of the original French edition of this book] during sabbatical leave from the University of Geneva.

The professors, colleagues, friends, and fellow travelers whose advice and encouragement have nourished my research are too numerous to mention by name. Some will recognize themselves in the notes. I shall make only the exception of mentioning those to whom this book owes its present form, without, of course, their being responsible for it or even aware of it. I must mention Jean Rudhardt, of course, and also Walter Burkert, Claude Calame, Marcel Detienne, the late José Doerig, Nicole Durisch and Youri Volokhine, Stella Georgoudi, Erhard Grzybek, Fritz Graf, François Hartog, Maurice Olender, John Scheid, and Jean-Pierre Vernant, as well as Jean Bottéro, James Redfield, and Froma Zeitlin.

The friendly confidence of Nicole Loraux has patiently accompanied this itinerary from its beginning. I thank her from the bottom of my heart.

Mother of the Gods

CHAPTER ONE

An Itinerant Mother

A Forgotten Kingdom

Phrygian stories that were heard by the Greeks hark back to the most ancient times: the long past, legendary era of the Phrygian kingdom and of Midas.[1] Based on local traditions throughout Lydia in the time of Croesus, the Greeks developed narratives depicting Midas as the founder of numerous Phrygian cities: Gordion, Ancyra (Angora, Ankara), Celenes, and Pessinos. Pacifier and unifier of Phrygia, Midas was above all a royal figure. We shall see him appear as such within the central myth of our corpus, the story of Agdistis of Pessinos. An ancient tradition, which has come down to us through Tyrtaeus, Aristophanes, and Plato, holds that Midas was fabulously wealthy. This attribute, added to the motif of a king who sees his empire overthrown by the Cimmerians and commits suicide, makes of Midas a pessimistic mythical precursor of Croesus. Freely confusing Lydia and Phrygia, the legend goes on to say that it was the gold of the Pactolus—a river flowing through Sardis, Croesus's capital—that ended the curse that caused Midas—king of the high plateaus near Gordion—to turn everything he touched into gold.[2]

As early as the end of the seventh century B.C.E., the Greek poet Tyrtaeus, who was writing in Sparta, a city with close ties to Lydia, evokes Midas the Phrygian and Cinyras of Cyprus side by side, equating their royalty and wealth.[3] This comparison can also be found in Plato. It becomes clearer when placed into the larger symbolic perspective, since both of these Orientals were kings who founded cities and were dedicated to the cult of a goddess. Aphrodite of Paphos (the Paphian or Cyprian Aphrodite) is to her priest Cinyras what the Phrygian Mother in Pessinos or Gordion is to King Midas.[4] Linked to fabulous wealth, the monarchy of these barbarians is also connected to a goddess. Far from being perceived as warlike, which it most certainly was, that monarchy appears in the "memory" of myth as theocratic, under the sign of the female.[5] She foreshadows in myth what the Greeks and Romans would actually encounter in the heart of Phrygian territory, in Pessinos, the power held by the magistrates who were the Mother's priests, designated by the names Attis or Battakes. Midas's power, to use Dumézil's term for it, is marked by a third function. We should not be surprised then to find that the Gordian knot that symbolized this power, kept at Gordion, the ancient capital until the time of Alexander, referred to a peasant's implement, a harness whose yoke tightly connected to that of a plow.[6]

There is a kind of ambivalence constituting the Greek outlook on Phrygia. At the heart of the specifically Greek reception of these Anatolian echoes, there are two postulates. What for the Phrygians who were contemporary to the Greeks was a prestigious, but irretrievably lost, origin became in the Greek imagination something both foreign and constitutional. Central characters came into Greece from this legendary royal Phrygia. Pelops, for example, before founding the Olympics, imported the music referred to as "metroac,"[7] according to the fifth-century author Telestes.[8] Conversely, "Midas's goddess," as the Greeks sometimes called the Anatolian Mother, received a young Dionysus in her home to cure him of his madness and initiate him into her own rites. In fact, when Dionysos is shown in Thebes, his country of origin, he is depicted as a foreigner coming to these regions, arriving after a long voyage.[9]

One should therefore not simply call it an issue of alterity with Phrygia, but rather of a recollection where both the chronology and the difference between Greek and barbarian are blurred. At the heart of the Greek world, there is an empty throne attesting to this recollection, the one where Midas sat to dispense justice and that, as the first barbarian to consult the oracle, he dedicated to Delphian Apollo.[10] Midas's throne at the foot of Mount Parnassus evokes the throne of Pelops on Mount Sipylos (Manisa Dagi), above Magnesia, today called

Manisa, not far from Smyrna, very close to Sardis, which Pausanias describes,[11] a mountain throne associated with what the Greeks identified as the most ancient image of Cybele (it is actually a gigantic royal figure from the Hittite period, sculpted into the cliff above Akpinar, a few kilometers from Manisa) and believed to be the work of a brother of Pelops.[12] Phrygia, in the widest sense of the term, is actually Cybele's land. In the Greek tradition, Cybele took her name from a mountain in this region, an unidentified spot where her first epiphany took place.[13]

Phrygia is thus the object of a double discourse: on one hand, it is an entity that is forever lost, the legendary kingdom of Midas; and on the other, the relatively miserable survival in this same land of a culture, a language, and a religion. In classical Greece, Midas sometimes designated the great king from long ago whose epitaph one liked to improvise, and sometimes, as in Aristophanes, the name refers to a comic slave.[14] As we are embarking on the itineraries of the Mother of the gods, it is important to emphasize the fact that we are confronted with the evanescence of her place of origin. As a cultural and historical reality, Phrygia remains for the most part unattainable outside of its mediation through the Greek perspective. It seems that this result is not simply due to a lack of other information. In fact, the archaeology of the Mother, resulting from digs at Anatolian sites, leads us to the same sort of difficulties.

Old Phrygia, the only one that had experienced any kind of political unity, was short-lived, lasting perhaps one hundred and fifty years. Constituted after the breakup of the Hittite empire by a population from the Balkan regions speaking an Indo-European language, a first Phrygian kingdom was established around Gordion during the middle of the ninth century b.c.e. At the end of the eighth century, the Phrygian state controlled a vast region, the extent of which has been revealed by archeological evidence from sites as distant from one another as Sinope (now Sinopi) on the Black Sea, Ankara, Alaça, Pazarli, Bogazköy (the ancient Hittite capital Hattusa), Konya, and finally, even farther east, Malatya. On Assyrian tablets, the Phrygians were known as the Muski and, toward the end of the eighth century, we can identify Midas in the king they call Mita. In approximately 695 b.c.e., emerging from beyond the Caucasus, the Cimmerians invaded this region. According to Greek tradition, Midas committed suicide by drinking bull's blood.[15] When the Cimmerians retreated, Phrygia, despite its disintegration, continued its existence in the shadow of a new power, the Lydians from Sardis. Alyattes, the first king of the Lydians, reconstructed Gordion. In 546, after Cyrus's victory over Croesus, the last of the Mermnadae (the race of

Lydian kings), Lydia became a dependent of the Persian empire up until Alexander's time.

During this momentous history, whose continuity is orchestrated by the Greeks, the Gauls (Galatians), and then the Romans, Phrygian culture never disappeared. Both the cults and the vernacular language persisted in this region, where Christianity made its first moves, until the fourth century c.e. As we shall see, the worship of this goddess, the subject of the present study, underwent a marked revival during the Hellenic period at the very sites of her most ancient sanctuaries.[16]

On the high plateaus of Phrygia, to the north of Sardis (Sart), in the region of Afyon Karahisar and Eskisehir, on the western border of the route linking Izmir (Smyrna) to Ankara (Ancyra), we encounter monumental forms cut into the rocks. This is the primary evidence of an image and a cult whose emergence I shall attempt to analyze through its periodic reinventions in the classical, Hellenistic, and Christian worlds. Rooted in a desertlike landscape, into which they blend, situated in most cases away from agglomerations and roads, the most ancient of these monuments attesting to a significant archaic faith go back as far as the end of the seventh or beginning of the sixth century b.c.e. In other words, the oldest monuments date from a period far later — almost a century later — than the disintegration of autonomous Phrygia.[17] Cut into the rock along with the votive façades, there are inscriptions in an alphabetic writing of Phoenician origin and Greek importation,[18] naming Matar (the Phrygian equivalent of the Greek Mētēr, "Mother") and Matar Kubileia or Kubeleia ("Cybelian Mother").[19] The most impressive sanctuary of this type is at Yazilikaya, not far from Afyon. It takes the form of a monumental door with a flat surface decorated with geometric patterns, suggesting a supernatural presence inside the rock to which it blocks access. There is an inscription naming the Mother, who is a part of this rocky mass and whom the monument identifies as living in the cliff, if not as the cliff itself. A second inscription mentions the dedication to Midas, a century after the death of the sovereign of Gordion. Midas had therefore become a cult hero connected to the Mother in Phrygia.[20] These rupestrian monuments sometimes contain the effigy of a goddess standing up in a kind of niche, surrounded by lions. The most famous example is the sculpted rock at Aslankaya.[21]

One of the most recent specialists to have dealt with this subject from the iconographic perspective as a whole, Friederike Naumann, rightly insists on the fact that this type of representation developed during a period when Phrygia, having long lost its independence and its unity, was strongly influenced by the

Greeks. Since Greek civilization flourished on the coasts of Asia Minor during the sixth century,[22] it is clear why the Anatolian prototypes of the goddess the Greeks called the Mother of the gods were already highly Hellenized from a stylistic point of view. The image and some of the lasting attributes of the goddess,[23] even if we know of their existence elsewhere and their more distant Middle Eastern antecedents, are thus crystallized here in an exchange between the Phrygian world, itself a mediator between the old Middle Eastern world, and archaic Greek culture. This complex relationship begins between the end of the seventh and the beginning of the sixth centuries in the countryside, under the domination of Sardis. The high Phrygian plateaus were dependencies of the Lydian Mermnadae dynasty, which reigned from 680 to 547 B.C.E. and maintained cultural and commercial relationships with Egypt, Assyria, and Babylon. During the first part of the sixth century, throughout the reigns of Alyattes and Croesus, Greek artists were attracted to the court of Sardis.[24]

It was in this same city of Sardis that the Greeks historically found one of the most ancient figures of a foreign and divine Mother. The Ionians admitted their guilt in setting the famous fire in this goddess's temple, an act that constituted, at the dawn of the Persian wars, a very serious pretext for the Persians to take revenge against the Hellenic world. Behind the Cybebe mentioned by Hipponax and Herodotus, and attested to in Lydian under the name of Kuvav-, there is a hidden theonym (divine name) directly inherited from the old Anatolian religion of the second millennium, the form Kubaba, mentioned in the Old Assyrian, Ugaritic, and Hittite cuneiform texts, designating a goddess of Carchemish who is guardian of the city.[25] Thus, it is by way of Lydia that the ancient Near Eastern Kubaba meets up with the goddess called "Cybele," a divinity whose first two appearances are almost contemporary, although situated at opposite ends of a vast space already marked by the presence, or influence, of the Greeks. In the paleophrygian inscription at Yazilikaya, near Afyon, mentioned above, from the end of the seventh or beginning of the sixth century B.C.E., we encounter the adjectival form *kubileia* qualifying the noun Mother (Matar), while on a shard from a vase from the same period offered ex voto in a sanctuary at Locri Epizephyrii in southern Italy, we find the word *Qubalas* (a genitive meaning "possession of Cybele"), apparently designating the divinity to whom the vase was consecrated. A group of toponyms transmitted by way of Greek tradition allows us to affirm nonetheless that the name "Cybele" was originally only an epithet, one of many possible names given to the goddess more simply referred to as the Mother: Matar in Phrygian. This epithet also refers to the name of a mountain.[26] The

Matar Kubileia, or "Cybelian Mother," of the paleophrygian sanctuary is a nick-name that is part of a long series of Anatolian Greek extensions. We find Mētēr Dindumene, Mētēr Sipulene, Mētēr Berekuntia, Mētēr Idaie, and Mētēr Angistis, or Agdistis (or Agdestis). These names translate as: "Mother" of Din-dymus, "Mother" of Sipylus, "Mother" of Berecyntus, "Mother" of Ida, and "Mother" of Agdus . . . which are all mountains. The best generic term, some-times used by the Greeks, would be Mētēr Oreia or "Mountain Mother." It is therefore not necessarily "Cybele" whom Cybebe runs into, but rather a Mother who is sometimes, but not always, Cybelian. Claude Brixhe formulated a very fine hypothesis years ago to explain this. If the Greek language often used the noun "Cybele" for the noun "Mother," and not only as an epithet among so many others, the reason for this might very well be this encounter with the old, original deity of Carchemish. "*Kubele* would then be a compromise between the Phrygian adjective *kubileia (Matar)* and *Cybebe,*" Brixhe reasoned. "The phonetic proximity of the two terms would have favored such a crossbreeding. It also would have powerfully contributed to the expansion of *Kubele* in Asia Minor and finally to her triumph in the Greco-Roman world."[27] In fact, to Brixhe's credit, ancient sources can be used to connect Cybele to a toponym. This name, however, is rare. Used in a limited way, it is a poetic term,[28] not often evidenced in ritual practice. The Greeks first venerated the goddess as "Mother" or "Mother of the gods," and the goddess whose image spread from Anatolia thus more often than not remains completely anonymous to us.

The Diffusion of an Image

Thus everything begins with the formidable task of making an inventory. In this case, it is a spatial and temporal one of the way of perceiving a divinity whose importance is only evidenced in iconography from the beginning of the sixth century B.C.E. The space involved extends from the high plateaus of Phrygia and the Ionian and Aeolian coasts of Asia Minor, via the isles of Chios and Samos, into the heart of the Peloponnesus, as well as in southern Italy—Locri Epize-phyrii—and the Phocian colony of Marseille.[29]

The image spread according to a relatively clear itinerary. From Anatolia toward the Greek mainland, a first path led the Phrygian image into Laconia, probably through the intermediary of the old Lydian kingdom, Croesus's city of Sardis. A second path, contemporary with the first, carried this same image, this time through the intermediary of the Greek cities on the Asian coast, toward

Italy and the south of France, from Phocis to Marseille. Later, starting in the second half of the fifth century, the Anatolian prototype of the goddess surrounded by lions, transmitted through Ionian iconography, was transformed by the great Athenian art of sculpture. The cult statue sculpted by Agorakritos, a student of Phidias, represents the new version of the goddess. This statue was located in a sanctuary connected with the *bouleuterion*, the headquarters of the Council of Five Hundred, on the Agora in Athens.[30] The image thus became more and more widespread: more minor (and popular) artisans produced an increasingly greater number of replicas. The National Museum in Athens alone holds at least fifty-two votive reliefs. These are representations of a goddess inside a temple niche, or *naiskos*, where she is seated on a throne holding a large drum (or *tympanon*) in one hand and a cup for libations (*phialē* or *patera*) in the other. In each representation, the goddess is shown either with a small lion on her knees or seated on a throne framed by two of these docile beasts.[31]

The piety manifested during the fourth and third centuries B.C.E., especially in Greece, through the abundance of these votive offerings and their redundancy, is not anything new. In the sixth century already, in Marseille, the Ionian prototype of the anonymous Athenian Mother of the gods received repetitive and monotonous homage from her faithful followers. Chance would have it that in 1863, during the construction of the rue Impériale (later rue de la République), close to fifty votive stelae were found near the top of the rue Négrel. Of forty-seven archaic votive stelae excavated, forty-six represented a female figure seated in a *naiskos*, sometimes with a lion on her knees. The finders of this little treasure of piety could not have known of the Ionian and Aeolian parallels, which were discovered much later during the archaeological digs led by Salomon Reinach in 1881 in Aeolian Cyme, on the coast of Asia Minor. They knew, nevertheless, that without being able to identify the goddess, they could very precisely locate the origin of her image. Describing the find to the Académie des Inscriptions for the first time in 1863, Adrien de Longpérier observed: "We know that Miletus and Phocis belong to Ionia, and the community of origin of the peoples should account for the conformity of their works. One of the stelae in Marseille represents a woman holding a lion on her knees; this animal, seen on the coins minted by the Phoceans of Velia and of Marseille, is one of the symbolic attributes of the Asian Diana."[32]

In thinking of the Ephesian Artemis [Diana], Longpérier was close to the right solution. Although he did not have all the iconographical and paleographic documentation that allows us to confirm it today, with a few nuances, we can concur with the interpretation advanced twenty-six years later by Reinach. This divinity, remarkably widespread throughout the archaic period, is in fact a "Cybele," that is, a Mother.[33]

An Anonymous Goddess

This divinity, whose image is dominant as of the beginning of the sixth century B.C.E., does not have a proper name. She is a generic Mother, whose authority is easily extended and whose epithet, when she has one, is satisfied with localizing her significance. This is a salient point. Referring to a toponym, the epithet functions as an epiphanic means of recognition and local appropriation.

The wording "Mother of the gods" is not sufficient in itself to designate a personalized divine entity who is distinct, differentiated, and definable in the framework of a pantheon. To accomplish that goal, it is necessary to have an ulterior motive, or to be in the presence of a speaker with a religious image or cult symbol that would require resorting to this expression. "Mother of the gods" is a generic term, which can be applied to several divinities. The fact that this qualifier ends up becoming, in a specific place on the Agora of Athens, at a time we herein undertake to determine, the official name of a powerful divine object of worship presents us with a problem. How can one go from a signifier to a referent that is a priori plural to the development of a cult dedicated to an anonymous Mother of the gods (*Mētēr theōn* or *Mētēr tōn theōn*)?

This question leads us to clearly distinguish two stages in the literary documentation, for the moment considered apart from the rest of the iconographical, archaeological, and epigraphical evidence. In the first stage, we observe how the epithet functions for the poets who first use it to address the Earth, according to Hesiod's teachings: "One, the race of men, one that of the gods. But we breathe, as we each and every one come from one, single Mother."[34] This common Mother is identified with the Earth as early as the ancient reading transmitted by the scholia on Pindar. This evidence is actually inscribed in a series. According to Aeschylus, "Earth gives birth to all beings and after having nourished them takes from them the fertile seed." Sophocles and the Homeric *Hymn to Gaia* explicitly describe the Mother Earth of the gods. One also recalls a famous observation by Solon: "She can better than any other give witness in the court of time, the very great Mother of the Olympian gods, black Earth."[35] This epithet, shared by Rhea, also considered to be the "mother of the Olympians," but from another point of view, therefore calls out to an ancient primordial power of fertility and justice.

Mother of the gods, Mother of the gods and men, Mother par excellence, splitting this up is a delicate task. Take away *theōn* and *mētēr* remains, a mother who can just as well sometimes designate Demeter. The Homeric hymn addressed to the Mother of the gods retains the anonymity to better render it universal and salutes her, at the end, by associating her with all the other goddesses: "I salute you in this song, as well as all the goddesses together." The formula is remarkable and rings out respectfully with the traditional custom: "I shall think of you in all my other songs." Yet there is only one more appearance of this formula in the entire corpus of the Homeric *Hymns*. This time, and it is certainly not by chance, it is applied to Artemis of Ephesus.[36]

The Homeric hymn to the Mother of the gods nevertheless specifies that the Mother of the gods and men likes to hear the sound of rattles and tympanums, as well as the noise of flutes. She loves the howling of wolves, lions' roaring, mountains filled with echoes, and small wooded valleys. Here we can recognize the reference to a primitive figure, a precivilizational and partly exotic being. Localized in a mountain landscape among the wild beasts, she loves a music that is frequently found in the Dionysian context, as well as in that of Zeus's childhood in Crete, and in the entourage of the Asian Great Mother. Cymbals and rattles sound off in Pindar (fr. 48) near a *Mētēr megala* whom the poet once calls Cybele, qualifying her as *Mētēr theōn*, "Mother of the gods," or simply *Mētēr*, "Mother," which connects her back to the Arcadian landscape where she was accompanied by Pan, guardian of her sanctuaries.[37] Situated on the edges of an original land, the Mother appears to partake in both a spatial and a temporal register. This Mother precedes the law-making grain goddess Demeter. Is she prepolitical too?

Listening to Origins

To Athenian ears, her fame seemed to come from somewhere else. According to Plutarch, when Themistocles left Susa in 464 B.C.E., he saw the Mother of the gods in a dream. At the time, he was in the land of the Anatolian Matar, in Upper Phrygia. The goddess warned him in person to watch out for the Lion-Head, Leontocephales, perhaps the place the Turks later called Afyon Karahisar, the "Black Castle of Opium," where a trap was waiting for him. When he arrived safe and sound in Magnesia ad Sipylum in Lydia, another great site of the Phrygian Mother, Themistocles had a sanctuary built for the "Mother of the Gods" and appointed his daughter as priestess there.[38]

One should not gather from this evidence, if it can be considered historical, that the Athenians felt this to be the expression of a foreign, barbarian religion. It was just the opposite. The memory of a metroac religion, when it appears in an account by Herodotus, situates the rite, addressed to a divinity recognized as Greek, in a familiar context, that of a ritual vigil, a *pannuchis*. Thus, in book 4 of the *Histories*, when he is heading home for Scythia after having discovered Hellenic civilization, Anacharsis stops one last time on Greek soil, in Kyzikos on the Propontis (the sea of Marmara):

> For when Anacharsis, having seen much of the world in his travels and given many proofs of his wisdom therein, was coming back to the Scythian country, he sailed through the Hellespont and put in at Kyzikos; where, finding the Cyzicenes cele-
> √ brating the feast of the Mother of the Gods with great pomp, he vowed to this same Mother that, if he returned to his own country safe and sound, he would sacrifice to her as he saw the Cyzicenes do, and establish a nightly rite of worship. So when he came to Scythia, he hid himself in the country called Woodland (which is beside the Race of Achilles, and is all overgrown with every kind of wood); hiding himself there Anacharsis celebrated the goddess's ritual with exactness, carrying a small drum and hanging about himself images. Then some Scythian marked him doing this and told it to the king, Saulis; who, coming himself to the place and seeing Anacharsis performing these rites, shot an arrow at him and slew him. And now the Scythians, if they are asked about Anacharsis, say they have no knowledge of him; this is because he left his country for Hellas and followed the customs of strangers.[39]

It is possible that this barbarian shows his barbarism by importing from the Greeks that which is least Greek. It is nevertheless from Greece that the importation occurs. Apollonius Rhodius later also mentions this cult of the Dindymene Mother at the gates of Kyzikos. He affirms that this ritual, which he considered exotic, had nonetheless been founded in an ancient prehistory by the Argonauts, that is, by Greeks, but as they were passing through, after a local epiphany in a foreign land.[40] A Greek figure is thus constituted in conjunction with the Anatolian interior, from which nothing filters out except the image of a goddess and the costume of her priest Anacharsis.[41]

CHAPTER TWO

In the Athenian Agora

A Sanctuary

In order to find a cult in Greece dedicated to the Mother of the gods under no other name, unless it is simply that of the Mother, we have to go back to the end of the fifth century and the Athenian Agora, clearly political turf. There, the Mother of the gods (*Mētēr tōn theōn*) had a sanctuary called a *mētrōon*, specifically said to be situated next to the *bouleuterion*.[1] A law dating from 403–402 B.C.E. informs us that it was customary to erect stelae of the written laws in front of this sanctuary.[2] In this same *mētrōon*, also in 403 B.C.E., a decree was displayed mentioning the honors conferred by the city on those who brought back the exiled members of the demos from Phyle.[3] There are also some records dating the founding of Athens's public archives from this same year.[4] Finally, an anecdote concerning Alcibiades, to which I shall return further on, leads us to believe that trial records or court proceedings (*tōn dikōn hai graphai*) were also kept inside the *mētrōon* in the second half of the fifth century.[5]

In the fourth century, the evidence is even more specific and more abundant, especially from the orators and epigraphic documents. In 323, Dinarchos spoke of a decree deposited "with the Mother of the gods who established herself as guardian of written justice for the city."[6] In 330, Lykourgos declared in court: "Come now, citizens, if someone entered the *mētrōon* and erased even one single law, defending himself with the pretext that this law represented nothing for the city, would you not have him put to death?"[7] Pseudo-Plutarch, in his *Lives of the Ten Orators* (842 f.), affirms that when this same Lykourgos was on his deathbed, he had himself transported to the *mētrōon* and to the *bouleuterion* to recite an account of his political activities in public. It is obvious in this context that he went before the Council of the Five Hundred. However, the specific mention of the *mētrōon* in connection with that council indicates that he was not only trying to obtain an official audience. It was a matter of his staging his political last will and testament in a space where the truth of the collective was archived under the guardianship and authority of the Mother of the gods.

The *mētrōon* was the place where one could also claim justice for oneself. Although this may seem strange at first glance, evidence of such claims being made indicates that this was the case. Aeschines describes how in 345 B.C.E., Pittalakos was furious at having been beaten up at his home by his former lover Timarchos and the latter's new boyfriend, Hegesander. The next day, Pittalakos went up to the Agora completely naked and seated himself at the altar of the Mother of the gods. A crowd began to gather, and Hegesander and Timarchos rushed over and begged him to get up, blaming the violence on their drunkenness. In the end, they persuaded him to leave the place, lending credence to the idea that Pittalakos was to regain at least some of his rights. The altar of the Mother does not function as a place of refuge here but rather as a busy public place situated at the heart of community life, where Pittalakos came to provoke a scandal. It is a space where one can make accusations and express a desire for vengeance.[8]

The documents available to us establish the relationship between the sanctuary of the Mother, the *mētrōon*, and the building of the Council of the Five Hundred, the *bouleuterion*. This close relationship is confirmed by archaeology.[9]

The texts indicate that the *mētrōon* was adjacent to the *bouleuterion*. At least in the fourth century B.C.E., these two structures and the *tholos* (a rotunda built around 465, in which the members of the standing committee of the council, the *prytaneis* [presidents], lived and took their meals)[10] formed a whole. American archaeological excavations in the Agora have shown that what the Athenians called the *mētrōon* by the end of the fifth century was actually the ancient *bouleuterion*, situated directly next to the later one and very close to the site of the future *tholos*. The most recent interpretations[11] reiterate Homer A. Thompson's conclusions and establish the following chronology for this site:

(a) First, there was the old *bouleuterion:* a square building with steps inside it. Constructed between the end of the sixth century B.C.E. and the beginning of the fifth, after the reforms enacted by Kleisthenes, it served both as the meeting place for the new Council of the Five Hundred and as an archive.[12]

(b) During the same period, adjacent (and probably connected) to this first *bouleuterion,* a small temple was erected, which was later destroyed by the Persians in 480 and never rebuilt. We do not know the name of the divinity to whom it was dedicated.[13]

(c) Between 415 and 406, a new *bouleuterion* was built next to the old one.

(d) The ancient *bouleuterion* did not disappear. After the construction of the new one, it continued to function as an archive and received a new name. It was called the *mētrōon* to distinguish it from its neighbor, which was reserved for meetings of the *boulē* (council).

(e) This was its function up until approximately 140 B.C.E., when a Hellenistic *mētrōon* was built. This last building, explicitly called the *mētrōon* in our sources, replaced the ancient complex (*bouleterion* and *mētrōon*) and served as the council's meeting place, an archive, and a sanctuary alike.

If we consider these points, we begin to question the original placement and authorship of the famous sculpture of the Mother. Visitors in the Roman period could still admire the cult of Mētēr in the Hellenistic *bouleuterion.* Arrian's description of it is confirmed by later iconography (reproductions, imitations, and variations). The goddess is seated on a throne framed by lions; she is holding a drum (a tympanum) and a libation cup (*phialē*). According to Pausanias and Arrian, Phidias sculpted this work. However, according to Pliny, Agorakritos was the sculptor.[14] There is a similar discrepancy between Pliny and Pausanias with regard to the attribution of the Nemesis of Rhamnous, which we know to be the work of Agorakritos because of the inscription on the base found there. Sensitive to the partial, fragmentary rediscovery of the goddess of Rhamnous, archaeologists now lean toward attributing the Agora Mētēr to Agorakritos. If the work were by Phidias, it would have to have been produced before 432 B.C.E., when that great artist stopped working. By recognizing it as a work by Agorakritos, we can date it from the last third of the fifth century, a period during which this disciple and lover of Phidias's was still very active. This is precisely the period to which the American excavations have dated the new *bouleuterion's* construction, leaving the previous building to serve as a sanctuary and archive, which it did until the second century C.E.

The consecration of a religious statue sculpted by Agorakritos in the old *bouleuterion,* now turned *mētrōon,* at the end of the fifth century signifies at the very least a resurgence of the cult of the Mother, if not (which I do not believe) its reestablishment de novo.

In truth, we know nothing about the Athenian goddess before this period. There is no epigraphical or literary evidence allowing us to affirm anything. After carefully considering the matter, Giovanni Cerri has proposed three scenarios to explain how the cult of the Mother began at the *bouleuterion* complex:

(a) The little temple at the end of the sixth century was already dedicated to the Mother of the gods.[15] According to Cerri and this first hypothesis, the ancient *bouleuterion*, contemporary with the little temple, would have served as both the meeting place for the Council of Five Hundred and as a space in which to celebrate the cult of the neighboring goddess. Cerri imagines this cult as originally oriental and, in essence, part of the mysteries. When the Persians destroyed the little temple, the old *bouleuterion* survived and then began to function as both a sanctuary and a meeting place for the *boulē*. In the last quarter of the fifth century, with the new *bouleuterion* built, the ancient one ceded its function as a meeting place for the *boulē* but remained a sanctuary *(mētrōon)* and an archive. H. A. Thompson and M. P. Nilsson had already opted for this hypothesis, situating the introduction of the cult of the Mother of the gods, considered to be of foreign origin, toward the end of the sixth century.

(b) The second scenario is much more probable. The cult of the Mother of the gods, for which we have no earlier evidence, was first introduced with the building of the new *bouleuterion*. This innovation does not necessarily mean that the new cult was dedicated to a foreign goddess or to an unknown female deity, as assumed by Cerri, who treats as historical the later story (which does not in any case date from before the Hellenistic era and may even be Roman) about Agorakritos's statue being erected in the *mētrōon*.

(c) The third scenario proposed by Cerri is not incompatible with the second one. The cult of the Mother of the gods, already known at the end of the sixth century, experienced a revival at the end of the fifth century B.C.E. At this point, she was iconographically likened to a foreign goddess from Phrygia.[16]

It is not impossible that the Mother had a sanctuary at Athens that disappeared in 480 B.C.E., and that was later remorsefully remembered during the last decades of the fifth century, after what seemed like a long period of neglect. The rare archaeological finds connected to the first sanctuary, some of which evoke Eleusis, point us in this direction. The period when the ancient *bouleuterion* became a *mētrōon* in which Agorakritos's cult statue was erected corresponds perfectly well with the earliest available Athenian commentary. We shall return further on to the hymn to the Mother of the gods that Euripides composed for the chorus of his *Helen* in 412 B.C.E. Nevertheless, the first Mother, for whose having been forgotten the "new" cult makes up, remains beyond our reach. She may have had a name. We know nothing of it. In any case, what we do know is that the Mother of the gods, ritually installed at the political center of Athenian memory at the heart of the archives of the ancient *bouleuterion* toward the end of the fifth century, deliberately retains her anonymity. Moreover, despite appearances to the contrary, she is not at all a foreigner.

A Political Cult

In the ancient sources and direct evidence, there is no indication of imported Phrygian mysteries being involved in the Athenian *mētrōon*. This legendary tradition, marked by the influence of the Mater Magna and her *galli*, did not take hold until the Roman era. (We shall come back to it.) Conversely, the cult of the Mētēr tōn theōn in the Athenian Agora appears to have been completely traditional, linked to the political status of a manifestly ancestral power.

The relationship of the *mētrōon* to the *bouleuterion* is not only topographical, it connotes a political cult. Depositing certain archives in this sanctuary, as well as counterfeit money, served more than practical purposes. Under Athenian influence, the *mētrōon* in Delos also housed archives.[17] According to Demosthenes and Theophrastus, the *prytaneis* made sacrifices to the Mother of the gods, going in procession to the festival of the Galaxia, at which the *epheboi* dedicated a *phialē* to the goddess for the welfare of the city.[18] This holiday was an official, but minor, festival celebrated without much ado and usually in a mechanical fashion. Theophrastos ridicules the Vain Man by describing him as one who gets the *prytaneis* to announce the sacrifices made in its name to the demos. Crowned and dressed in a bright cloak, he steps forward to proclaim: "O citizens of Athens! We, the *prytaneis*, have made the sacrifices of the Galaxia for the Mother of the gods; the sacrifices are favorable; receive all benefit from them!" In Immanuel Bekker's *Anecdota Graeca* and in Hesychius, we read that a *galaxia*, a kind of porridge (*poltos*) made from barley and milk, was boiled during this festival.[19] The Roman tradition, leaning on the word *puls* (which Varro links with *poltos*),[20] recalls that this type of food is older than bread. Barley was the predominant cereal in Attica, better suiting the climate there than wheat, which was introduced later but found to be better for making bread.[21] In Attica, barley blooms between the end of March and the middle of April, the exact month designated as *Galaxion* — the equivalent of the *Elaphebolion* in Delos.[22] A repast for the autochthons, or for citizens "nourished on the same milk" and members of associations claiming a spotless heritage,[23] the barley-and-milk *poltos* seems to fit with a goddess often identified with Rhea. Without being pre-cereal, she seems nonetheless to precede Demeter in the Greek imagination of the origins of agriculture.

She is a primordial figure. Her anonymous character makes her resemble those divinities to whom Epimenides sacrifices in consequence of a plague caused by the pollution of civil conflict (*stasis* and *loimos*).[24] Reconnecting with the depths of the earth, our goddess ensures the joint functions of justice and fertility. Epimenides's altars were thus numerous and scattered all over Attica. Like the Hestia of the Prytaneion, the Mother of the gods reigns in her enigmatic singularity at the political center. Her power, like that of the city's center, radiates beyond the place where her cult is rooted.

Far from being a deity whose exotic ritual originated in an ecstatic practice, she appears to have been endowed with a function that cannot be dissociated from that of the Council of the Five Hundred instituted by Kleisthenes. Her sanctuary was located only a few meters from the monument of the eponymous heroes. She was the privileged guardian of written justice.

Even though Athenian discourse likens her to a "savage" Demeter, and we see her progressively assimilated to a Phrygian foreigner, the cult practice maintains her in a political role. The fact that she was not the only one to play this role, and that other divinities also guarded other archives, changes nothing. In the fourth century, the texts of laws and many other official documents were preserved in the *mētrōon* under the guardianship of the goddess and a *demosios*, a public employee acting as her assistant. As of the end of the fifth century, the Mother had her treasurers, her *tamiai*, selected from among the members of the *boulē*.[25] There are also inscriptions indicating that there was an *antigrapheus*, that is, a secretary responsible for providing copies on demand, for example, for the engraver who had to reproduce the text on a stele. The documents protected by the Mother were evidently sufficiently interesting to tempt a rich and famous collector who lacked scruples: Apellikon of Teos, a great buyer of libraries (notably Aristotle's), later stole the originals (*ta autographa*) of the ancient decrees deposited in the *mētrōon* of Athens.[26]

Although she was the guarantor of justice, if not even the guardian of the city's memory preserved in writing, the Mother seems to have been powerless in the face of the somewhat dubious tradition of deriding her function. Hegemon of Thasos, an author of comedies who had just been handed down an adverse judgment, gathered his colleagues and went with them to Alcibiades's house to ask for help. With the artists trooping after him, that prince of Athenian youth seems to have gone into the *mētrōon* and erased the minutes of Hegemon's trial with a wet finger. Although furious, the bailiff and archon kept quiet because it was Alcibiades. The accuser, it is said, ran off.[27] This anecdote shows, of course, how Alcibiades was above the law and piety, able to do whatever he wanted. His behavior reminds us of a situation that was not exactly democratic, where justice was at the mercy of a small group of aristocrats or oligarchs.

The Council of Five Hundred, to which the *mētrōon* is linked, appears to have been a democratic council, and its conflicts with the much more conservative Areopagos council lasted throughout the fifth century.[28] The Mother of the gods at the *bouleuterion* counterbalanced the power of other divinities who were also conceived of as very ancient, but more aristocratic, whose shrines were located elsewhere, near the Areopagos.

For Athenians, the name "Mother of the gods" had evoked the Earth ever since the time of Solon. A divinity with known oracular powers, the Earth, Gē [Gaea or Gaia], was closely related to justice in Athens. In *Prometheus Bound*, Aeschylus treats Themis and Gaia as a single entity.[29] The cult of a Gē-Themis is also evidenced by inscriptions mentioning her priestess on the seats at the theater of Dionysos.[30] On the Areopagos, the Semnai, or "Venerable" or "Holy" ones, that is to say, the Erinyes-Eumenides [the Furies], were close to Pluto, Hermes, and Gē.[31] Moreover, it is precisely in this area that a great number of votive reliefs have been found. These *naiskoi*, dedicated to the Mother of the gods, are today in the National Museum of Athens.[32]

The invention of the singular Mother is nonetheless also a reference to the ancient functional split between a plurality of goddesses guaranteeing justice (Gē, Themis, Erinyes: each in her own way, according to her abilities). The rediscovery of the Mother of the gods in the Agora at Athens toward the end of the fifth century thus amounts to recalling the importance and perhaps also reinforcing the influence of these ancient female divinities. Yet is she not, then, by the same token, a rival alongside these impressive guardians of justice?

A Wild Demeter?

On the Areopagos, a change in attitude that marked a turning point for the city took place in ancient times under the auspices of the law. Summoned to the city's tribunal, the Furies (the Erinyes) abandoned their anger at Orestes and turned into Eumenides. As such, they became part of the land of Athens by forever guaranteeing the fertility of the fields and the herds, albeit through the use of threats. That the Mother of the gods was associated and contrasted with Demeter through myth, at a time corresponding to the period of the ancient *bouleuterion*'s transformation into the *mētrōon*, has a revelatory function for us in this context. This counterpoint emphasizes an aspect of Demeter where the Eleusinian goddess is very close to the Erinyean one. However, Athenian discourse does not go so far as to name this rediscovered figure Demeter.

In a famous chorus of *Helen* in 412 B.C.E., Euripides addresses a hymn on the theme of reconciliation to the Mother of the gods, not to Demeter.[33] The interpretation of the second of the three *stasima* punctuating the end of the play poses a real problem in terms of the work's overall structure. The ritual error alluded to, and felt by Helen with regard to the Mother, seems disconnected and is not explicitly followed up anywhere in the rest of the play. This observation led Henri Grégoire and Louis Méridier, following F. A. Paley, A. C. Pearson, and Ludwig Radermacher, to seek out some kind of external motivation.[34] According to these scholars, Helen's fault, in this play produced after the disaster in Sicily, would connect to crimes of impropriety committed in 415 on the eve of the departure of the Sicilian expedition that Alcibiades first helped lead and then betrayed. These crimes included the mutilation of the Hermae and the profanation of the mysteries, celebrated before the uninitiated in a private house. It is certain that a play produced in Athens in the spring of 412 on the theme of Helen's ghost, and therefore implicitly referring to a reflection on the war, could not help but ring true in connection with the contemporary vicissitudes experienced by the city. The response to the question posed by the introduction of a reference to the Mother in this context depends entirely on an examination of the historical record. Without eliminating the possibility of a relationship to religious events that marked the preparation of the Sicilian expedition, it nevertheless seems that the most obvious reference made here is to the cult of the Mother itself, recently revived on the Agora after a period of neglect.

In Euripides, the reconciliation with the Mother of the gods is envisioned as the paradoxical inversion of anger into laughter. This marks the end of an ancient suffering, that of the goddess whose daughter was wrested from her, but who let herself be distracted from her bereavement, however unforgettable, by Kypris [Aphrodite], who, at the instigation of Zeus, offered her the musical instruments that became her own attributes. The chorus of Helen's Laconian companions in Egypt introduces this ancient drama as the paradigm to which the abandonment of a more recent anger refers. Helen, in this context, would have neglected the cult of the goddess, but will be able to repair this "error" by jubilating as a maenad. The "Mountain Mother of the gods" (*Oreia matēr theōn*)[35] was implicitly connected to the Cretan Rhea (an allusion is made to Ida)[36] and to Gē, the Earth become sterile when the Mother holds herself aloof.[37] Sometimes as Deo[38] and sometimes as Mētēr,[39] she was presented as a divinity whose myth was borrowed from Demeter's. Yet the names she shared with the latter (Deo, Meter) in some way disconnected the two constituent elements of a name (Demeter) that she refused to bear:

> Before, the Mother of the gods ran down into the small, wooded valleys, to the rivers, to the groaning sea, in her desire to find her lost daughter, the one whose name no one pronounces. The busy castanets clacked away, while the wild animals pulled the goddess's chariot. The child had been seized in the midst of her companions.[40]

But Zeus had foreseen another destiny, aside from this Eleusinian one, of the reunion between Mother and Daughter:[41]

> Weary of running around looking for the kidnapper who had stolen her daughter from her, arriving atop the snowy peaks of Mount Ida, where the Nymphs were on the guard, she fell down in desperation into the snowy thicket of the rocks. Then and there, she left to humankind the fields without greenery! No fruit came out of the furrows: the human race would disappear! She refused to allow the grass to flourish and the herds to graze. . . . Life left the cities; there were no more sacrifices to the gods, no more cakes to burn at the altars. She prohibited the foamy waters from running from their sources. Nothing could make her forget her loss. When she had finally ended all celebrations for gods as well as for men, Zeus wanted to attenuate her disastrous wrath. "Go then," he said, "august Graces, take her sadness away with your ritual cry,[42] Deo, you who are furious about what happened to her daughter,[43] and you Muses, with your choruses and songs." Then Kypris, the most beautiful of the graced ones, sounded the deep-pitched bronze[44] and the tympanum[45] strung with leather for the first time. Charmed by the ritual song, the goddess laughed and reached for the flute with the deep vibrations.[46]

The rest of the *stasimon*, verses 1353 to 1368, which have come down to us in a very corrupted text, allude to Helen's tragic error. Apparently, she had not respected the sacrifices due to the goddess and had thus provoked the Great Mother's anger (*menis megalas Matros*). The chorus advised that in order to repair this negligence, the guilty woman should let herself be led into a nocturnal, Dionysian-type celebration. Here, it is said explicitly that Helen had to behave like a suppliant by flipping her hair around in honor of Bromios.[47] The presence of a group of familiar elements — narthex, fawn skins, ivy, bull-roarers — refers to the same model.

Mourning for a lost daughter, wrath, peace of mind. The sequence was the same as at Eleusis. Yet even though the reference was obvious,[48] the narrative of the Mother of the gods was constructed as systematically distinct from the Eleusinian story in terms of its emphasis on the wild and precivilized. Euripides' Deo ends her wandering in a high mountain landscape, not at the edge of a wheat field. Worshiped with the sound of castanets, a Dionysian type of music, she drives a chariot drawn by lions. Closer to the Arcadian Demeter known as Erinys or Melaina, she retreats and grieves in the snowy thickets of the woodlands, thus choosing a place evoking the Phigalian valley more than the palace at Eleusis. The climax of both stories is nevertheless the goddess's change in attitude: from irritated to magnanimous; from passive to active; from sterile anger to nourishing fertilizing activity. The end, nonetheless, proposes a new contrast, since there is no question of this Mother getting her daughter back.[49] Condemned to mourning without forgetting (*penthei alastoi*) the daughter whose name cannot be pronounced, she finally lets her anger disappear, defeated by the cry of the Charites, the hymn of the Muses, and, finally, by Kypris, who makes the Mother laugh by playing the tympanum. Kypris mimes a role that is not Aphrodite's, but that will become precisely that of the Mother, who accepts the musical instruments that will become her attributes. This transformation through laughter signifies the resumption of the functions of life: labors, fruits, fecundity of the herds, activities in the cities, and sacrifices. Aphrodite acts on the orders of Zeus, that is, the boss.[50] Helen, likewise, is apparently guilty of having neglected the Mother.[51] Like Aphrodite before her, to whom she is still linked here,[52] Helen will have to borrow the ritual attitude of the female companions of the goddess. In Helen's Asian setting, these eastern women constitute an entourage similar to that of the maenads around her.[53]

A change in attitude through laughter exploding into a comic reaction, if not sarcastic ritual, is already a theme in the Homeric *Hymn to Demeter*, in which the servant Iambe and a grotesque dance persuade Demeter to participate in palace life at Eleusis. In a version considered to be Orphic, the role of Iambe was played even more explicitly by the famous Baubo.[54] The involvement of Pan, sometimes considered to be the father of Iambe (in an Arcadian version), also constitutes more documentation of the same.[55] In Euripides, after the Charites and Muses get involved, it is the strange behavior of the goddess of loving desire, Kypris, playing the tympanum, that lightens the Mother's mood.

A choral text, known through an inscription from Epidaurus, difficult to date but certainly as old if not older than Euripides' play, includes the Muses addressing the "Mother of gods" again called the "Great sovereign mother of Olympus."[56] The chorus evokes a mythic episode during which the goddess, wandering in the mountains and the valleys, keeps away from the world of the gods until Zeus intervenes in a burlesque fashion. This was probably imitated by an actor who threw bolts of lightning and played a tambourine, beating rocks to the rhythm of a surprising dance before addressing the fugitive in the present tense: "Come back to the home of the gods, Mother, stop wandering in the mountains, for fear that something might happen to you, with the hungry lions and gray, furry wolves." The goddess answers: "I shall not return home to the gods before obtaining my shares [*ta mere*], half the sky, half the earth, and a third of the sea. Then, I shall return." Before having thus made plain her claim to cosmic sovereignty,[57] she receives greetings from the chorus. Nothing is said either of causes or circumstances connected to her retreat or of the final result of the negotiations. As shown in Robert Wagman's detailed analysis, this text, whose composition goes back to an ancient period (at least the fifth century B.C.E.), was recopied during the imperial era on a votive monument in Epidaurus, alongside other hymns. It was thus situated especially close to a hymn to Pan that can be dated to Hadrian's time and to a similarly late hymn to "All the Gods." This later recontextualization comes from a resemanticization that no longer recognizes the grotesque character of the original document and instead endows the Mother's "strike" with cosmic dignity, underscored by being framed between Pan ("Everything") and "All the Gods." The light tone of the poem and Zeus's appearance in a role analogous to the one Euripides attributes to Aphrodite suggest that the original text was probably poorly understood by the copyists of the imperial period. It was, moreover, a caricature of the myth of anger and reconciliation otherwise found in popular music and burlesque dance. Wagman recognizes evidence of "sacred Dorian farce" in this song: "a poetic form evidenced in the Peloponnesian sanctuaries as early as the end of the seventh century B.C.E."[58] Euripides' chorus addressed to the Mother, the Arcadian versions of the Demeter myth, as well as the "Orphic" version involving Baubo, may all at least partially relate to a common heritage connected to those ritual practices. This would explain the farcical way in which the Mother is evoked in *Helen*. The playful aspect of farce connects to a ritual element and in no way contradicts the seriousness respected in these activities. It is important to recognize the apotropaic value of laughter and jubilation, which dispense with the dramatic effects of the Mother's absence. Sterility, famine, depopulation, and finally, impiety — since the sacrifices could not be made—were the consequences of her voluntary exile. Strangely enough, these are similar to the consequences of war.

Whatever the distant ritual or literary origins, the Mother's laughter in Athens in 412 occurred in a specific context whose implications we can easily guess. Produced for the Great Dionysian festival in the month of March, in 412 B.C.E., *Helen* was not only chronologically linked to a cult revival of the Mother of the gods in the Agora, she was also created immediately after the Sicilian disaster, exactly when the Greek cities in Asia and the islands were beginning to defect and abandon their alliances with Athens. During the winter of 413,[59] the Spartans began negotiations with Chios and Eretria, which the Athenians knew nothing about during the spring of 412.[60] It was not until the Isthmian games at Corinth,[61] at the end of April,[62] that the defection of Chios and Erythrea, then of Clazomenae and Miletus, began to become an established fact.[63] We can observe that the list of cities coincides with that of the major cult places dedicated to the Mother of the gods in Greek Asia during the archaic and classical periods.[64] This is enough to understand that the reference to this divinity in the spring of 412 should be situated in the context of the anguished mourning that overtook Athens after the Sicilian disaster and at a time when it was being abandoned by its Ionian allies. The introduction of the Mother as a figure of reconciliation in a play dedicated to Helen and her ghost thus referred to two cults at once. On one hand, it addressed the civic cult of a recently revived ancestral goddess of justice, thereby correcting a tragic error, in the mode of palinodes (or recantations).[65] On the other hand, it referred to Asia Minor, the world of the allies, in terms of both its poetic discourse and the image of the cult.

At the same time, the assimilation of the mother to Demeter[66] favors the strange connection drawn in Athenian discourse between the political goddess of the *mētrōon* and a goddess of foreign origin, an Anatolian Mother sometimes called Cybele. This formidable, wild deity was also a maternal figure who, in the Phrygian myth, suffered intolerable grief as a result of the death of her consort Attis.

The Recognition of a Foreigner

In his *Philoktetes* (405 B.C.E.), Sophocles mentions a figure seemingly inspired by the cult statue sculpted by Agorakritos. He describes a goddess on a throne, drawn by lions, who is designated as the mountainous and nourishing Earth, but also as the mother of Zeus and sovereign of the great Pactolus River, on which

Sardis lies.[67] The image of the Mother of the gods in these verses refers both to Gē and Rhea, which is not surprising, but also to the Anatolian Matar, which requires an explanation.

In Attica, as early as the last quarter of the fifth century, Aristophanes jestingly noted the presence of a group of foreign cults. In *The Birds* (414 B.C.E.), an individual appears next to Cybele called Sabazios the "Phrygilian" — a name that makes him sound like both a Phrygian and an ostrich.[68] The poet denounces this religiosity as a recent importation. Nonetheless, it must subsequently have gained greater importance, to judge by the discovery, made in 1971, of the Moschaton sanctuary near Piraeus, where the cult statue was inspired by the one made by Agorakritos. This sanctuary was built at the beginning of the fourth century.[69]

In a 1944 study, William Scott Ferguson found that the most ancient epigraphical evidence of a cult of the Mother of the gods practiced by foreigners in Attica was an inscription in Piraeus that can be dated to the end of the fourth century.[70] This dedication was found on a votive statue:

Manes Metri
Kai Mika Metri theōn.

Manes to the Mother
And Mika to the Mother of the gods.

This double apostrophe reflects a special conception of the divinity in terms of two perspectives, rather than as a double (a point to which I shall return).

Also in Piraeus, in 284–283 B.C.E., an organization of *thiasotai* was honoring two of its members, Soterichos of Troezen and Kephalos of Heracleia. One of them was a priest and the other was an *epimelētēs*, that is, a building superintendent. The sanctuary from which this inscription came was likely situated on the Aktē peninsula.[71] Later inscriptions no longer speak of *thiasotai*, but of *orgeones*.[72] So it seems that there was a development in the organization of the cult, as Ferguson observed, such that after the *thiasotai*, who were of foreign origin, there were *orgeones*, who were citizens.

This does not mean that the specifically Phrygian cults tended to disappear. Agdistis, a Phrygian name and more precisely the Pessinontian name of the goddess, appears next to Attis on a relief from Piraeus that can also be dated, like the one mentioned by Ferguson, from the end of the fourth century. Inasmuch as the comparison can be made with the better-known cult of Bendis, another foreign divinity established in Piraeus during the second half of the fifth century, there was a double process of integration and distinction. A foreign cult was being poured into the mold of Athenian institutions and representations at the same time as an Athenian fad was attracting citizens to an exotic movement.

We have observed the strange epigraphical doubling of "Mother" and "Mother of the gods" accompanying the dedication of a single figure. Other inscriptions[73] speak of goddesses, or mention two thrones. Although Cybele and Attis have been noted in this connection, should we not rather think of two Mothers? Or the Mother considered according to both aspects, indigenous and foreign? Among the numerous votive reliefs discovered in Attica, many are in the form of double *naiskoi*. Two niches are represented side by side with the same, or almost the same, goddess seated in each one. The only slight difference might be that one has the lion on her knees, while the other has it at her feet; but the attributes, the *phialē* and tympanum, are identical. The divinity on the left holds a scepter and a *phialē*, while the one on the right has the tympanum and the *phialē*. Friederike Naumann counts eleven Attic examples out of eighteen double *naiskoi*. Moreover, a double relief from Isthmus reveals the following inscription addressed to a single goddess: Mētēr theōn Ourania: "Ouranian Mother of the gods."[74]

Various interpretations have been proposed: a mother-daughter relationship, as in the Eleusinian myth; a double aspect in the cult itself, based on the example of the two Athenas — Athena Polias and Athena Parthenos — or even the reinforcement of power and the exaltation of the divinity.[75] According to I. N. Svoronos, one of the two associated figures in the frame of the Attic reliefs dedicated to the Mother of the gods would refer to the cult statue of the *mētrōon* in the Agora, and the other to the *mētrōon* in Piraeus.[76] In this way, one would be Greek and the other Asian. This hypothesis, which recognizes two contrasting but connected aspects of a single divinity at the origin of the double *naiskoi*, puts us on the right track. By following it, we can understand the very official role that an autochthonous Mother of the gods was able to play in Macedonia where freed slaves were periodically dedicated to her in exchange for services rendered.[77] Prohibiting *galli*, who were certainly foreigners practicing the itinerant religion of the Mother, from entering the sanctuary of a local divinity in Eresos, a town of Lesbos,[78] was part of opposing two perspectives likely to focus on the same, sometimes foreign, sometimes native, divine entity. Peter Frei has recently demonstrated how a strange narrative in Ovid's *Metamorphoses* relating the transformation of Lycian peasants into frogs, performed by Leto, carries with it the memory of a conflict between the old local religion in the valley of Xanthos and the cult of the mother of Apollo and Artemis, imported by the Greeks.[79] These examples outside Athens, and later in time, confirm what we begin to see: the concern for maintaining a religious separation, even as religious feeling was tending to recognize the oneness of the divine figure.

Officially introduced in Athens between 431 and 429 B.C.E., the cult of Bendis offers us a further useful basis for comparison. With Bendis, we observe one of the ways in which a bipolar organization could be established around a new cult of foreign origin to unite citizens and foreigners in honor of a single divinity through the ritual of a double procession. In fact, Athenians recognized a form of Artemis by integrating a deity originating from Thrace.[80] With the Mother, we observe the reverse process. An ancient Greek figure with renewed value is united in a simultaneous relationship of solidarity and opposition to a foreign figure recognized as being, ideally, the same.

Starting out with a local figure, an anonymous, but ancient and formidable, representative of the powers of justice on Earth, a discourse arose around the cult image of the Mother of the gods in the Agora, which tended to identify her as a foreign, Lydian or Phrygian goddess, but fell short of actually doing so. There was definitely an attempt made to frame an exotic setting for the native goddess, sketched in the metaphors of the tragic authors, around the iconography of the cult statue, from the last third of the fifth century on. We find a good example of this argument in Aristotle's positing of the notion of metaphor, in the etymological sense, as the "displacement" of meaning. From the characters named in the example selected, Aristotle goes back to the first half of the fourth century B.C.E. We discover that the goddess's ambivalent status — she is sometimes considered autochthonous and close to Demeter, sometimes a foreigner — was common knowledge. Iphikrates mocked the Eleusinian priest Kallias by calling him a *mētragurtēs*, that is, one of the Mother's wandering beggars. Kallias could only respond flatly that Iphikrates was speaking as a layman. If Iphikrates had been an initiate, he would have called him a *daidouchos*, a torch bearer, one of the priestly functions reserved for the Eleusinian aristocracy. The two terms are applied to the goddess, "but one [*mētragurtēs*] is dishonorable, whereas the other [*daidouchos*] is honorable," Aristotle notes, adding that this "metaphor" is analogous to that in which actors are called "Dionysian sycophants" (*dionusokolakes*), whereas they considered themselves professionals, or "artists" (*technitai*).[81]

The foreign cult of the Mother in Attica developed away from the city. It only gained importance later on and ostensibly under the influence of the political cult. It was first of all practiced in Phrygian communities, *metics* (residents of foreign origin) in Piraeus, then by mercenaries in Rhamnous, who worshiped the goddess under the name Agdistis, her name in Pessinos. Along with these sedentary communities, there were itinerant ones who collected funds for the goddess, the *mētragurtēs* who were the objects of sarcasm.

Even though they were run by the members of religious associations controlled by the state, the Phrygian cults of Athens did not divulge their secrets. The citizens who were introduced into them were only privy to bits and pieces. Thus the practice of the Corybantes, an initiation ritual with psychotherapeutic objectives, where strident music and frenetic dancing around a patient played a liberating role, is well documented in Plato.[82] Sometimes there was membership in a *thiasos* that included a group of foreigners, slaves, and lower-class citizens. The orator Aeschines, according to his adversary Demosthenes, participated in his youth in these less than glorious initiations. His mother Glaukothea led the rituals, crowned with fennel and white poplar while participants manipulated plump serpents, which they swung over their heads screaming "Euoi Saboi" and dancing to the tune of "Hyes Attēs, Attēs Hyes." Strabo already recognized the evocation of Sabazios and Attis in these cries. Both figures were completely Phrygian and part of the cult of the goddess in Anatolia.[83] But these are only names. If these names are evidence of the presence of a foreign discourse in Athens, which was certainly well informed about things Phrygian, that discourse did not take hold. It has remained outside of literature, as if it were indecent to report. We can observe the same kind of resistance in a different, Hellenized context, in Persian-occupied Asia. There is an inscription in Sardis showing us the local satrap forbidding the priests of Zeus Baradates (the Iranian Zeus, Ahura Mazda), from participating in the mysteries of Sabazios and Agdistis. The Phrygian cult was not forbidden; rather, it was kept separate and controlled.[84]

The name Agdistis, which the inscription in Sardis associates with Sabazios, is well known. Numerous documents apprise us that it was a name given to the Mother in Phrygia. Agdistis is named, next to Attis, on a votive relief deposited around 300 B.C.E. in a Phrygian sanctuary in Piraeus. This relief was dedicated by a certain Timothea for the welfare of her very young children (*huper tōn paidiōn*), following a divine prescription (*kata prostagma*).[85] This appearance of Attis and Agdistis inscribed in the tradition of foreign cults in Athens remains an exception. Although they were instigated by the success of Phrygian religious practices, the numerous votive reliefs coming from Athens assumed a completely different iconography. Furthermore, they were not dedicated to Cybele or Agdistis, even less to Attis, but rather to the Mother of the gods, a divinity conceived of as totally Hellenic.

The Mother of the Gods Is Also the Mother of Humankind

The late fifth-century revival of a maternal and divine figure representing both Justice and the Earth manifested the need to reaffirm origins and foundations. The issue of social integration interconnects with the issue of an original guarantee, and in this politically charged atmosphere, the prestige of a great foreign deity quickly becomes evident. A Mother at the heart of the political realm and the guardian of the justice of the written word: is this a paradox in a city as patently patriarchal as Athens? In the last chapter of her book *Mères en deuil* [Mothers in mourning] (1990), Nicole Loraux proposes this fine explanation: "Acclimatized to the city, the Mother of the black angers watches over the imprints of the political just as a mother is supposed to keep the paternal marks inscribed inside herself." Thus, the maternal envelope housed the writings of male power. A formidable guardian, she is also a disconcerting figure. The revival of the importance of her cult during this next-to-last decade of the fifth century responds to this apprehension. She is determined by the desire to connect back to a primeval moment, more all-embracing and more anonymous than the deities in the familiar pantheon. As Loraux observed so well, the city must finally satisfy the needs of its own "mothers in mourning," those who lost their sons during the war.

Next to the cult administered by the magistrates, and in the background in relation to the official propaganda, but just as important in reality, if not more so, are the private rituals. We would like to learn more about these individually initiated rites in which feminine piety played such a significant part. Linked to long-standing practices, they date back to a tradition that escaped the literary record. We have to content ourselves with a few, rare allusions in classical texts to which we can connect later, quite abundant documentation from Asia Minor. In Attica and Greece proper, dreamt injunctions or other oracular prescriptions are mentioned where reference is made to "paramedical" beliefs.[86] These situate the Mother at the heart of speculations and popular practices of purification aiming at the treatment of afflictions we consider today to be psychiatric in nature. The ancients classified these in the vast category of phenomena of possession, enthusiasm, or *mania:* "This goddess can exorcise madness," a scholiast informs us.[87] The chorus in Euripides' *Phaedra*, whose love-sickness appears to be a crisis of melancholy, informs us that she behaves like a woman possessed, guilty of a ritual fault committed against the Mother or a similar divinity.[88] Considered by the ancients as medically close to melancholy, epilepsy was also often connected to the Mother of the gods in popular beliefs.[89] Here, once again, the goddess causes the crisis out of her negligence; a ritual forgetting (or a forgotten ritual) makes her mad. The fault must be rectified in order to soothe the goddess and find the way back to health through cathartic rites. One could also invoke the Mother, alongside Hermes Katouchios, Hecate, and Earth, to destroy an adversary, whose name one inscribed on a lead tablet that was buried in the greatest secrecy in a place appropriate to the ritual of magical cursing.[90] A document from Asia Minor (but whose content allows the interpretation of a curious Athenian practice),[91] attests to another type of "magical" recourse to the Mother: it speaks of the depositing in her sanctuary of a tablet asking for the Mother's vengeance on unknown guilty parties who have stolen the believer's gold. In some way, the Mother assumes the anger of the human victim who identifies with the Mother, and she takes care of the matter.[92] Numerous texts from Asia Minor called "confessions" were addressed to a goddess whose resentment is acknowledged by the worshiper, even as he recognizes his own guilt and praises her vindictive power, attesting to the angry and frightening nature of this Mother, who nonetheless remains nurturing.[93] The goddess is not only "skillful singer of hymns" (*sophē humnoidos*) — that is, competent in casting spells and incantations — but also a healer (*iatros*).[94] Already presented as such in the fifth century in ancient Hippocratic literature criticizing this type of popular belief,[95] she reappears later, in a myth reported by Diodoros, in the form a woman endowed with the power of curing children and young animals. Without a doubt, this Mother's main function was to protect small children and babies. In the near-silent realm of individual practice, we shall find this Mother playing the role of wet nurse in myth.[96]

The name "Mother" can refer to two ideas. The first is maternity in the sense of direct filiation: this Mother is a "mother" because she has a given number of children, whom we can name. Second, there is the respect linked to "maternal" status in general. All female divinities, in this sense, were theoretically likely to see themselves called "Mother." The exceptions — Artemis and Athena — were remarkable and sometimes ambiguous.[97] Considered from the point of view of this alternative between actual filiation and simple matronly authority, the appellation Mother of the gods that the goddess received in Athens, and then in Rome, appears intentionally problematic. Is this Mother at the origin of the pantheon? Can she be assimilated, then, to Earth, to Hesiod's Gaia? And in a more limited way, to Rhea, Kronos's wife, mother of the Olympians? Or does she figure in the pantheon among the gods, who are not her children, as one in whom maternity designates power and sovereignty in the guise of a woman, making her more like other feared and honored females such as Demeter or Leto? The two interpretations coexisted in both Greece and Rome. The second refers to a notion already found in Mycenaean times, when Linear B texts speak of the cult of a "divine Mother."[98]

The Mother of the gods who reigns over the Agora in Athens lends herself to many interpretations. She is a divinity without a proper name. As the guardian of the city's archives, she is the focus of an official cult whose ritual symbols lead us to believe that she is understood both as an original figure, analogous to Gaia, and as a bringer of justice, similar to Themis. Simultaneously with the development of this political version, a tradition appeared identifying the goddess with a foreign deity from Phrygia, Lydia, or Crete, a Mother of the mountains, a primitive without genealogy, understood to be Gaia, Rhea, and Demeter all at once. Supported by the appearance of the statue in the *mētrōon*, this tradition finally developed in the Hellenistic period, or perhaps under Roman influence, into a veritable legend concerning the origin of the cult, involving a missionary priest.

After having returned to her origins in the form of a wrongfully neglected ancestral figure, the Mother reworks herself as a foreign deity. In so doing, she resembles Dionysus—who, moreover, arrives in Thebes from her country. The Dionysian epiphanies or frenzies are also apparently returns from exile, retribution for forgetfulness.[99] In any case, as opposed to Dionysus, who is intent upon affirming, and even emphasizing, his genealogy, the Mother, whose territory we must not forget is the land of exile, maintains all the advantages of her anonymity. She is therefore ready and able to play both sides of the field. Simultaneously national and exotic, native and oriental, she becomes dual, if not plural. Like her friend and companion the god Pan, she manages to escape the restrictions of the genealogical framework of the Olympian family. She excels at this game, which she plays at different times in different contexts. This is first evident in the existence of so many ex-votos and double *naiskoi*. There is a doubling of the representation for the purposes of magnification, of course, but also to signal the double definition and, at the same time, the singularity of the one who is revered in contrasting rites by immigrant communities and citizens of local origin alike.

In Rome, we shall rediscover a strikingly similar phenomenon when the Mother of the gods is introduced at the end of the Second Punic War. The cortège of *galli*, a Phrygian ritual, will be seen to go back to an exotic practice that contrasts strikingly with the aristocratic practice of the exchange of communal meals and with theatrical spectacles. This practice is nevertheless addressed to the same goddess, the Idaean Mother of the gods, conceived of both as a foreigner, come with her clergy from the high Anatolian plains, and as the ancestor of the Roman people, originally from Trojan Ida.

The Mother of the gods is also the Mother of humankind and the protector of cities. The fact that she is both from here and from elsewhere must be seen in relation to a questioning of their origins on the part of the political communities that rediscovered her. This questioning constituted one of the conditions for this goddess to appear. All in all, her cult only takes shape much later and under special conditions, after crises force the city to rethink, not only its identity, but its unity as well.

CHAPTER THREE

The Invention of a Mythology

Attis Before the Fact

The Mother of the gods is only exceptionally the subject of narrative in Greece during the era we call classical. She has neither a genealogy nor, apparently, a history, aside from allusions in Euripides and the Epidaurus Hymn connecting her to mourning and reconciliation, expressed in terms that recall Demeter, a figure firmly anchored in the most ancient of narrative traditions. In the heart of the classical Greek polity, the Mountain Mother evokes a mute landscape of ancient liminality that is at once foundational and disquieting. Her ancestral marginality is both fundamental to her nature and disconcerting at the same time. Even when they approach her on foreign, Asian soil, from the point of view of Anacharsis or Themistocles, the Greeks have virtually nothing to say about this divinity, whose powers and cult seem to be self-evident to them. Except for the myth Euripides reiterates and the epigraphical Epidaurus Hymn, we know of only two instances in which the goddess has a role in a narrative developed before the Hellenistic period. Both relate to an epiphany and its ritual consequences. The first explains the death of a missionary priest, Anacharsis, and the second relates the origin of a priesthood through the dream of Themistocles's daughter in Smyrna. These are on the face of it entirely Greek stories, but each is also concerned with a return, inherent in the relationship opposing two spaces: a Greek land in Asia (Anacharsis departs from Kyzikos and Themistocles returns to Smyrna) and a land situated at the extreme frontiers of Hellenism (respectively, Hylaia and the high plateaus of Phrygia).

When their imagined original space is confronted with the reality on the ground, the Greeks only understand what they care to understand. For them, it seems to be the mystery of it all that remains dominant. Sardis, in close contact with the Greek world, nevertheless stands out as a place of significant development where not only the iconography but also the main features of the Greek discourse on the Mother of the gods were established.

It will be recalled that Sardis is where the eastern Kubaba (Kuvav) and the Phrygian Matar Kubileia meet. And it is precisely there, at the foot of Mount Tmolos, reflected in the golden waters of the Paktolos River, but toward the end of the ostentatious Lydian capital's glory days,[1] that the most ancient representation of the goddess's priest, aside from Anacharsis, is to be found. In Herodotus's famous account, this is Atys (spelled that way by the "father of history"): an Attis described as a son of Croesus who is killed during a collective hunt organized against a monstrous wild boar.

The story is as follows. After an oracular dream informs Croesus that the young man will die because of an iron weapon, the king keeps him away from his male companions, confining him in the back of the apartments, in the *thalamoi*, far from all instruments of war. Croesus is hoping to marry his son off when a Phrygian prince, exiled for having accidentally caused the death of his brother, arrives in town. Exonerated and purified by Croesus, this foreigner is given the responsibility of guarding his son Atys. Together, they manage to persuade the father to let him participate, this once, in an expedition of young people from Sardis intent on slaying a wild boar ravaging the region. To convince his father, Atys emphasizes that the wild boar has ivory tusks, not metal weapons, and that the prediction in the dream therefore has nothing to do with it. During the hunt, the Phrygian prince, who was to protect Atys, accidentally kills him with his javelin. Readers of Herodotus have long recognized the connection between Adrastus, a prince who could not escape his destiny as a murderer, and Adrasteia, a divine Mother whose name is often associated with Nemesis. The name of this goddess, who was the object of a cult in Anatolia, suggests inescapable decrees.[2] The Greeks heard this story in Lydia, although its Phrygian inspiration was manifest. Adrastus, the involuntary murderer of Atys, was the son of Gordios, himself the son of Midas.[3]

An elegiac poem written by Hermesianax in approximately 300 B.C.E. echoes Herodotus. Pausanias summarizes the narrative plot of this poem.[4] Attis is presented in it as the son of a Phrygian named Kalaos.[5] Apparently, Kalaos was born incapable of procreating, he is *ou teknopoios*, a "non-producer of children." Attis emigrates to Lydia, where he initiates the population into the rites of the Mother. This goddess bestows such honors on him that Zeus becomes irritated and sends a wild boar to attack the Lydians' farmlands. Attis participates in the hunting expedition and is killed by the animal.

In another, closely related version, given by the scholiast on Nikander's *Alex-ipharmaka*, the wild boar is sent by a Zeus who does not dare confront the formidable goddess directly. In so doing, Zeus hopes to end the goddess's love for a Phrygian shepherd.[6] Following Hugo Hepding, these versions (Herodotus, Hermesianax, and the ancient commentator on Nikander) were traditionally grouped together under the heading "Lydian," as opposed to other versions of the myth that were considered "Phrygian." In the Phrygian versions, the wild boar does not appear, but the theme of castration does. It is well to note that the Lydian group, which seems influenced by stories related to Adonis, is presented in Pausanias as the version known to the Greeks. However, it has no echo whatsoever in the Roman tradition and therefore can be considered minor compared to the whole group of Phrygian versions, which were more widespread. These Phrygian versions were also closely related to the cult rituals of the *galli* as practiced in Anatolia and then in Rome from 204 B.C.E. on. We would nonetheless be wrong to assert the autonomy of the Lydian group prompted by Hermesianax's odd contention that Attis was born unable to procreate. It does not seem here that the theme of castration was totally unknown, but rather that it was intentionally silenced. In other words, it was transformed into a surprising bit of information resisting the narrative logic. As for the version recounted by Herodotus, although it ignores the love between Atys and a goddess, it does indicate a threat from the outside impacting the inside. On one hand, there is the wild boar in the hunting scene (i.e., the goddess's traditional backdrop); on the other, there are the *thalamoi*, the palace apartments where Atys is protected and kept apart for his future marriage.[7] We can observe the same kind of opposition at work in the most ancient versions in the Phrygian group. The essential point, from this perspective, is the role played by the matrimonial artifice invented by Croesus to protect his son from the danger portended by the oracle. This artifice can be read as a transformation of the theme of Attis's marriage with a mortal. That union, in the versions belonging to the other group, constituted a betrayal ending his passionate relationship with the goddess and was the underlying cause of his death.

We shall return later to the historical context in which the *galli*'s discourse emerged. For the moment, especially because the inquiry in this chapter is myth-ographic, and its aim is to put in place the different elements of a dossier to be considered further on, we can adopt the attitude of observers.

As others have noted,[8] one is obliged to recognize that Attis, in the Anatolian iconographic and epigraphical documentation, was not known as a cult figure before the Roman imperial era. In Anatolia, from time immemorial, Attis (or rather the name "Attis") seems to have designated a particular type of priestly function connected with the Mother, although it simultaneously from its first appearance retained the status of a proper name — it was a common anthropo-nym, one of many.[9] When it first appeared on Greek soil, this name referred to a character of supernatural status. On the previously mentioned votive relief from Piraeus dating from the last third of the fourth century B.C.E., Attis is represented as the object of the dedication, along with Agdistis, the Pessinontian goddess facing whom he is seated.[10] The most ancient literary evidence of Attis is in a fragment from the comic poet Theopompus and can be dated between 410 and 370 B.C.E. Like the relief, it appears to allude to the love between Attis and the goddess.[11] The detour through Greece, or simply through Greek eyes, was therefore enough to transform the priest into a supernatural being with an am-biguous status at the dividing line between priestly and divine. Moreover, he was involved in a passionate relationship with the Mother. Thus, Attis becomes a character not unlike Phaeton in his relationship to Aphrodite, as told by He-siod.[12] Considered in terms of the Greek interpretation of the Mother in Rhea, Attis is also one in the series of numerous companions of the goddess of the mountains that included Curetes, Corybantes, and sometimes also the Cabiri, whose existence, like that of the Nymphs, was both ritual and mythological. These names actually designate the titles of priesthoods or members of religious associations, as well as the divine acolytes in the narratives concerning the gods.[13]

As opposed to these figures, who are essentially collectivities, Attis, in his new role, affirms a clear-cut individuality. He is introduced through a story where the priesthood has become a love affair ending with the death of the lover and a ritual act. The sorrows of the Mother, Rhea, crying over Attis, a lover designated as a priest,[14] appear as of the Alexandrine period in a poem previously attributed to

Theokritos.[15] Nikander, for his part, alludes to a place of Attis worship connected to a sanctuary called the "chambers of Rhea Lobrina," which we know is located in the region of Kyzikos.[16]

A New Paradigm: The *Galli*

The influence of the Lydian group of stories where Attis dies like an Adonis began to wane as soon as the Greeks discovered, or rather directly observed, which usually had to mean in their own land, certain ritual practices that had until then been repressed.[17] The sanctuary to which Nikander alludes was near the very Greek city of Kyzikos, a Meletian colony, from which Anacharsis took the image and the cult of the Mother to Scythia. It was the scene of a ritual, as eruditely reported by the scholiast on the *Alexipharmaka:* "The chambers of Rhea are the sacred underground places where those who practice the cult of Attis and Rhea deposit the testicles [*ta mēdea*] that they have cut off [*ektemnomenoi*]" (themselves).

A remarkable change in vocabulary soon appeared that can appropriately be connected with this second discovery of Phrygia by the Greeks and then by the Romans. The word *gallos*, a new term, does not appear in the literature until the end of the third century B.C.E.[18] This term, which turned out to be enormously successful, emerged as a new technical appellation for the Mother's priests, who were until then known under other names, referring to other functions. Among the pre-Hellenistic designations, we find *kubebis*[19] and *kubebos*.[20] Both refer precisely to Cybebe of Sardis (Kubaba-Kuvav) and designate a particular type of devotee possessed by the goddess. The *kubebos* is to Cybebe what the bacchante (*bakkhos;* perhaps also *bakelos*) is to Dionysus.[21] Hipponax attests to Kubelis, a name that refers to Cybele and also derives from a place, or a "city."[22] Cybebe disappears in favor of the Mother of the gods and the habitual designation of this type of character becomes *mētragurtēs* and also, owing to a frequent confusion between the devotees of Men, a moon god of Thracian origin, and those of Mētēr, *menagurtai*.[23] In addition, there are the *bakeloi*, especially linked to Sardis for the Greeks,[24] who apparently get their name from the Lydian form of Dionysus (*baki*).[25] In the literature, they are readily associated with tympanums and Mother rituals. The *bakeloi* seem principally to have been sacred dancers connected with the sanctuaries. For the Greeks, the *mētragurtai* were part of a vast category of *agurtai*, who are the object of Platonic contempt.[26] An *agurtēs* was literally "one who reunites, who invites," or an "assembler."[27] Sometimes sounding a trumpet, the *agurtēs* recruited from the crowd those who were called to partake in a collective enterprise. He appears with this name and function in the iconography depicting Achilles on Skyros. Hidden among the daughters of Lykomedes, disguised to avoid the expedition against Troy, Achilles was unable to resist the trumpet call.[28] In the realm of religion, such a role might have been part of the ritual recruitment practice, the *agurmos*, as evidenced for example in the great assembly of the *mystes* marking the first day of the Eleusinian mysteries in Athens.[29]

Very early, however, next to these official functions, the *agurtēs* was metaphorically attributed the less than glorious tasks that were part of private ritual practices and became an object of contempt. This slide down to the pejorative register originated in one of the ancient functions of religious assembly: the collection for the gods (for the Nymphs, for example,[30] or for the hyperborean Virgins).[31] Since the *Odyssey*, the verb *agurtazō* has signified "trade, search for wealth."[32] The idea of material profit, with a hint of charlatanism, gradually became associated with the religious function. In Sophocles' *Oedipos tyrannos* 388, Tiresias the sage is called a "sneaky charlatan" or *agurtēs dolios*. In Plato's *Republic*, the *agurtai* are mentioned in the company of sacrificers, enchanters, and purifiers. Not only individuals but also cities referred to them by these names for practicing buffooneries that they called initiations (*teletas*).[33] In the *Laws*, Plato proposes the creation of separate prisons for a type of character similar, if not identical, to these wizards or sages in the entourages of tyrants, who were actually atheists whose practices abused human credulousness.[34] The Hippocratic treatise *On the Sacred Disease* lists the *agurtai* among other healers:

> Those who were the first to sanctify this illness [epilepsy] were in my opinion those who are today magicians [*magoi*], expiators [*kathartai*], charlatans [*agurtai*], and imposters [*alazones*], all of whom feign piety and superior science. Hiding their ignorance and their inability to do anything useful under the cloak of [divine origin], these people pretended that this illness was sacred. Using suitable arguments, they came up with treatment where they were on safe ground, prescribing expiations and incantations, and forbidding bathing and various foods. Hippocrates, *De morbo sacro* 1.22–31

The author concludes, like Plato, that these people were atheists. We have no information on the social origins of these "specialists of the sacred." Perhaps they were quite varied, like their activities. They were involved in the tyrant's court and the public square, with both individuals and the city as a whole. No one knows what proportion of these people were foreigners or Greeks during the classical period. In a more specialized form, showing how connected they were to the Mother of the gods, they can be discovered at a very remote date referred to by the noun *mētragurtai* or the verb designating their ritual behavior collecting offerings: *mētragurteō*.

The evidence is not plentiful, but it is interesting. First of all, there is Aristotle, who makes *mētragurtēs* into the pejorative equivalent of "Eleusinian priest."[35] Then there is Plutarch, who writes of Ptolemy Philopator being called a miserable effeminate *mētragurtēs* by the Spartan king Kleomenes.[36] The metaphor becomes reality when we approach the verb. A disciple of Aristotle's, Klearchos, reports that the tyrant Dionysius the Younger tragically ended his life as a destitute *mētragurtēs*, begging with his tambourine. Aelian confirms this tradition and specifies that he "became a bum" in Corinth.[37] Designated by the participle of the verb *mētragurteō (hoi mētragurtountes)*, the *mētragurtēs* appears again in comedy, in Antiphanes, in an invective where the pedagogues and the nursemaids are considered—insult of insults—as having acted worse than a *mētragurtēs*.[38] In Dionysius of Halicarnassus, finally, they are called *galli*.[39]

A perceptible evolution gradually transposes the image of the *mētragurtēs*, thought to originate in a marginal religious community, in the direction of the itinerant *gallos* whose portrait is painted in famous passages by Apuleius and Lucian.[40] These *galli* are nomads who go from public square to public square, talented in drawing a crowd. Purifiers, fortune-tellers, or magicians, these charlatans collected offerings and money, carried their idol on a chariot, and sold their magic. A fragment from Babrius preserved by Natale Conti describes the *galli* in their role as *agurtai* going from village to village, shouting out: "Who among you villagers does not know the blond Attis and how much he was loved? Who has not yet deposited in Rhea's sacred tambourine the first of their vegetables and victuals?"[41]

With the *galli*, a more specific type appears and the evidence of castration asserts itself. Until then, the Greeks had known of ritual castration only as something that occurred in very faraway places or in specific local contexts (e.g., Scythian eunuchs [*enarees*] or the chaste attendants [*megabyzoi*] of Artemis of Ephesus).[42] The classical *mētragurtēs* was essentially a healer working on his own. He was not associated with castration and did not evoke the idea of a religious collectivity. Evidence appears only relatively late, in Anatolia, of priests of a particular type — saintly characters who were far from being marginal — to whom the terms *galli* and Attis, in their proper meanings, were linked, as the names of functions.[43]

The Realistic Attis

If the overview of the literary documentation relating to Attis as a proper noun has allowed us to follow an evolution leading from the mythological representation of the goddess's priest-lover to that of the god, this should not obscure the equally literary and not exclusively religious existence of another Attis. This other parallel Attis was faithful to the Anatolian context in which he was only known as a human priest. The literary appearances of this "realistic" Attis, from the end of the third century until Catullus, almost eclipse the mythological character for two centuries, while maintaining a relationship of near identification with this character.

According to our sources, it all began when Atys,[44] who was designated as a *gallos*, journeyed from Pessinos to Sardis. The reference is in a series of five short poems in the *Palatine Anthology*, of which the most ancient is by Dioscorides. The poems date back to the period during which the Romans were aided by Attalus in the search for the image of the Mother in a city controlled by the clergy of Attis, that is, Pessinos itself.[45] Attendant "in the service of the chamber" of Cybele *(thalamēpolos)*,[46] the chaste Atys runs around in a trancelike state, his hair in the wind, until nightfall, when his passion cools down. Entering a grotto where he thinks he will lazily be able to spend the night, forgetting the goddess, he is surprised by the roar of a lion, the Mother's animal, which reminds him of his duty to maintain his trance.[47] Under the effect of a miraculously rediscovered inspiration, he takes hold of his tambourine, the *tympanon* belonging to the cult of the Mother. The sound drives the animal away. In Catullus's admirable poem 63, Attis is once again a priest who travels and falls asleep, forgetting the Mother and regretting the irreversibility of his dedication, until the lion reminds him of his "vocation," that is, his ritual madness.

In classical Greece and under Lydian inspiration, the Mother's priest was introduced furtively yet remained identifiable behind his "technical" name: Atys, in the historical genre. The remarkable silence about his ritual castration arises from the cultural repugnance for practices that remained marginal,[48] or that were remote until after Alexander's visit to Gordion. The theme of the *galli*, notwithstanding its scandalous nature, ends up becoming as poetry, in which it can be traced from its first Hellenistic appearances down to Catullus. It concerned a religious practice, that of very real priests designated by the title "Attis."

Mystical Exegeses

The writing of the name Attis (and of his myth) underwent a metamorphosis. From mythical lover-priest, mourned by the goddess, he was recognized by the Greeks and the Romans as the prototype of the modest *gallos* described by Dioscorides and Catullus. From this conjunction of human and divine, a veritable reinvention of Attis gradually takes place through a long process for which there is explicit evidence throughout the fourth century c.e.[49] From his echo in old Anatolian stories of the second millennium b.c.e. concerning heavenly royalty to his resurrection as the Mother's lover, he finally emerges as a pagan response to Christian apologetics. This reelaboration of the figure and the story occurred in light of Greek paradigms at the heart of a philosophical type of exegesis concerning ritual. We see this exegesis explicitly referring to an intangible "indigenous discourse" (*logos epichorios*), which it actually produces itself. Its only visible extensions are limited to commentaries of a mystical nature. We can follow the tracks of this new "text," continually being developed in light of our unfortunately inadequate information. The witnesses to this long hermeneutic work include first Timotheos of the clan of the Eumolpidae, who worked on adapting the Eleusinian themes into the framework of the Alexandrine religious reforms under Ptolemy I Soter, around the year 300, and Neanthes of Kyzikos, author of a *Treatise on the Mysteries* (ca. 180).[50] The great tradition of the Neoplatonist commentaries on Attis by Porphyry, the emperor Julian, and Sallustius continued the exegesis. In Athens, in the fifth century c.e., Proclus still respected the tradition of the young metroacs, as passed on to the Romans by the Phrygians.[51] A true friendship linked him to Pan and the Mother of the gods from whom he received goodwill and protection on several occasions. To learn more about Proclus's relationship to the goddess, Marinus of Neapolis says, we need only read his book on the Mother, in which her entire theology, the whole group of myths and rites linking her to Attis, will be found set out in an inspirational and philosophical manner, clearing up concerns about the strange laments and tales alluded to in this connection.[52]

We would have no version of this account before the fourth century c.e., which only exists in relation to philosophical commentary, if it had not been introduced during the Hellenistic period in the historical fiction of the euhemeristic sort that the historian Diodoros Siculos has recorded for us.[53] Ovid, in the *Fasti*, will create the illusion of conferring poetic stature on the mysterious *logos epichorios* in a unexpurgated version. Moreover, the *logos* thus reconstituted by poetry was in turn able to feed the exegetes' reflections as well.

The Euhemerist Story

Let us return to our story, not where we left off with Catullus, but a little later, with Diodoros Siculos, who gives the first sufficiently explicit version of the mystical-fictional Attis.[54] This leads us to Samothrace, the island dedicated to the Mother of the gods by the Amazons. Here we find the esoteric cult of the Cabiri established, like the one in Eleusis, by the goddess herself, since she set up her own sons, the Corybantes, as colonizers. Diodoros tells us that the identity of their father is something passed down "in the secret of the ritual."[55] We learn a little more in Diodoros's book 5, where he writes of the violent and incestuous loves of the Mother (both Demeter and Cybele) and Iasion. Their union results in the birth of Korybas, the eponym of the Corybantes.[56] Accompanied by Cybele and Dardanos, Korybas leaves Samothrace and goes to Asia, where he establishes the Phrygian mysteries of the goddess. The involvement of Dardanos, ancestor of the Trojans, and therefore also of the Romans, can only refer to a Roman assumption that the Mother had originally come from the island of the Cabiri via Trojan Ida.

After having presented the long story of the Amazons introducing the cult of the Mother of the gods, named Basileia,[57] in Samothrace, Diodoros reports a second version, which he qualifies as a local Phrygian tale. From the union of Meion, a local king, and Dindymene, a daughter is born. Meion brings the girl to the top of Mount Kubelos, where she is exposed to the elements, suckled by wild beasts, and cared for by a shepherdess, who names her Cybele, for Mount Kubelos. Cybele survives and grows up. Remarkably beautiful and intelligent, she invents the syrinx (Pan's pipe), cymbals, and the tympanum, as well as charms effective in curing cattle and small children, upon whom she dotes. Her virtues merit her being called the Mountain Mother (*oreian mētēra*). A deep friendship links her to Marsyas, an impressive character in terms of his intelligence and temperance, who remains chaste until his death. Once she has grown up, Cybele falls in love with Attis, later nicknamed Papas, an adolescent whom she has met in the country. They meet in secret, and she becomes pregnant. It is then that she is recognized by her parents and taken back to the palace. When her father discovers that she is no longer a virgin, as he had believed, he kills the wet nurses, along with Attis, and abandons their bodies without burying them. Because of her love for the young man, Cybele goes mad and runs away to the country. Playing her tympanum, she travels alone throughout the land, screaming in a sinister fashion, her hair disheveled. Later, Marsyas joins her, full of compassion.

They arrive together in Nysa, at the home of Dionysus, where they meet Apollo. The famous joust opposing Marsyas and Apollo occurs in this context. After the flaying of Marsyas, Apollo dedicates the lyre and the flute in the cavern belonging to Dionysus. Then, having fallen in love with Cybele, he accompanies her in her wanderings as far as the land of the Hyperboreans.[58] In Phrygia, an illness causing sterility is spreading among men and over the land. The oracle prescribes burying the body of Attis and giving Cybele the honors due to a goddess. Since the body of Attis has disappeared, the Phrygians set out to sculpt an image of the adolescent, before which they practice their lamentations and attempt to seek his favor by performing the appropriate rites. For Cybele, they first build altars, where they make annual sacrifices. Then, at Pessinos, Midas has the Phrygians construct a magnificent temple in her honor.[59]

In this last version of the story, the death of Attis is not the result of castration. There is no such theme, although it is alluded to in Pessinos, the *galli*'s metropolis, and in the eternal chastity of Marsyas. The death of Attis is also not the unfortunate outcome of a boar hunt. Instead, the young lover dies a victim of his mistress's father. His abandoned corpse disappears in the end. This detail, linked to the fact that Attis becomes the object of frequent ritual lamentations under the name Papas (see the beginning of the story), corresponds rather precisely to what Arrian reports in his work on Bithynia. There the faithful followers of Attis-Papas identified him with Zeus: climbing to mountain tops, they called him a god.[60] This type of ritual, observed by Arrian on the eastern shore of the Black Sea, extends a well-evidenced scenario from a bit further south on the banks of the Propontis. The Greeks knew of these rituals through stories of the disappearance (*aphanismos*) of Hylas, Heracles's young lover.[61] Without actually being a search for the lost Attis, Cybele's wanderings echo both Heracles' search for Hylas and, of course, the search by Demeter, or simply Mētēr, for her lost daughter.

The writing of the name Attis, although it is presented as originating in the Phrygian ritual from Pessinos, uses the assonances valued in the Greek literary tradition. This does not, however, prevent us from reading Diodoros's account as also the result of a reflection on the Phrygian ritual. It suffices to observe from this point of view that Cybele, in the economy of Diodoros's account, occupies a place that one would "normally" expect to have been given to Attis. It is Cybele who is abandoned, not Attis; she who is brought back to the palace; she who goes mad, not because the king wants to marry her off, as he would have done with Attis, but rather because he refuses to accept her union with Attis. This story is presented by Diodoros as a *logos epichorios*, and as tainted as it is by euhemerism, it does remain faithful on many basic points to Anatolian cultural tradition.

Cybele's father, Meion, thus bears the name of the ancestor of the Meionians, precursors of the royal Lydian line.[62] His name is also that of a river. Underpinning his union with Dindymene, we recognize the old binomial river-mountain,[63] ever-present in the stories where Phrygians like Marsyas, Gallos, Sangarios, and other characters give their names to rivers and accompany a Mother who is described as Berecynthian, Dindymene, Sipylene, Idaean, or Agdistis, names deriving from those of famous mountains. As for the obvious obscurity of Diodoros's text, which never mentions the child Cybele is carrying, but notes the wet nurses murdered at the same time as Attis, it seems to mark the logical limits, and consequently the awkwardness, of a story attempting to synthesize a complex, heterogeneous literary tradition. The youth Attis, the goddess's lover, cannot be said to be her son. Led, despite itself, in this direction, Diodoros's account has to remain silent on this point. Attis is not, in fact, the son of the Mater Magna. He was only exceptionally purported to be such, after a long evolution.[64]

The success of Hellenized writing specifying and mastering the irreducible otherness of Attis is found less than a generation after Diodoros in Ovid's *Fasti*.[65] The goddess loves the beautiful child encountered in the woods with a love the poet describes as chaste, although he compares it to the passionate and liturgical liaison of Aphrodite and Phaeton in Hesiod.[66] Swearing to always want to remain a child, Attis enlists himself in the exclusive service of the goddess. Yet his error, a marriage, is also a betrayal of his love. The nymph, daughter of Sangarios, for whom (literally, "in whom," *in nympha*)[67] he ceases to be what he was, dies the death of the hamadryades. The wounds that the Mother inflicts on her tree correspond to the fault committed. They equate to a sexual penetration, since *in arbore*, in verse 231 responds to *in nympha*. As for Attis, he goes mad in the nuptial chamber *(thalamos)*, whose name evokes the sanctuary of Mētēr in Kyzikos,[68] but whose roof moves back and forth like that of the palace of Cadmos in the *Bacchantes*. He escapes to the top of Dindymus. Hallucinating, he sees flaming torches and whips and believes himself to be hotly pursued by the "Palestinian goddesses."[69] He lacerates his body with a sharp stone, practicing on himself the type of bloody mortification that the *galli* will later imitate. He lets his long hair down, thus designating the spoiling of his betrayed virginity,[70] and is heard uttering: "I deserved it, I am paying exactly for my error with the price of my blood. Oh! May the parts [of my body] that have made me do wrong, yes, may they disappear!" He removes the burden from his groin, and no sign of his virility remains.[71]

It was a complete castration, ablation of both penis and testicles, as appears to have been practiced by the *galli* in Rome.[72] This rite was performed in a trance state, in enthusiastic fervor, as part of a ritual where the "candidate," encouraged by the other participants, was under the effect of the flute music, incense burning, and drunkenness.[73] The instrument used for the self-mutilation was a Samian potsherd (*samia testa*), which must have been particularly sharp.[74] Attis's castration, as Ovid notes, served as the unfortunate example for the effeminate, long-haired priests of Cybele. Although situated in the region of Mount Dindymus near Kyzikos, like its Hellenistic models, the myth concerned a fact that the Roman tradition, and Ovid himself,[75] connected to the region of the high plains of Phrygia. This story of Attis's betrayal in marrying the nymph appears to be the aspect most generally recognized in Rome until the time of the Antonines.

The Pessinontian Myth

A new version of the Phrygian myth of Attis was specifically presented as a story from the city of Pessinos on the origin of the cult practiced by the *galli*. It appears in our sources from the second century of the present era. This elaborated version amplified Ovid's emphasis and also referred to information from other traditions. All in all, it evidenced a significant transformation in the religious attitudes concerning Attis and the Mother of the gods. We know about two of these accounts. They are of unequal length but are, on the whole, remarkably similar in nature: one is by Pausanias and the other by the third-century Christian theologian Arnobius.

Everything about him leads us to believe that Pausanias was originally from western Anatolia, and more precisely from the region of Mount Sipylos or Pergamon, where the memory of ancient Phrygian stories remained intact. Pausanias handed down a story he specified was the *logos epichorios*, the local, Phrygian version from Pessinos, as opposed to the popular Greek version.[76] While sleeping, Zeus spreads his seed on the Earth. Fertilized, this seed produces a bisexual monster, Agdistis. Terrorized, the gods cut off the male parts of the monster. From the severed genitals, an almond tree springs up, bearing ripe fruit. The daughter of the Sangarios River plucks an almond and places it in the folds of her dress. The nut disappears and she becomes pregnant. An incredibly beautiful child, Attis, is born, but abandoned and left to be raised by a goat. Agdistis falls madly in love with Attis, but his relations intervene to separate them. He is sent to Pessinos to marry the king's daughter. While the wedding songs are being sung, Agdistis suddenly appears. Attis is seized with *mania* and cuts off his genitals. The king of Pessinos follows suit. Agdistis repents, but his regrets are too late: Attis is dead. Zeus grants Agdistis's wish that no part of Attis's body will ever rot or disintegrate.

Pausanias wrote the seventh book of his *Description of Greece* in approximately 170 C.E. We have Arnobius to thank for a second version of the same myth, recorded in his *Adversus nationes* between 300 and 310 C.E. However, Arnobius does not refer to Pausanias as his source, and his own version is much more developed than the first.[77] Arnobius instead cites Timotheos, "a distinguished theologian," whose account was confirmed by other no less savant writers on the Great Mother of the gods and her rituals. Timotheos ostensibly let it be understood that he took this story, which Arnobius entitles *origo*, from nearly inaccessible books on the "antiquities" and the practice of the mysteries. One of the authors evoked by Arnobius in addition to Timotheos is a certain Valerius, qualified as a pontifex. We know nothing about this Valerius.[78] Stephanos of Byzantium informs us instead that Alexander Polyhistor, a Greek mythographer living in Rome in the first century B.C.E., spoke of Attis and Gallos in his work *On Phrygia*. Both were supposedly punished, and the second went on to establish himself next to the river to which he gave his name. Those who cut off their genitals (the *galli*) also took their name from him. According to this same passage, Alexander Polyhistor was citing Timotheos and was probably, therefore, the theologian mentioned by Arnobius, given the context.[79] It is generally accepted that this Timotheos character was a specialist in the mysteries. Tacitus calls him a Eumolpid [one of the priestly family in Attica, descendants of the Thracian bard Eumolpos, the first hierophant and first to introduce the Eleusinian mysteries] and Plutarch calls him an exegete. He collaborated on the adaptation of the Eleusinian religion to the Alexandrine cult of Serapis with the famous priest Manetho under Ptolemy I Soter in approximately 300 B.C.E.[80] Therefore, the account handed down by Arnobius first goes back to Hellenistic sources connected with the Phrygian mysteries. Notwithstanding several discrepancies owing to the occasional use of sources other than Timotheos, this account demonstrates remarkable consistency.[81] Strongly influenced by Greek theological reflections at its roots, it is nevertheless colored later on by preoccupations inherent in the imperial period, as well as by Arnobius's Christianized writing. This complexity calls for an analysis on several levels. Before beginning such an analysis, it is advisable to introduce the content of this version, which most certainly constitutes the most important narrative document we have on Attis.

The Mother of the gods, according to this story, is a stone from the same rock from which Deucalion and Pyrrha took the stones that gave birth to postdiluvian humanity. The original rock, named Agdos, is located in Phrygia. The Mother, a stone extracted from this rock, was animated by divine will. Zeus attempted in vain to rape her. The sperm of the god rejected by the Mother spread over the original rock, from which a violent, bisexual monster named Agdistis was born. Agdistis threatened both gods and men. Dionysos managed to get him drunk and put him to sleep and then attach his sexual organs to the soles of his feet. Once awake, Agdistis springs up and castrates himself. Blood gushes out in great quantities, which the earth absorbs, along with bits of flesh. A pomegranate tree thereupon springs up, loaded with fruit.[82] Fascinated by the beauty of this tree, the daughter of Sangarios, eponym of the river flowing near Pessinos, gathers a fruit, which she places in the fold of her dress.[83] She becomes pregnant. Her father, believing her to have been dishonored, locks her up and attempts to starve her to death. But the Mother of the gods nourishes her with pomegranates and other vegetable food. The daughter of the river gives birth to a beautiful child, which Sangarios exposes to the elements. The child, Attis, is found by a certain Phorbas, who raises him on goat's milk.[84] The Mother of the gods loves Attis. Agdistis, although he has lost his virility, also loves Attis, homosexually. Attis hunts with Agdistis. King Midas of Pessinos, in his attempt to save the child from such an injurious union, offers his daughter to Attis in marriage. Lest any importunate arrival interrupt the joy of the marriage ceremony, Midas has the doors of the citadel closed. The Mother of the gods penetrates into the city by raising the walls with her head. Agdistis enters after her and instigates fury and madness in all of the guests. Attis takes hold of Agdistis's flute and goes insane. At the height of the bacchanal, he jumps up gesticulating, then cuts off his genitals under a pine tree, declaring: "Keep these for yourself, Agdistis, these things that made you foment such great perturbations of dangerous madness."[85] Life drains from him as the blood flows, but the Mother of the gods retrieves the organs. She washes them and covers them with earth, after having dressed them up in the costume of the dead. Violets grow from the blood strewn about, with which the pine tree is crowned. The young bride, named Ia ("Violet") by the pontifex Valerius, commits suicide, but not before having covered Attis's chest with soft wool and wept along with Agdistis. As she dies, Ia's blood is transformed into purple violets. The Mother of the gods also breaks down weeping. Her tears give birth to an almond tree, signifying the bitterness of mourning. She carries the pine under which Attis lost his virility into her cavern and adds her lamentations to those of Agdistis. She beats her chest and circles the now immobilized tree. Zeus does not resurrect Attis, as Agdistis requests, but he grants that Attis's body shall not decay; that his hair shall continue to grow; and that his smallest finger shall remain alive, incessantly moving of its own accord. Satisfied, Agdistis dedicates the body at Pessinos, where he has it honored by special priests in annual ceremonies.

First of all, we must emphasize that this story of Phrygian inspiration began to be developed in the form in which we have read it, at the earliest, at the very end of the fourth century B.C.E., in a Greek context. Many aspects of the Pessinontian story manifest a preoccupation with connecting Phrygian tradition to classical mythology. In particular, the oracular involvement of Themis is related to an allusion to Deucalion and to the new humanity born from stones that the survivors after the flood had thrown over their shoulders.[86] On the other hand, the ways in which Agdistis is conceived seem to echo the well-known Athenian tradition, of which Timotheos is an authorized representative,[87] involving the Athenians' ancestor Erichthonios being born from the Earth, fertilized by the seed of Hephaestos, who is chasing after Athena. The theme of the transfer of maternity, from the Mother who rejects Zeus's advances to the rock Agdos, fertilized with the god's semen, is told in terms evoking an ancient Greek theme of autochthony. The fruit of this "displaced" union nevertheless holds a very different meaning, depending upon whether one considers it in the Athenian context, where Erichthonios is a human ancestor, or in the Pessinontian context, where Agdistis, before being stopped, is a cosmic monster who threatens the gods.

Echos of the Second Millennium

Walter Burkert and other researchers have demonstrated that Arnobius's account can also be analyzed in a convincing way by comparing the episode centered on Agdistis (the sequence leading from the conception to the castration of the monster) with an Anatolian myth of the second millennium, the Hurrian myth of Ullikumi, adversary of the sovereign god Teshub, the functional equivalent of Zeus. Ullikumi was born from the union of Kumarbi, the Hurrian Kronos, ousted by Teshub, with a rock. Placed on the shoulders of the giant Ubelluri, who held up the sky, earth, and sea, the monster begins to grow and grow, until one day he is brought down, separated from his base of support by cutting his feet off with an old copper knife that had originally separated the sky from the earth.

While the Hurrian myth of the monster born from stone prefigures some of the aspects of the Anatolian story of Agdistis, it still has extended connections to twentieth-century legends from the Caucasus.[88] If the entire comparative research is considered as a whole, we can see that behind the myth of Ullikumi, there is an echo of the Hurrian story of succession of heavenly kingdoms, to which Hesiod's theogony responds.[89] As an aside, this unknown part of Sir James Frazer's research resolves, but from an entirely different perspective, the problem he introduced in *The Golden Bough* relating to a possible relationship between the *galli*'s castration in the myth of Agdistis and Attis and the castration of Ouranos in Hesiod.[90]

It is undeniable that this vast group of structural connections appears to be reinforced by the redundancy of precise narrative elements indicating a certain continuity. We are therefore able to postulate the transmission of a heritage of narrative propositions, conveyed in a discourse in slow mutation over more than three thousand years in a relatively limited geographical area. It appears somewhat vain to attempt to establish a strict genealogy of these stories, however, since each comes from a specific cultural field and is determined by very different emphases. It would be useful to underscore the difficulties of a simultaneously diachronic and transcultural perspective in a given symbolic sector. Far from proving the permanence here of a system of thought or behavior, postulating the continuity of a religion of the "Great Mother" from Çatalhöyük to the taurobolic altars of the Vatican, the pursuit of such a path would at most allow us to state the recurrence and the reuse of certain mythic formulas, both iconic and ritual, in a space where direct contact and borrowing cannot be doubted. For this type of analysis, we should observe that the precise ways of "neutralizing" Agdistis — drunkenness and being tied up, but not, it is true, self-castration — are evidenced, not in the Hurrian myths of Ullikumi and the heavenly kingdom, but in other stories from the second millennium B.C.E. These other stories were also Hittite, but of purely Anatolian origin, such as the traditions connected with the dragon Illuyanka, another adversary of the storm god. From Illuyanka, we are immediately led to Typhon. Thus, we can clearly identify certain narrative elements present in Anatolian mythology of the second millennium that are also found in the Greek myth of the succession of divine sovereignties, in certain traditions concerning Typhon, and in the episode concerning the generation of Agdistis in the Pessinontian myth reported by Pausanias and Arnobius. What circulates and is handed down appears to be a group of independent systems of thought. In this sense, one might rather speak of fragmented memory.

If we seek a real Near Eastern illustration of the meaning of the traditions concerning Attis, it is not to the apparent structures of these narratives, but rather to the central figure of the *gallus* that we should turn. This figure has real precursors, not directly in Anatolia, but in the ancient Mesopotamian traditions. Here again, Walter Burkert leads the way. Burkert analyzes Arnobius's story in his book *Structure and History in Greek Mythology and Ritual*,[91] where he underscores that the myth of the Mother, Agdistis, and Attis is completely oriented toward the figure of the emasculated *gallus*, the Mother's priest. He then suggests that the entrance of the goddess into the city to stop the marriage is strikingly close to the Mesopotamian story in the Sumerian version describing the return of Inanna liberated from the world of the dead. The goddess returns to life escorted by infernal demons, the *gallu*, who will end up seizing the vegetation god Tammuz, or Dumuzi, to return him to the Underworld.[92] Burkert thus proposes, in the form of a hypothesis to be developed, that these infernal *gallu* should be recognized as the temporary companions of the goddess and as both the semantically and etymologically distant origin of the Phrygian *galli* who were companions of Agdistis-Cybele. In a note, he adds that, by strange coincidence, a category of Mesopotamian priests were called *kalu;* in Sumerian, *gala*.[93] These priests, tympanum players, were involved in bull sacrifice, Burkert notes, and *taurobolē* (bull sacrifice) and the tympanum are also elements present in the cult of Mētēr. A careful review of what we know reveals that the path of inquiry thus embarked on by Burkert does not pan out as such, but as a working hypothesis sprung from fertile intuition, it can nevertheless lead us to a very interesting result. The major difficulty comes from the fact that the Sumerian *gallu* who pursue Tammuz are neither priests nor eunuchs. As for the *kalu* or *gala*, except for the illusion of a relative homophony and the fact that they play the tambourine, a relatively commonplace instrument in the Mesopotamian religious context, there is nothing to connect them with the Mother's *galli*.

However, Burkert's intuition has the merit of attracting our attention to a particular type of character. It gains from being extended, without any etymological pretensions, in the direction of another category of Mesopotamian priests, the *assinnu, galatur,* and *kurgarru*, who were clearly the functional precursors of the Mother's *galli*. These individuals, whose priesthood or métier, as Jean Bottéro puts it, constituted an art learned through true apprenticeship, had a sacred function. They participated in liturgical rites, during which they were costumed and masked. They played music, sang, and danced, most often in ceremonies dedicated to Ishtar, the goddess with whom they were most closely linked. The erotic nature of their ritual activity was manifest. These masculine transvestites were associated with the courtesans and prostitutes who devoted themselves to Ishtar. They are described as having dedicated themselves to passive homosexuality, and some of them were eunuchs or had been castrated. They were spoken of as "not being males," or as "half men," and their behavior was effeminate. As Bottéro discovered, "as an institution" the role of these sacred prostitutes was recognized as necessary to civilization, but "as individuals" these same characters were the object of deep collective contempt.[94] Their mythic prototype was Asu-shu-namir, a being neither male nor female, created by Ea to search for Ishtar in Hell, in the Accadian version of the descent into the Underworld. Obliged to release her prey, the queen of Hell, Ereshkigal, pronounced a curse on this character, who proved to be the mythic model for many successors: "From now on your means of sustenance will be that produced by the plows of the town, and your drink that taken from the canals in the town. You will only stay in the buttresses of the ramparts and only live at the thresholds of gates. Drunkards and thirsty men will slap you around as they please."[95]

Note, then, the completely ambiguous status of this mythic character and his like. Mendicants condemned to lead a beggarly existence for having brought back life to Earth, they were inscribed in a transcultural series of analogous person-ages, including Scythian eunuchs, the *galli* of the Roman empire, the *hijras* of the Mother goddess in India, North American berdaches, and the *skoptzy* in Russia (a Christian sect that practiced castration). For them, transexuality was both an object of disdain and part of a supernatural capacity to surpass the limits desig-nated by the cosmic and human order.[96]

Ancient Readings

Although it emerged on the ancient Near Eastern horizon, the myth of Attis took shape in a Greek context. It is therefore by the standards of that context that the comparative interpretations should in the first place be assessed. Let us return for a moment to Frazer, the precursor in this domain. He proposed an interpreta-tion assimilating the destiny of the "dying god" to that of vegetation. This view was apparently prefigured by classical speculations by Lucretius and Varro, to name the most ancient of them. These two authors, who say nothing about Attis, but who knew of the *galli*, saw in Cybele the Mater Magna Deum, an allegory of the land productive of animal and vegetable life. There is, however, no mention of a resurrection of Attis in our sources prior to the third-century Roman presby-ter Hippolytus and Firmicus Maternus in the fourth century, and it is further-more not found in the account that the latter cite — in which Attis well and truly dies — but in their commentaries, which adduce "physical," which is to say, allegorical, interpretations. As Firmicus Maternus puts it: "It is supposed that Attis is specifically identified with the fruit of cereals; and the punishment he endured is supposed to be identified with what the harvester armed with his sickle inflicts on the ripe grain. He is supposed to have died during the grain harvest and to live again, according to the annual cycle, once the grains are reintegrated into the earth."[97]

We are not familiar with the pagan sources used by Firmicus Maternus. According to Porphyry, Attis means the flower (and not the spike or the ear), which dies before the grain appears.[98] For him, in any case, it seems that the grain is represented by Adonis and not by a revived Attis. It is therefore only between the third and fourth centuries, and most likely under Christian influence, that the ideology of Attis's resurrection was developed. As formulated by the emperor Julian and Sallustius, the last pagan version of the myth ignores resurrection. Attis, after his madness and castration, simply returns to live with the Mother of the gods.[99] There is an evolution, but it involves forgetting the death episode. In reading the older version handed down by Arnobius, this oversight appears to be the result of what was originally presented as the rejection of an irreparable death, followed by a cult dedicated to a corpse with supernatural characteristics. If myth is finally led to silence the death of Attis, it is to emphasize the dedication to the goddess.

Only some of the commentaries of the myth explicitly account for the resurrection. The account itself, in its different versions, remains very close to the tradition inaugurated by the sources of Pausanias and Arnobius. In Julian and Sallustius, the Mother of the gods, who is born without a mother, discovers Attis abandoned on the banks of the River Gallos. Seduced by the beauty of one who grows like a flower, she loves him and forbids him to love anyone else. But he descends into a cavern, where he begins an affair with the nymph. Driven mad, he mutilates himself. The Mother abandons her anger and summons Attis to return to her. The commentary that Sallustius adds to the account is clear: death, in this story, does not occur as a result of castration, but before it, and allegorically, as the consequence of the abandonment of the immutable divinity, the Mother, in favor of the generation that embodies the future, the nymph. As a renunciation of the power of reproduction, castration instead allows the divine to be reintegrated. In this interpretation, there is no explicit death episode—it is simply mute on the subject—and one detects here the desire of certain writers, who were acutely aware of the Christian problematic, for the traditional account, in which there was absolutely no resurrection theme, to concur allegorically with their own interpretation of the ritual of the holy week of Attis, developed later under the empire. Thus, Sallustius, in articulating the various episodes of the myth and how they were allegorized into the various stages of the ritual (*canna intrat, arbor intrat, sanguem, hilaria*) was able to conclude as follows:

> We celebrate a festival according to the following rituals: in the first place, since we too have fallen from the sky and are living with the nymph, we remain prostrate and abstain from bread, as well as any heavy and impure food, since both are contrary to the soul. Next, the mutilation of a tree and fasting mark our ablation of the last stage of generation. After that, we nourish ourselves with milk to mark our rebirth. Finally, there are manifestations of joy, crowns, and something of a reascent to the gods.[100]

In the most ancient Roman ritual dedicated to Cybele, it was the *lavatio* performed on the image of the goddess, and not the resurrection of Attis, that ended the Mother's mourning. This concurs with the unavoidable fact of the Arnobian version: Agdistis is not granted that Attis be brought back to life.[101]

The destiny of Attis's dead body has only rarely been studied by modern scholars. Hugo Hepding refers simply to several stories concerning bodies miraculously preserved from deterioration,[102] citing a study by Erwin Rohde on the Sleepers of Sardinia (the nine Thestiades), as well as Christian traditions relating to the bodies of Saint Catherine of Bologna and Saint Augustine. Although Rohde does not mention Attis in this study, Hepding suggests a possible interpretation by citing him, given that the "Rohdian" theme par excellence is disappearance and immortality after a divine rapture (see his *Psyche: The Cult of Souls and Belief in Immortality Among the Greeks*).[103] Is this not perhaps a framework in which to explain Attis's destiny? The founding heroes, such as Rohde presents them, do not die. They sleep. Or rather, like the "Happy Ones," they are taken away to live with the gods, in a superhuman afterlife. Such a perspective on the myth of Attis is not without pertinence, provided we stick to what is explicit—a refusal to accept death—and do not orient the analysis toward the theme of becoming immortal or divine. Sometimes, notably in Diodoros, the corpse even disappears.

Is it a question of a cadaver that cannot rot or of a lost body? It appears that these two propositions are on the same level, equivalent in their refusal of the inevitable. The texts unanimously convey that Attis ends up dead. Most definitely dead. Resurrection only becomes a factor under Christian influence. The incorruptibility of the corpse, hair that continues to grow, and a little finger that lives on and moves are paltry substitutes. Agdistis's attempt fails; it runs up against Zeus's refusal.

Neither W. H. Roscher[104] nor the article on Attis in the Pauly-Wissowa *Realencyclopädie*[105] say anything about this paradoxical corpse. In his commentary on Pausanias 7.17, Frazer contents himself with referring to Arnobius, and he adds nothing in his *Adonis, Attis, Osiris*. The *Realencyclopädie* article on Agdistis mentions the hair that keeps growing and the moving finger, but without any analysis.[106] Even Franz Cumont remains silent on this issue.[107] There is nothing in Henri Graillot or M. P. Nilsson. Recent authors are just as reserved.[108] Otto Gruppe is one of the rare scholars to give us something to reflect on.[109] He proposes interrogatively that we see in this body that cannot rot, with a moving finger, an object of mantic observations deposited in an oracular sanctuary. As is often the case in Gruppe, the genesis of this hypothesis is complex, if not ambiguous. The idea of the oracle is suggested to him because of the incorruptibility of the body, which would evoke the idea of sleep more than death. From sleep, we are led to incubation. As for the movement of the little finger, it would be connected to a kind of divine observation. M. Fritze, in a 1909 article, believed he had identified a remarkable finger on a coin from Kyzikos from the imperial period representing a statue of the cult of Attis.[110] As for Maarten Vermaseren, he wrongly attributes a sexual interpretation of the finger to Hepding,[111] an interpretation in vogue in general, rather than that of any particular author. (Vermaseren backs up this idea with quotation marks in his summary of the myth in his 1977 study *Cybele and Attis*, in which he speaks of "the 'little finger' [remaining] alive" and moving continuously.)

In the meantime, another finger had caught the attention of researchers. After committing matricide, Orestes had cut it off to satisfy the Erinyes, who were pursuing him in his madness. The tomb of this finger used to be visited in Arcadia during the time of Pausanias.[112] In 1869, the folklorist Felix Liebrecht sought to explain this "finger tomb" by means of parallels taken from popular European beliefs, in particular German and Norman lore.[113] Inter alia, he cited this passage by Amélie Bosquet: "In lower Normandy, it was believed that dead children stuck their arms out of their tombs when in life they had raised a hand against their parents. A maternal correction was needed to purge their sin, and the mothers, with merciful care, would go to whip these small tormented cadavers in the cemeteries."[114] Liebrecht added that another explanation of Orestes' finger tomb could be advanced: a legend of origins might have been grafted onto a misinterpreted object, or one that was no longer understood. A slightly used Arcadian

Hermes or better yet a stone phallus on a tomb could have given rise to the account of the finger tomb. Other ancient and modern parallels exist: Dionysus planting a phallus on the tomb of Prosymnos, images of Priapus next to tombs, funerary phalluses in Norway.

Commenting on the passage from Pausanias mentioning Orestes' finger tomb, Frazer refers to Liebrecht but prefers a more economical and careful explanation of the Greek phenomenon. The self-mutilation practiced by a matricide is an expiatory sacrifice. The finger functions here as a substitute for the person, a part for the whole. Frazer recalls a variation of the myth of Lykourgos, who attacked Dionysus and only regained his sanity after cutting off his own extremities.[115]

Frazer's interpretation of Orestes' finger places us on the path leading to the interpretation of Attis's finger. The death of Orestes' finger, a part equivalent to the whole body, whose tomb is shown, is enough for the Erinyes, who turn from black (irascible, quick-tempered) to white (placated, soothed). In the case of Attis, the process is analogous, but inverted: only the finger escapes the death of the body, and it therefore represents Attis alive. The dead man's hair continues to grow and his little finger continues to move constantly as a concession, which becomes a simulacrum of life, accorded to a corpse that will never decompose. It is a matter of emblematic elements referring to the lost wholeness of the living body. Abundant hair is in fact a traditional attribute of the *gallus*,[116] whereas the finger, *daktulos* in Greek, might designate Attis, the companion of the Idaean Mother, as one of the Idaean *dactyli*.

To measure the distance separating the problematics described by Julian and Sallustius from the problem raised by those who developed the Hellenistic version of the same myth, we should return to the text by Arnobius. Michel Meslin[117] and especially Ezio Pellizer[118] have, I believe, demonstrated that it is first of all a matter of representing the relationship between the sexes. The *fabula* (fable), as Pellizer shows, is "a complex apparatus, articulated in a symmetrical fashion, with the function of alternatively exploring exclusionary hypotheses. Sometimes the exclusion concerns the female gender, sometimes the male. Through the atrociously complicated results of all these hypotheses, the fable seems to strive to define the norms of integrating the two sexes in the reproductive act. . . . It is a matter of observing the consequences of a global and symmetrical negation of the masculine and feminine qualities, as well as their possible union. This appears to be the nuclear meaning, the problem at the heart of the whole story." Pellizer is not concerned with the ritual, which involved what he calls the "conclusive segments" of the story. These had the subordinate function of accounting for a variety of botanical, institutional, and ritual phenomena. Others, however (and without contradicting the semiotic approach), have read in this story the myth of the foundation of a cult. This religion was the cult of Pessinos, which spread as earlier as 204 B.C.E. to Rome through the *galli's* practice. The myth refers to Pessinos precisely in terms of the meaning of these practices. Carsten Colpe proposes that in this story, and the ritual following it, there is an underlying nostalgia for the lost unity of androgyny.[119] That is why Agdistis, after his castration, actively pursues Attis, who would represent his masculine side, since he was indirectly engendered by him. It is true that we can find no trace of this nostalgia in the account as we read it. Agdistis's double sexuality is negative and clearly condemned. As for the union of Agdistis, after his castration, with Attis, this is not a union of male and female. The doubling of Mētēr and Agdistis is not, in fact, a doubling of the same twice over. Agdistis, although he bears the old Pessinontian (female) name of the Mother, becomes masculine in the versions by Pausanias and Arnobius. Thus, we conclude, in terms of the ritual fact proposed by all the evidence on Agdistis, that there was a reversal of the character. One might expect that, first conceived of as bisexual and then deprived of his masculine sex organs, he became purely and simply female, a double of the Mother. By insisting on designating him, despite this, as male, the words of the story suggest apprehending in this being who castrates himself, albeit involuntarily, the realization of the impossible ideal of the *gallus:* a male truly becoming female, a totally successful sex change (i.e., a berdache). This explains why, despite the fact that he was really, and not metaphorically, endowed with female genitals, his relationship with Attis is presented as being homoerotic.

Ezio Pellizer grasps this very well: what the king condemned was the union of a castrated person visibly endowed with feminine attributes with a young man who had just reached marriageable age, that is, the age at which a boy should no longer be the object of loving attentions from another male. This allows us to understand the expression applied to Agdistis, lover of Attis: *blandus adulto comes.*[120] We can then read a version of the myth handed down by Servius in this perspective:

> Attis, a beautiful child, while he was presiding over the rituals of the Great Mother, became the object of loving desire of the king of the city. But when he understood the violence that the king wanted to do to him, he ran away and hid in the forest. When he was discovered and saw the violence he was going to be forced to submit

to, he cut off the genitals of the seducer, who, as he lay dying, cut off the same body part on the child. When the ministers of the Great Mother found him half dead under a pine tree, he was transported to the Temple of the Goddess in a vain effort to revive him. When he died, he was buried. So that his memory remain eternal, the Great Mother established annual mourning in her rituals and took the pine tree under which he fell under her protection. Finally, she established that those faithful to her [the *cultores*] would cut off their virile parts and these were called the *archigalli.*[121]

As surprising as it may seem, this version presents the essential aspects of the propositions constituting Arnobius's account:

(a) The opposition between the space of the city and that of the forest, an opposition like that between the king and the goddess, but presented in an inverted relationship. Attis has a religious and chaste relationship with the Mother inside the city. It is in the forest where he escapes and is pursued by the king that the castration takes place;

(b) The homosexual relationship, with, once again, a reversal: while the version by Arnobius has Attis responding to Agdistis's love, a goddess manifested underneath the features of a perverted character, and while King Midas, by locking the young man within the city walls wanted to put an end to this "scandal," Servius's version attributes the homoerotic desire to the king of the city by in some way conferring Agdistis's role on him.

Everything occurs as if the goddess, in her purely maternal guise, had a solely religious relationship with the young man who was her main priest. The presence of the homoerotic theme in this version, which ignores the Mētēr-Agdistis doubling, leads one to think that this doubling is not the result of any awkwardness on the part of Arnobius, but rather, on the contrary, an intentional feature of the story.

If one returns to the narrative as told by Arnobius to consider it in terms of the most obvious articulations — in terms of transformation opposing the initial situation to the final situation — one notes that we move from a state where Agdistis is characterized by a double sexuality to a state where, from bisexual turned man-woman, he goes hunting with the young man, Attis. As for Attis, he goes from being a late-blooming adolescent who hunts with Agdistis to being a bridegroom. Yet the marriage is a wedding injected with madness and reintroduces the theme of sexual confusion. The king and his companions witness the mutilation leading to the death of the wedding couple. This destiny is commemorated by an annual ritual under the direction of a clergy established by Agdistis. In Pessinos, this clergy not only fulfills a priestly role but also constitutes the main tribunal in this theocratic state, directed by Attises. Whereas the castration of Agdistis functions to reestablish order by weakening, without managing to specify this, a being who had up until then been a cosmic menace, Attis's castration instead functions to put an end to his madness, while reestablishing the ambiguity. This is specified as taking place in a well-established location: in the city, with its ramparts, its closed gates, and its king organizing the marriage ceremony. From then on, everything seems to be built on the opposition between the savage and the civilized, between hunting and marriage. Yet this Hellenistic version of the story not only makes an inventory of deviances in terms of which a Greek order is defined but also signals the insufficiencies through which this apparently dominant order would be subverted from within. In fact, this order is effectively subverted in a ritual in Pessinos that turns out to be truly connected to power.

Entitled *origo*, this story concerns the origin of a political system directed by the *galli*, while addressing itself to those Greeks and Romans who asked about the unusual rites of the adherents of a sovereign Cybele. No longer a justification of a norm aiming at the reproduction of the social body through marriage and the procreation of legitimate children,[122] the myth was, nonetheless, a justification of a political norm. In a "city" displaced into a barbarian context, the myth of Attis expressed an ideal that remained the prerogative of a scandalous and dominant mystical minority: the *galli* and the Pessinontian Attises.[123]

CHAPTER FOUR

The Mother's Entrance into the Roman Republic

The Sybilline Oracle and Senatorial Debates

At the end of the third century B.C.E., a well-documented period in history, the Great Idaean Mother arrived in Rome. She was towed in up the Tiber River following a voyage from Pergamon, the capital of Attalus's kingdom in Asia Minor. Summoned by the Senate and set up on the Palatine Hill, the goddess came into the city accompanied by an exotic priesthood, who remained by her side. She was immediately associated with the scandalous practices of the *galli*, her oriental acolytes. Although well-tolerated and even ritually indispensable, these practices were usually kept at a safe distance from the official procedures of a renewed cult tailored to the use of the Roman people according to norms dictated by custom and inspired by Hellenic models. Our task is to investigate how the one whose official name was and remained Mater Magna Idaea Deum (MMID = "Great Idaean Mother of the Gods") was integrated into Rome.[1] We know that her introduction included references to her Anatolian origin, her status as an already Hellenized goddess, and her being identified as an ancestral Roman goddess whose cult went back to the legend of Trojan origins. Just what importance was accorded to each aspect of her background defines the subject of our evaluation.

The story begins in 205 B.C.E., in the Senate, at the end of the Second Punic War. At this time, there was a discussion of reports of "frequent falling rocks" over the course of the year, a phenomenon that had since become widespread. In the mind of the Roman citizen, this caused a particularly acute feeling of religious fear. After evaluating the rumor, and in light of its rigor and concern for controlling what we call public opinion, the Senate decided to respond to these signs in an appropriate manner. It proceeded to do what the technical vocabulary of the Roman region designated with the verb *procurare*, to "take care" of these wondrous occurrences by asking that the Sibylline books be consulted by the decemvirate. This commission of ten then returned to the Assembly after having secretly composed an oracle (a *carmen*) in Greek acrostics. According to this oracle, it was necessary to go to Pessinos to find the Idaean Mother in order to rid Italian lands of the foreign invader.[2] The city fathers connected this prophecy to earlier, analogous ones along the same lines. They connected it to a prophecy from Delphi and yet another oracle concerning a man named Scipio.[3] The deliberation centered on discovering how to give a favorable follow-up to this group of supernatural warnings, *fata, omina, oracula, portenda.*

The introduction of the god of healing, Asclepios (latinized as Aesculapius), was recalled, an encouraging precedent because it involved the naturalization of a foreign divinity without a prior treaty between Rome and his city of origin, Epidauros. It was remembered too that on the Greek side, King Attalus was waging a war against Philip V of Macedonia, just like the Romans, making him a de facto ally. Attalus was Pergamon, that is, the power closest to both Pessinos and the Trojan Mount Ida, which the decemvirs' *carmen* designated as the Mother's place of origin.

The Senate thus decided to send a very aristocratic delegation to Pergamon.[4] However, before meeting with Attalus, the delegation would first make a detour to Delphi, where a new oracle, meant to clarify the first, still in Greek, was pronounced and a new interpretation was offered. It turned out that it was not enough simply to bring the goddess to Rome; it was necessary that the *vir optimus*, the most virtuous man in the city, be found to welcome her there. Conceivably following a new debate on the interpretation, once in Pergamon, the delegation obtained from Attalus a sacred stone from Pessinos in Upper Phrygia, where the inhabitants called it the Mother of the gods.

Why Pessinos? The Greek aorist infinitive *pessein*, from which the name Pessinos is believed to derive, signifies "to fall," and it thus evoked the idea of a fall to

Hellenized ears, which tied in with the original portent of the falling rocks. Decades ago, moreover, following Pergamon's intervention, the settlement at Pessinos had come under Galatian domination. So, in speaking of the foreign invader, the decemvirs' *carmen* was evidently alluding to the Gauls, allies of Hannibal and the Carthaginians.

However, while en route to Rome with the goddess (or rather the stone representing her), the delegation sent an emissary, Valerius Falto, to hasten on ahead and alert the Senate of the need to find the *vir optimus*. More speechifying followed, during a session dedicated to organizing the reception of the Idaean Mother.[5] The young Publius Cornelius Scipio, called Nasica, was selected as the *vir optimus*, and he proceeded to Ostia accompanied by all the Roman matrons — the perfect intermediaries because, as "indispensable strangers," in John Scheid's phrase,[6] they were welcoming a goddess who was both ancestral and foreign, a "Trojan" Mother presented as the divine paradigm of their own role in the city.

The Young Man and the Matron

The young Scipio was charged with conveying the stone off the ship in which it had traveled with the delegation and entrusting it, once ashore, to the matrons, who would pass it from one to the other in a procession leading to the sanctuary of Victory, the temporary home of the goddess on the Palatine.[7]

This is when the enigmatic Claudia Quinta appears in Livy's account.[8] This matron — to others, a vestal virgin — saw her dubious reputation (*dubia fama*) transformed by a burst of indisputable respectability (*clariorem pudicitiam*) in the shape of a scrupulously performed ritual service (*tam religioso ministerio*). Livy gives no other details of this service, which Roman tradition presents as a miraculous feat. What Livy does say, however, is enough for us to understand the basic facts. The matrons in Rome acted as spokespersons for the land as a nation.[9] Doubts about the chastity of any one of them, like doubts about the chastity of a vestal virgin, could become a problem affecting the very foundation of the city. Claudia Quinta's *dubia fama* echoed doubts about the chastity of the mother of the twins who founded Rome, Rhea Silvia (whose name in Greek, be it said in passing, calls to mind the Mother of the gods, often identified with the Cretan Rhea, mother of the Olympians).[10] The matrons were thus all concerned here, and Claudia Quinta's ritual test endorsed them in some religious sense. The young man, on the other hand, was by definition beyond suspicion, having been recognized as the *vir optimus*. He could therefore transmit the image of the divine Mother to the human mothers so that they in turn could introduce her into Rome.

Other sources inform us that this medium-sized stone, which a man or woman could lift without any trouble, was black. Apparently, it was a meteorite,[11] and it was later embedded in the face of the cult statue. The goddess was kept for thirteen years in the Victory sanctuary on the Palatine Hill, until the completion of her own sanctuary, also built on the Palatine, and dedicated by the *praetor urbanus* M. Iunius Brutus on April 10 in 191 B.C.E.[12] The decision to build this sanctuary had been made as early as 204 B.C.E., the year of the goddess's arrival in Rome, after a decree in the Senate.[13] The location was designated by the censors Marcus Livius and Caius Claudius, in the consulate of Marcus Cornelius Cethegus and Publius Sempronius Tuditanus.[14]

Livy does not emphasize the Claudia Quinta episode at all; instead, he underscores the role of the matrons responsible for carrying the goddess to her residence on the Palatine. The young Scipio was only in charge of the very initial contact, carrying the divine idol ashore and passing it along to the female community. Diodoros Siculos, who wrote his *Bibliothēkē historikē* before Livy, alludes to a scenario where the male and female roles seem to be divided in a more clearcut fashion. The whole Roman collectivity is supposed to receive the sacred objects coming from Pessinos. Thus, there is the men's group led by Scipio, the best man, and the women's group, led by Valeria, the most virtuous. In this version, Valeria plays the role that usually belongs to Claudia Quinta.[15]

Ovid also emphasizes this balance. Scipio only participates in the *Fasti* at the entrance to Rome, near the Capena gate, in the procession accompanying the goddess's chariot.[16] Before embarking on the story of Claudia Quinta's miraculous feat, the poet specifies that in order to welcome the Mother, the people went to Ostia accompanied by the corps of *equites* and the Senate, along with a procession of mothers, daughters, daughters-in-law, and vestal virgins.[17]

There are therefore differences in the details given in the various versions. These show some flexibility in the manner in which the Romans organized the Megalesia during the April festivals dedicated to the Mother. Ovid explicitly described the festivals as theatrical representations of this episode.[18] The basic structure is constant. The entire city of Rome at its most aristocratic embraces the goddess. Her reception is orchestrated by dividing the people into their two essential components, male and female, each incarnated by an exceptional individual: on one hand, Scipio, and, on the other, Claudia Quinta.

Compared to the account given by Livy, the long development in Ovid's *Fasti* on Claudia Quinta[19] can leave us with the feeling that we have now left "history" for true "myth":

The men busily exhaust their arms on the straining towrope,
but the foreign ship barely makes headway upstream.
The earth had long been dry, drought had singed the grass:
the ship ran aground and settled in the muddy shallows.
Everyone on the job did more than his share and helped
by shouting encouragement to the strong laborers.
But she settled like a steadfast island in mid-ocean; dumbstruck
by the portent the men stood and quaked.
Claudia Quinta traced her descent to noble Clausus[20]
(her beauty was a match for her high birth).
She was chaste but no one believed it; unfair gossip
had hurt her and she stood indicted on a false charge.
Her elegance and the way she appeared in a variety of hairstyles prejudiced
the inflexible old men, as did her quick retorts.
Her clear conscience laughed off rumor's falsehoods, but we
are a bunch ready to believe the worst.
When she advanced from the ranks of the chaste matrons
and scooped pure river water up in her hands,
she sprinkled her head three times, raised her hands three times
to heaven (the onlookers thought she was out of her senses),
and on bended knees she fixed her gaze upon the image
of the goddess, undid her hair and said:
"Fertile mother of the gods, kindly heed the prayers of your petitioner with this
    stipulation.
They say I'm not chaste: if you condemn me, I'll admit I deserved it;
I'll pay with my life if convicted with the goddess as my judge. But if the charge
    doesn't stick, give proof of my honorable life
by action, and chastely follow my chaste hands."
She spoke and pulled on the towrope with a slight effort:
It's a miracle, but one the stage attests to:
the goddess was stirred, followed her guide and vouched for her
by following; a cry of joy rose to the stars.[21]

The scene has become a theatrical fiction, but Claudia Quinta's "miracle" operates in writing in such a way as merely to amplify an already fantastic story. The ritualization of the reception, after a long debate on the interpretation of oracles reported by Livy, made her the subject of both politics and myth. The recollection of the Trojan origins of Rome and the foundation of the city implicitly mesh with the preoccupation with establishing eastern alliances. These were times when Rome was attempting to open up to the Greek world. Welcoming the Mother, after the wars against the Carthaginians and the Gauls, equated with joining the prestige of ancestry and the risks of alterity in a single gesture.

In this way, Rome invites us to investigate our own conditioning as historians. We reflect on the origin of the dualism inhabiting our desire to oppose myth and history with such constancy. It is true that ritual procedures indispensable to the realization of political aims necessarily develop from something memorable. Inextricably linked to the genesis of the historical account, myth originates from a debate blending the political and the oracular. It would be useless to oppose these as two mutually exclusive entities when we witness their complicity in both Livy and in Ovid.

A Double Ritual

Before returning to the mythological substructure of the historical narrative, let us look more closely at what we know about the ritual involved. Another historian whose writings are almost contemporary with Livy's, Dionysius of Halicarnassus, invites us to do so. By introducing the example of the cult of the Idaean goddess to explain Rome's surprising resistance to the divine myth, this time from the Greek perspective, he provides an unusually precise definition of the cult of the Mother, observed with the distance he maintains as a foreigner. I believe it deserves our full attention:

> The rites of the Idaean goddess are a case in point; for the praetors perform sacrifices and celebrate games in her honour every year according to the Roman customs, but the priest and priestess of the goddess are Phrygians, and it is they who carry her image in procession through the city, begging alms in her name according to their custom, and wearing figures upon their breasts and striking their timbrels while their followers play tunes upon their flutes in honour of the Mother of the Gods. But by law and decree of the senate no native Roman walks in procession through the city arrayed in a parti-coloured robe, begging alms or escorted by flute-players, or worships the goddess with the Phrygian ceremonies. So cautious are they about admitting any foreign religious customs and so great is their aversion to all pompous display that is wanting in decorum.[22]

Each aspect of this account is confirmed by all the Roman sources on the Mother of the gods. The duality of ritual customs is noteworthy. Lucretius had already written of the *galli*'s ecstatic and bloody procession that accompanied the chariot, drawn by two lions, that carried the goddess, wearing her crenelated crown, through the great Greek cities, "in the middle of the pulsating crowd":

> Tambourines were held out and sounded under the shock of palms, concave cymbals rustled around the statue, trumpets menaced with their raucous song as the Phrygian flute rhythm threw delirium into everyone's hearts. The procession brandished arms, emblems of violent furor, terrorizing the ungrateful and impious souls in the crowd with the sacred terror of divine power. Thus, as soon as she rode on her chariot through the great cities, the silent image of the goddess gratified the mortals with her mute protection. The faithful made generous offerings in the form of bronze and silver strewn about over the entire road she traveled. Roses rained down, covering the Mother goddess, as troops escorted her. In addition, armed groups, Phrygian *curetes*, as the Greeks call them, jousted capriciously among themselves. Together they jumped up and down in sheer joy, full of the blood that inundated them. The movements of their heads shook their horrifying plumes. Thus, they remind us of Dicte's Curetes of ages ago, who, according to legend, encircled Jupiter to cover up his wailing cries in Crete. Surrounding the child god to hide him from view, the armed youths formed agile circles and played in rhythm, bronze against bronze, for fear that Saturn would discover his son and eat him up, inflicting a mortal wound on his mother's heart.[23]

During the procession, there was a great deal of begging for alms, which, as Dionysius of Halicarnassus states in his text, was part of the regular ritual practices of the Greek followers of the Mother. In Greek tradition, we have seen that the *galli* are *mētragurtes*, itinerant charlatan diviners, who gather the good people around an idol of the goddess and ask for alms. Whereas this ritual was common among oriental populations and practiced by sectarians of the Mother or the Syrian goddess, the Romans barely tolerated it. Nevertheless, in the case of the Idaean Mother, this natural repugnance for mendicancy cedes to respect for the ritual. It is enough to see how Cicero, in discussing the framework of the rules conceived of as traditional ones, presents as an obvious exception that servants of the Mother be allowed to beg for alms. It is true that this was only acceptable on the days set by Roman ritual.[24] Ovid, who also equates the Mother of the gods with Rhea, alludes to such a procession in Rome:

And at once the curved Berecynthian flute will blow and the festival of the Great
  Mother of Ida will commence.
The eunuchs will parade and strike their hollow tambourines,
and cymbal clashing on cymbal will jingle.
Riding on the soft necks of her followers she will be carried
through the city's streets amid their howling.[25]

Ovid does not neglect the traditional allusion, already made by Lucretius, to the
tame lions under the power of the goddess.[26] Yet he prefers to describe a properly
Roman practice, like the one Dionysius of Halicarnassus comments on, finding a
model for it, as does Lucretius, in the *curetes'* covering up the wailing of the
young Zeus with their noisy dancing. Ovid dates this exotic ritual as occurring on
April 4, just a bit before the anniversary of the dedication of the Palatine sanctuary (April 10). Official festivities included the games, theatrical representations,
and reciprocally shared meals (*mutitationes*) preceding this date. The end of
Ovid's description, however, introduces an episode directly connected to the
legend of Claudia Quinta, that is, the "historical" advent of the Mother. After the
miracle of the ship's being extricated from the mud, and following a restful night
during which the goddess's boat, secured to an oak tree,[27] was docked in an elbow
of the river called "Tiber's place," Ovid specifies that at dawn preliminary rites
were performed at the Capena gate, the entrance to the Urbs. He cites the
sacrifice of a heifer and bathing the divinity at the confluence of the Almo and
Tiber Rivers:

A white-haired priest in a purple robe came there and bathed
Our lady and her holy things in the Almo's waters.
Her followers howled, the maddening flute was blown
And soft hands struck the cowhide drumskins.[28]

This second description of a procession could only allude to the properly Phrygian ritual of the *lavatio*. This was when the procession of the *galli* led precisely to
the junction between the Almo and Tiber Rivers where the goddess was carried
on a chariot to be bathed.[29] Ovid's reference to two different ritual processions in
a single festival is an attempt to give a global Roman interpretation to everything
connected to the Mother. This concern for synthesis led to a confusion, or,
rather, attraction, between two rituals that were in fact heterogeneous.[30] Yet this
allowed him simultaneously to give new, Roman meaning to the Phrygian ritual
of the *lavatio*, which occurred on the last day of the metroac liturgy, that is, March

25.[31] Already practiced during Ovid's time, but not official until the reign of Claudius, this ritual festival was the most visible and spectacular conclusion of a series of liturgical practices reserved under the Republic to the foreign service of the goddess. As part of the Roman interpretation, this procession to the Almo could only serve to manifest the goddess's presence outside the confines of the Urbs, that is, in a territory that she was symbolically responsible for protecting.[32] This would agree with her original vocation, defined by the historical context of her translation. We know through Arrian that this ritual bath in fact marked the end of the mourning for the goddess and referred back to the Greek myth and eastern liturgy of Attis.[33]

Phrygian practices in keeping with a foreign myth, just like the *lavatio* itself, the bloody procession and the *galli*'s solicitations signaled the beginning of the official festivals dedicated to the Idaean Mother in Rome. This exotic prelude appears to have been a concession happily granted to the undeniable otherness of the goddess. It is nevertheless clearly distinguished from the exclusively Roman and aristocratic practice of the Megalesian games, or *ludi megalenses* (Megalesia), which began on April 4, the anniversary of the temporary installation of the goddess in the Victory sanctuary on the Palatine Hill.[34] Financed by the State or by rich citizens, these games lasted until April 10, the date of the dedication in 191 B.C.E. of the goddess's own sanctuary.[35] Originally, the Megalesia included circus games, and, soon afterward, theatrical performances. Plays by Plautus and Terence were put on in a theater constructed facing the Palatine sanctuary.[36] These *ludi* were reserved for Roman citizens; foreigners and slaves were excluded. On this occasion, aristocratic families, grouped according to fraternities, would exchange invitations in order to reinforce ancient communal ties around a ritual meal. These *mutitationes* honored the ancestral goddess of Trojan Ida.[37] In particular, the celebrants would eat a dish composed of herbs, garlic, cheese, salt, oil, and vinegar, called *moretum*.[38]

As Dionysius of Halicarnassus mentions, there was also a legal ban excluding the participation of Roman citizens in Phrygian rites. It should be understood that this was especially, but not exclusively, related to the Phrygian practice of castration. Two observers are particularly eloquent on the subject. One is Julius Obsequens, who writes of a slave who castrated himself for the Idaean Mother and was banned from Rome and exiled across the sea (*trans mare*) in 101 B.C.E. The other is Valerius Maximus, who mentions a freed slave stripped of his inheritance in 77 B.C.E. on the grounds that he had voluntarily amputated his genitals and could no longer be considered either a man or a woman.[39] These two events indicate that despite the Roman repugnance and official reaction, there was no lack of curiosity about this kind of religiosity.

Indeed, the Roman attitude to the Idaean goddess was characteristically ambiguous, if not paradoxical. She was a goddess with a double ritual, both national and foreign, and not quite able to accept that the exotic part of her religion be abandoned to strangers living in Rome. In any case, the priest and priestess directing the Phrygian ritual were established inside the *pomerium*, located on the Palatine Hill, in a sanctuary built according to the Senate's orders, where there were numerous examples of Roman piety.[40]

Double Goddess, Double Language

The goddess's name (Mater Idaea) designated her as Trojan, that is, linked to the origins of the Roman Urbs. She was therefore not an unknown figure coming out of Asia Minor. In poetic representations, she remained as much Phrygian as Trojan, introduced by way of Pergamon, a city whose name evoked that of Troy, thus making her an Idaean ancestor. She is truly a figure similar to the Penates. According to Ovid, she refused to accompany Aeneas and ended up settling in Rome in the most ancestral space linked to the city, near the hut belonging to Romulus.[41] For Roman history, in which the Trojan plain and the high Phrygian plateaus are not confused, she nevertheless remained a strange, if not foreign, figure. In fact, Roman historians are unanimous in telling us that this goddess brought to the Romans by King Attalus did not really come from Trojan Ida, but from the sacred town of Pessinos.[42] There, the people worshiped a Mother who bore the name Agdistis in a religion linking her to Attis. Furthermore, this goddess is accompanied, as we have seen, by a Phrygian clergy constituted by *galli*, around the priest and priestess mentioned by Dionysius.

The Trojan identity of a national Roman goddess of Pessinontian origin is a hesitation, or rather, a double postulate referring back to a basic characteristic of the Mater Magna. Essentially, she is a double goddess from the beginning, to whom, as Dionysius of Halicarnassus specifies, a double religion is dedicated. Yet why does he refer to this in an explanation concerning the absence of divine mythology in Rome? In his discussion of the rites of the Idaean Mother, Dionysius was far from forgetting about myth. He had not lost track of his subject while describing the religion of the Mater Magna. The conclusion of his explanation about this goddess is proof of this, because he indicates his awareness of the traditional justifications for mythological discourse:

Let no one imagine, however, that I am not sensible that some of the Greek myths are useful to mankind, part of them explaining, as they do, the works of Nature by allegories, others being designed as a consolation for human misfortunes, some freeing the mind of its agitations and terrors and clearing away unsound opinions, and others invented for some other useful purpose. But, though I am as well acquainted as anyone with these matters, nevertheless my attitude toward the myths is one of caution, and I am more inclined to accept the theology of the Romans, when I consider that the advantages from the Greek myths are slight and cannot be of profit to many, but only to those who have examined the end for which they are designed; and this philosophic attitude is shared by few. The great multitude, unacquainted with philosophy, are prone to take these stories about the gods in the worse sense and to fall into one of two errors: they either despise the gods as buffeted by many misfortunes, or else refrain from none of the most shameful and lawless deeds when they see them attributed to the gods.[43]

In the interpretation by Dionysius, the Roman attitude toward the Mother of the gods is a paradigm of Romulus's attitude toward divine myth, which is also Rome's attitude. According to the Greek historian, the founder of Rome behaves as though he had read Plato's *Republic*. He decides to prohibit all the traditional accounts of the gods inherited from the literature or liturgy of the mysteries. This theory, the first to account for the absence of any original, unborrowed mythology in Rome, depicts Romulus, not as the inventor, but rather as the reformer. The consequence of this is that far from ignoring myth, the Romans, according to Dionysius, are still thoroughly Greek. Myth is relegated to the realm of the unspoken, the unusual and the scandalous. In the case of the Mother of the gods, although he does not specifically mention it, Dionysius indicates the existence of a mythical source that can be recognized and pinpointed in the *galli's* practices. These suppose a reference to a founding myth, which, according to Dionysius's theory, has to be Greek. The Greek historian believes that the Romans had nothing to do with this original myth, which does not mean that in their rushing to see the *galli's* processions, they were not influenced by it.

Dionysius's interpretation portrays a perfectly Roman reality, although emanating from the theory that the Romans were a particular kind of Greeks, so that the domination of the Greeks by the Romans could be justified to Greek eyes.[44] Until the end of the Republic, the cult of the Mother of the gods flourished without any legend, aside from the account of her introduction to Rome. It is not that Rome ignored the existence of the goddess's Greek or Phrygian narratives, but rather that the city did not recognize any significant ritual practices connected to these accounts. Only ritual practice counted in Rome. That the priest and priestess inside the Mother's sanctuary were Phrygian could and must have linked their liturgy to an exotic mythology, but this did not interest the city. Rome left foreigners all discretion regarding their national customs. Having introduced this goddess into the heart of the Urbs because of an oracle, thereby recognizing her as ancestral, the Senate reserved all commentary when it allowed her authentic face to be seen a few days each year. The *lavatio* of March 27 was not the subject of an official exegesis connecting her to the myth of Attis, any more than the procession of the *galli* announcing the Megalesia on April 4. When the Romans before Ovid sought to explain the etiology of these processions integrated into their own traditions, they turned to the Greek interpretation of Cybele as an allegory of the productive earth. Lucretius and Varro both make this explicit choice.[45] As for the most aristocratic part of the festivities, the *ludi megalenses*, the commentators are not much more loquacious. Ovid simply suggests that the gods ceded their presidency over these games, the first of the Roman year, to their Mother, the goddess identified with the Greek Rhea. As for the *mutitationes*, for lack of anything better, he connects these to the good omen for Rome represented by the goddess agreeing to change residence, leaving Phrygia and coming to Rome.[46] What would this mean, if not that, as John Scheid puts it, only orthopraxy counts here? The interpretation of this narrative remains open.

Why did Dionysius choose the Mater Magna as an example? I shall not attempt to prove it, but it seems to me that one of the bases for this choice, aside from the fact that she is an important national divinity within the Augustan milieu, is precisely the ambiguous character of this figure.[47] It turns out that the double ritual developed is both Phrygian and Greek, as well as popular and aristocratic. Faced with the censure of the Phrygian myth and the obvious absence of an old, properly Roman narrative tradition (since, as we know, the cult was only introduced as of 204),[48] one was forced to choose between patriotic legend (Claudia Quinta) and erudite speculation (Lucretius and Varro).

If Dionysius chose the Mother, it was because he recognized that she was in reality the subject of a myth that the city condemned. In this, his example illustrates Rome's fidelity to Romulus's "reform." Yet it is also because, as part of his whole theory of the origins of the Urbs, the Trojan Mother of the Idaean gods had originally come, via Samothrace and Dardanos's route, from Greece. Dionysius had to have been encouraged by Roman influences in his interpretation. According to Varro, the official name of the festival (Megalesia) was known to be

Greek. The rituals organized around a cult image were handed down by a Hellenistic sovereign, Attalus, after oracles from the Sibylline books were pronounced in Greek.[49] The theater, which was inspired by Greece, was also an essential ingredient of these *ludi*. As for the *mutitationes*, they too were borrowed from the Greek-inspired ritual relating to Ceres.[50] Finally, Servius relates that the hymns the Romans dedicated to the goddess were also composed in Greek.[51] Thus, the Greek character of these rituals, especially with regard to language, confirms what emerges from the whole investigation of the Roman Mother. We have here a divinity whose official religion was practiced by the most aristocratic and cultivated people of Rome. Under the empire, the *taurobolium* was the ritual sacrifice of a bull, practiced to safeguard the emperor's health. This new rite would then remain faithful to the original purpose of the goddess, since it was by her entering Rome that the safety of the state was preserved. What then can we make of the troubling figure of Attis and the shady world of the *galli?*

The Metamorphosis of Myth into History

In the ninth book of the *Aeneid*, Turnus insults Aeneas's troops, mockingly portraying the ancestors of the Romans as effeminate *galli:* "For you, then, garments embroidered with saffron and bright purple, and laziness but appetite for dancing, and long-sleeved tunics and miters with knotted ribbons! O veritable Phrygian girls, for you are not Phrygian men, go up to the heights of Dindymus where you are used to hearing the flute with two sounds! The tambourines of the Idaean Mother and the flutes of Berecynthia call you: leave arms to men and renounce all weapons!"[52]

Here Virgil constructs a polysemic image by linking an ancient Homeric given, falling under the rhetoric of invective,[53] with a Hellenistic topos that consists of using the word *galli* in the feminine form to designate the eunuch priests of the Phrygian goddess.[54] A bit earlier on, at the beginning of the ninth book of the *Aeneid*, Virgil has evoked the prayer the Idaean Mother dedicated to Jupiter. This prayer concerned the gift of her sacred wood that she gave to Aeneas for the construction of the ships to bring the Trojans to Italy. This prayer was answered by the prodigy of the ships, which, escaping Turnus's torches, plunged into the sea as dolphins and reappeared metamorphosed into sea-goddesses similar to the Nereides. The comparison of these two episodes shows the ambivalence of the Phrygian reference, which can easily be reinterpreted otherwise. From the high sacred place of the ancestral territory,[55] we are quickly reminded of the fairly disreputable connotations. Virgil associates this ambivalence with the Trojan origin of the myth, just as in Livy the birth of the founding twins of Rome, Romulus and Remus, refers back to the unresolved issue of the Mother's purity. It is not known whether or not Rhea Silvia received the god Mars or had darker and more obscure relations.[56] The historical account connects the Mother to the most distant origins of the city and thus reiterates the deepest, darkest inclinations of the Roman imagination. The goddess who enters Rome in 204 is both national and foreign. She is the object of the deepest respect, even though she manifests strange relationships. She is celebrated by both upper-class citizens and the *galli*, but according to two clearly distinct ritual procedures.[57]

On the official side, a special type of narration emerges very early and takes on great significance during the Augustan age. This is connected, not with the vicissitudes of the goddess, considered as part of a primitive, foreign scene, but rather with her official introduction into Roman history. Jan Bremmer earlier supposed that the episode of the slow and difficult arrival of Cybele in Rome, on a boat that gets stuck in the mud until the famous intervention by Claudia Quinta, should be compared with other stories. Such a comparison reveals the mythological inspiration of this highly moralizing legend, which shows how the Mother is one of the goddesses of a matronal aristocracy.[58]

We could go further. It can be assumed that the scenario described by this legend presupposes a recognition of what the city pretends to want to keep separate. The reception is staged like an interpretation — or, more precisely, like a ritual performance — of a romanized Greek myth of Phrygian origin, which the Romans do not want to hear when they welcome the goddess. Rome, since it cannot ignore Attis, introduces the curious episode of Scipio, a young man, in the middle of a procession of matrons whose temperance and moral perfection is underscored by Claudia Quinta's miracle. Emphasized by Claudia Quinta in this episode, chastity appears to be an essential quality, not only of matrons, but also of the Mother of the gods in the whole of Roman tradition.[59] In the myth of the goddess from Pessinos, the Mother of the gods is incensed by the treason committed by her young protégé, Attis, who leaves her to be with a mortal woman, thus sullying his ministry. The cult dedicated to the mutilated body of Attis at the end of this drama inaugurated the practices of the priests, whose self-emasculation defined how they consecrated themselves to the exclusive service of the goddess. In Rome, through an amazing and somewhat misogynous reversal, Claudia Quinta, representative of the matrons, becomes the subject of dangerous suspicion. A statue of Claudia Quinta was erected at the entrance of the Palatine sanctuary,[60] just as Attis's statue welcomed the visitor to the Greek sanctuaries of the Mother.

The Greek literary myth is therefore transformed into the Roman ritual practice of welcoming into the city. This ritual only exists for us in the historical account.[61] Through the respective roles played by young Scipio and Claudia Quinta, the arrival of the Idaean Mother in Rome was introduced as a metamorphosis of the story of the Mother's entrance into the sacred town of Pessinos in Phrygia.[62] It will be recalled, finally, that the Mother of the gods in the Pessinontian myth comes into the Anatolian town by raising the city walls above her head. From the Roman perspective, this theme is both a foundation myth and the underlying reason for the well-known image of the crenelated crown on the head of Cybele, protector of the Urbs.

The Roman form of the myth can be situated in the protected space separating the rites dedicated to the two figures of the same goddess. Attis is thus not mentioned in Latin literature before the reign of Augustus, even though he was present in the enclosure of the Palatine as early as the Republican era.[63] Even in Catullus, his name only designates Cybele's priest, a *gallus* among *galli*, and not the mythic lover of this goddess. It was not until Ovid that the strongly Hellenized Pessinontian myth received its Latin expression.[64] Yet the simple fact that the Phrygian liturgy was included as part of the official Claudian calendar sufficiently proves that the Hellenistic Greco-Phrygian account, despite official reticence, was widespread and circulated beyond the Palatine enclosure.

This myth certainly originated in distant Anatolia and concerned a Phrygian goddess, but one could not hear it retold in Rome without Greek mediation. The references to Pessinos at the origin of the Roman destiny of the Mother of the gods are linked to the fact that there were embassies to both Delphi and Pergamon at this time. As we shall soon see, too, this new divinity could not have been introduced in Rome without reference to Athenian memories.

CHAPTER FIVE

The Origin of the Mater Magna

Rome-Delphi-Pergamon, 205 B.C.E.: The Historical Context

The political situation and the game of forging alliances were particularly significant ca. 205 B.C.E. and therefore warrant a short historical summary. We are in the second phase of the Second Punic War. The great Roman defeats on the river Trebbia in 217 and at Cannae in 216 already belong to past history. Andalusia has been Roman for two years, but the Carthaginians and Gauls are still in northern Italy, despite Rome's historic victory over Hasdrubal, slain on the river Metaurus (Metauro) in 207. In Liguria, Mago's army razed Genoa, a city allied with Rome, in 205, and the enemy remained in southern Italy and Sicily until 203, despite the fall of Syracuse in 211 and Capua in 210. The memory of two thousand of Hannibal's cavalry arriving outside Rome at the Porta Collina in 211, the last forces to threaten Latium, was still fresh in the minds of one and all. The Sibylline oracle ordering that the Idaean Mother of the gods be brought from Pessinos to Rome, so that the foreign enemy (*hostis alienigena*)[1] could finally be driven from Roman soil, corresponded to the desire to gloriously put an end to a long, traumatizing war.

Such was the immediate context whose larger framework—the first Roman moves toward an eastern policy with pretensions to hegemony—must be outlined to better understand the facts of the oracle and its senatorial interpretation. From this perspective, the year 205 is a significant turning point.

Attalus I of Pergamon had established friendly relations and a military alliance with Rome in 210.[2] He had been solicited by the Aetolian league, headquartered at Delphi,[3] with which Rome had been allied for two years in the struggle against Philip V of Macedon, an ally of Hannibal since 215.[4] The island of Aegina, opposite Athens in the Saronic Gulf, which had been occupied by the Romans, now fell under Pergamon's control. Attalus's participation in this campaign was nevertheless interrupted in short order by more urgent local concerns calling him home. In 208, the troops led by Prusias I of Bithynia were invading Pergamon's territory. Attalus was nonetheless one of the co-signers, the *adscripti*, on the Roman side of the 205 B.C.E. peace of Phoenice, which temporarily suspended the hostilities between Rome and Macedonia. According to Livy, Ilium also signed on the Roman side.[5] The peace of Phoenice is the context in which we should see the senatorial mission sent to Attalus a little earlier, but in the same year (according to Livy), to seek the Mother of the gods. In Roman historical tradition, Pergamon and Ilium appear here as allies of Rome in the context of rediscovered peace. Erich Gruen, who presents this framework, nevertheless affirms that the mission sent by Rome to Attalus had no political implications for the East: "The object . . . was to rid Italy of Hannibal, not to expand contacts in Asia."[6] And yet. . . . If in 205 Rome aspired to peace, it was not without an ulterior motive. As André Piganiol observed, Rome's attempt to open up to an eastern politics could have been motivated by either fear or imperialism. Whatever the slight, and perhaps vain, nuances of this issue, it is not a debate that concerns me here. We know that the hegemonic objectives of Rome soon made themselves known in the east *nolens volens*. Whether this arose from fear or desire, under the pressure of events or according to an explicit, conscious plan of action, I have no idea. As one says in French, "L'occasion crée le larron" (The opportunity creates the thief). The only thing we can be sure of is that the Roman politics of expansion toward the east developed immediately after these two sets of concurrent events. On one hand, there is the peace of Phoenice, an episode generally deemed to be significant by historians of antiquity; on the other, there is the introduction of the Trojan Mother into Rome, an undoubtedly minor episode in the eyes of the same historians. This encounter between the political and religious realms was surely not a coincidence. The myth of Trojan origins, reinforced by the official introduction of the religion of the Mother, appears as providential ideological support for Rome's eastern strategy.[7]

Pessinos and the Galatians

Let us look at this a bit more closely. No one doubts the importance of Pergamon and Attalos's mediation. No one doubts the fact that the Romans felt that they were welcoming a Trojan divinity, the Idaean Mother (Idaea Mater). The only problem seems to be the exact provenance of this idol. Although explicitly said by Diodoros, Cicero, Livy, Strabo, Valerius Maximus, Arrian, Dio Cassius, Herodian, Arnobius, and Ammianus Marcellinus to have been Pessinos, this seems not always to have been found convincing, for three commonly mentioned reasons. The first of these is the "fact" that Pessinos was not part of Pergamon's sphere of influence until after the reign of Attalus I.[8] However, none of the skeptical historians doubt that Pessinontian priesthood remained on good terms with the Attalids, persuaded of this by Strabo, who is definite.[9] In addition, there were royal connections between the sovereigns of Pergamon and the Attis of the state temple of Pessinos from at least the time of Attalus II on. The case for minimizing the relationship between Pergamon and Pessinos is that the Galatians, although they had not yet entered Pessinos, would have nonetheless prevented any and all contact with that city. In 205, Attalus's emissaries would simply not have been able to cross a territory then controlled by the Celts to seek out the sacred Phrygian stone in Pessinos. The known history of Pessinos shows us, however, that as of 189 (during L. Manlius Vulso's expedition), this city constituted a special case. Even though the Roman consul was at war with the Gauls, the Galatians, the priest-magistrates of Pessinos, who were both *galli* and Gauls, were the ones who came to the Roman troops prophesying Rome's victory and conquest of the region. This indicates that in Pessinos, the sacred Phrygian city, the Galatians, who had been quickly integrated into administrative life, were predisposed to good relations with both Pergamon and Rome. We have no reason to doubt Livy when he describes the envoy leading the Roman emissaries from Pergamon to Pessinos in 205. His observation implies that such relations were already in place at that time. Nothing indicates that Pessinos, an ally of Pergamon, had been encircled by hostile tribes of Galatians, thereby cutting off all communication with Attalos's kingdom. The Gauls should not be seen as having all been, by definition, adversaries of the Greeks in Asia Minor. On the contrary, it appears as if they were much closer to them than the royal Hellenistic propaganda portraying them as almost cosmic enemies would have us believe. In fact, they were regularly involved, either as allies or as mercenaries, in the numerous conflicts among various Greek sovereigns in Asia Minor.[10] Far from being cut off from the rest of the world by the Gauls, who would have been the foreigners here, Pessinos belonged to an area in which the Galatians had been well-established for many decades by 205. Confined to Anatolia after many conflicts with Attalus I, running from 241 to 230, they mingled with the indigenous Phrygian populations.[11] In Pessinos, they belonged to the Tolistobogiae (or Tolistoagae), a Celtic tribe that had been allotted Aeolia and Ionia in the lottery of 277 dividing up Asia Minor among the three tribes for purposes of pillage,[12] while the Trocmae "received" the coasts of the Hellespont and the Tectosagae were awarded the Anatolian interior.[13] Recent research there has shown that Gordion, a Phrygian city not far from Pessinos, was hellenized relatively late, under the influence of Pergamon, when Attalos was pacifying the Galatians.[14] Alexander's passage left little or no trace in this region. The troubles caused by the multiple raids waged by the Galatians before Attalos's victory had provoked a decline in local Phrygian production. It was only in the second part of the third century B.C.E. that a cultural renewal became manifest. At that time, there was ethnic blending resulting from the integration of the Galatians into the political and religious life of the local communities, along with an accelerated process of acculturation.[15] When the Romans intervened militarily in the region under the consul L. Manlius Vulso, fifty or so years later, the Gauls of Asia Minor had long been *mixti*, having integrated into the local Phrygian populations, to whom they brought Greek knowledge and techniques. In a discourse Livy attributes to him, Vulso qualified these cultural half-breeds as Gallograeci ("Gallo-Greeks").[16] All of Galatia was traditionally referred to as "Gaulish Greece" or Gallograecia. This phenomenon of acculturation operated on two levels. The Gauls assimilated Hellenistic culture and in turn passed it along to the local populations. This particularly concerns the Tolistobogiae of the Pessinos region who, after having dominated the Greek coast of Asia Minor for decades, had become faithful allies of Pergamon.[17] To better understand the role of the Gallo-Greeks as a factor in hellenization, it should be kept in mind that the Celts had never ceased to mix with the Greeks since their arrival in Asia Minor. Whether this occurred during their raids or while they were serving as mercenaries, the beginnings of their hellenization probably go back much earlier than their actual entry into Greece and the unsuccessful sacking of Delphi.[18]

A second reason mentioned for doubting the Pessinontian origin of the goddess welcomed to Rome is linked to the specifically Greek character of the cult of the Mater Idaea, whose hymns were sung in Greek, not in Phrygian. In light of what has previously been said, this can only constitute a weak objection. The Greek character of the cult does not exclude a de facto Phrygian origin of the idol in the geographic sense of the term. The region of Pessinos had already been greatly hellenized by 205. As for the possibility of such a phenomenon, it is enough to think of Serapis, who was celebrated in Greek on Delos by an Egyptian family from Memphis, who had brought the cult image from Egypt.[19]

A third reason mentioned by those opposed to the idea of a Pessinontian origin of the goddess is that they consider it unlikely that the local clergy of the Mother would have accepted this separation from their idol. Such an argument, which, let it be said in passing, should also be true of Pergamon and Ilium, supposes an identification of the sign, the idol, and the signified, the divinity. Nothing indicates that this was the case. The Romans did not come to steal the goddess from the Pessinontian priesthood, who, in any case, continued to practice their traditional religion. What happened is analogous to the transfer of Asclepios of Epidaurus to Rome (where the god was called Aesculapius). The sacred stone functioned in the same way as the plump serpent (believed to incarnate Aesculapius) on the island in the Tiber. It existed in a separate place without the original sanctuary being profaned. Everything leads us to believe, in fact, that such "autoglyph" stones were numerous and famous in the region. Supposedly endowed with strange powers, they were capable of driving someone mad and leading to the irreversible act of self-castration.[20] Like Asclepios's snake, the black stone that arrived in Rome was far from unique.

All in all, only one piece of evidence seems explicitly to be invoked — Cicero, Livy, and Diodoros to the contrary — by those who claim Pergamon to have been the unique place of origin of the goddess and her cult. This is a text by Varro, which various editors over time have corrected, after a brutal verdict on it by Scaliger.[21] From the manuscript version, we learn moreover that "following the consultation of the Sibylline books, she [the goddess, or her idol] was sought out in Attalus's kingdom and brought to Troy, near the ramparts of a sanctuary of the goddess, or *megalesion*. From there, she was brought to Rome."[22] The fact that the sacred stone stopped over in Ilium due to the good graces of Attalus agrees perfectly with all the facts as Livy reports them. He too presents this idol as one with the Trojan Ida, since he has her come from Pessinos via Pergamon. This mediation erases all the difficulties created by the apparent contradictions in history and especially responds quite precisely to the nature of Attalus's role.

Only Attalus, king of Pergamon, would have been able to render this service, because of his friendly relations, not only with Delphi, through which the Roman delegation passed, and with Pessinos, but also with Ilium. Besides, although many sanctuaries of the Mother are known in Pergamon, none is situated "near the ramparts."[23] In Ilium, however, the *mētrōon* was located in the lower part of the town, near the *bouleuterion*, and seems to have been situated at the foot of the fortified acropolis, dedicated, just like the one in Pergamon, to Athena.[24] Thus it is possible to confirm Ovid's information, which, without ignoring Attalos, posits the Mother's origin in the Troad.

The fact that the antiquarian Varro does not mention Pessinos does not constitute a reason to doubt the entire historical tradition. His words relate neither to the cultic image — the Pessinontian stone — nor to the Phrygian ritual of the *galli*, but only to the Greek term used for the aristocratic Roman festival called the Megalesia, the festival of the *megalē*, the "great" goddess. Attalos's role and the probable passage through Ilium sufficiently explain the choice of this Greek word. Varro did not need to say any more about it. What he affirms does not contradict what is adequately specified elsewhere, that is, that the stone that came to Rome in 204 originated in Pessinos, as did the Phrygian ritual itself. Refusal to recognize this requires at least that one explain why Roman historians would have introduced Pessinos a posteriori to the tradition connected with the Mater Magna and were not content to keep Pergamon and (or) Ilium as her original sources. It makes no sense to think of Pessinos as somewhere that came up later on, after the fact.

It is therefore clear that if Pessinos was so unanimously cited by the ancients, it was because the idol of the Mother really came from there in 204 B.C.E. What did occur after the fact, and can be observed, is an effort on the part of ancient historiography to establish an explicit connection between Pessinos and Ilium through mythical genealogies linking the historical fact of the Phrygian origin and the Trojan legend. Whereas Theopompus still affirmed that Pessinos received its name from King Midas, thus emphasizing the Phrygian character of the site, other ancient historians, and also more recent ones, claim that the founder of Pessinos was Ilos, king of Dardania, son of Tros.[25] According to a version reported by Herodian, Ilos warred against Tantalos, king of Lydia, after a quarrel either about a right of way or a border, or because Ganymede had been kidnapped by Tantalos.[26] A long battle ensued, which was indecisive but saw many men fall (*pessein*). Hence the name Pessinos is connected to this etymology of "falling down."[27] In the version mentioning Ganymede, the body of the child disappears at this place, torn to pieces in the dispute between his brother and lover who literally rip him apart.

The better-known legend of the kidnapping by Zeus is only, according to Herodian's euhemerist view, the mythical transposition of this "historical" event. As C. R. Whittaker remarks, this attempt at rationalizing myth performs a synthesis between the legend of the Mater Magna localized in Pessinos and the accounts concerning Ilos, Ganymede, and the fall of the Palladium into the Troad.[28] In the same vein, we can point to a myth reported by Pseudo-Plutarch that situates a drama on the Trojan Mount Ida, where it is easy to recognize a transformation of the story of Attis, Agdistis, and the Mother in Pessinos. In this version, Agdesthios (*sic*), begotten from Zeus's seed, joins the nymph Ida in a love union, leading to the birth of the Dactyli. Before going insane inside the sanctuary belonging to Rhea, the Mother of the gods, Agdesthios gives his lover's name to the mountain. The Trojan mountain, previously called Gargaron, was henceforth called Ida.[29] These very specific stories attest to the care with which ancient historiography attempted to integrate the ideological affirmation of the Trojan origin of the Mother with the historical fact of her Pessinontian origin.

Finally, there is one last version of the story that should be noted: the city of Pessinos is said to have been founded by Dardanos, himself an ancestor of the Trojans and the most ancient initiator of the cult of the Mother in Samothrace. Thus his city, like Troy, was a distant relation to Rome. In this way, Dardanos also plays the role of the ancestor and prefigures Aeneas.[30]

Why Pessinos?

These hermeneutic exercises evidence a true virtuosity in the manipulation of genealogies. Although they are difficult to date, they were certainly posterior to the event concerning us here. Unfortunately, they do not reveal to us the sense that the reference to Pessinos might have had for the Roman Senate in the years 205–204 B.C.E. The task of discovering the significance of this is particularly difficult, because most of the documents directly relating to this Anatolian city are from after that date, and the archaeological evidence is slim.[31]

Let us nonetheless review the context. Pessinos was a Phrygian establishment on the high plateaus of Anatolia situated along with its nearby neighbors, Gordion and Ancyra, slightly northwest of the zone where rock-cut monuments such as those at Midas Sehri ("City of Midas") and Aslankaya attest to the most ancient cult of the Mother. We can suppose that even before Alexander's passage through this region, Pessinos, a priestly state of the Near Eastern sort, functioned like a great market, dependent on the sanctuary of a local goddess. This goddess named Agdistis was a Mother tightly linked to the rocky hill dominating the site, Mount Agdos, from which she took her name.[32] The Mother's priests also held political offices, the most important of them with the title of Attis or Battakes. The name of the local Mother, Agdistis, seems to have spread widely and rapidly, because it has been found, not only in different locations on the plateaus of Phrygia,[33] but also in Sardis as early as the middle of the fourth century.[34] In addition, this name is found a little later on in Athens,[35] as well as on a papyrus documenting the construction of a temple and sacred enclosure for Agdistis Epēkoos ("attentive to prayers") under Ptolemy II in Egypt.[36] The period during which this *naos* and this *temenos* were built by a priest named Moschos corresponds exactly to when Ptolemy II Philadelphos quashed the famous mutiny of four thousand Galatian mercenaries in Alexandria.[37] It is probable that the divinity designated as Agdistis had been introduced from Asia Minor into Egypt by the Galatian mercenaries themselves, since these Galatians were both familiar with the practices of Upper Phrygia and hellenized.[38] The fact that a sanctuary was built for her by a Greek priest was a remarkable precedent for Rome in 205, considering that the Galatians still constituted a threat to the empire. The ritual recognition of Agdistis is paradigmatic, given the context of the events underscored by the Hellenistic propaganda that was influencing the Romans in 205 in literary or poetic forms.[39]

We can therefore suppose that Pessinos, from before the reign of Attalos I, was already known as one of the high places of the cult of the Anatolian Mother.[40] Yet this does not explain why Attalos and Rome chose it. Other, less remote cities would have also been able to transmit the image of the Idaean ancestor to the Romans. Pergamon or Ilium would have been just as suitable. If Rome selected Pessinos in 205, it was not simply because of the etymology of this place-name. It is true that the name of the sacred city refers to the idea of an idol "fallen" from the sky. Since the idol was a stone, in fact, a meteorite, this popular etymology fortuitously agrees with the circumstances, that is, the falling rocks that led to consulting the Sibylline oracles in the first place. However, on the interpretative level, and in terms of the political and religious consequences for the Roman Senate, this connection simply reinforced a much more important fact: Pessinos was a Galatian city.

Galli and Gauls

In order to understand what we can call the function of Pessinos in introducing the Mother to Rome, it is necessary to track the role played by the Gauls in the hellenization of central Anatolia, a land barely touched by Alexander's passage to Gordion.[41] From this point of view, it first appears abundantly clear that in looking for the cult image in Agdistis's city, Attalus passed along to Rome a divinity simultaneously related both to ancient Phrygia — perceived as being, via Troy, and perhaps also Samothrace, the ancestral backdrop of Rome — and to the land of the Gauls, an enemy who in 205 still threatened Italian soil. Moreover, at the same time that Rome was welcoming the Mother, the latter had already begun undergoing a process of hellenization in her own homeland.

But we can go further. By addressing itself to Attalus, Rome was not only approaching its true eastern ally, but also, and perhaps first and foremost, the conqueror of the Galatians. It follows that since Rome was attempting to rid its soil of the "foreign enemy," it explicitly claimed its place in the ideological tradition of conflict with the Gauls, which was marked by a series of almost legendary out-and-out victories. Hellenistic monumental sculpture and poetry conferred heroic prestige on these victories. Each victory was considered a repetition of the preceding one, from present history back to the triumph of the Olympian gods over the giants, or of the Athenians over the Persians. This list includes the defeat of the Galatians at Delphi (279), Antigonos Gonatas's victory at Lysimacheia (277), Ptolemy II Philadelphos's victory over the mutinous mercenaries in Alexandria (between 275 and 269), the defeat of the Gauls by Antiochos I and his elephants (269–268), and, finally, the victory of Attalus I, celebrated in the famous monuments of Pergamon and on the Acropolis in Athens.[42] Rome claimed its "legitimate" right to be among the victors in this context by recollecting even more ancient and legendary conflicts with the same enemy. The legend of the Capitoline geese takes us back to the start of the fourth century B.C.E.

What remains enigmatic is therefore neither the recourse to Pergamon nor the reference to the Celtic threat made explicit by the detour via Pessinos. What strikes one as odd is rather the fact that the ancestral Mother, albeit Idaean and "Trojan," could have been conceived of as administered by an Anatolian clergy infiltrated by the Gauls.

The eunuch priests of the goddess, the *galli*, are designated by the same name in Latin as the Gauls (Galli).[43] In Greek, however, the word *gallos* exclusively designates a eunuch priest. The term, which did not appear until the arrival of the

Galatians in Asia Minor, is distinct from Keltoi and Galatai, which are names for the Gauls.[44] The first evidence of the word *gallos* is sometimes said to be in the feminine form, used as an insult. This is found in Catullus and in a fragment of two verses attributed to Callimachus: "Familiar *gallai* of the thyrsus, messengers of the Mountain Mother, whose pandemonium explodes from their swords and bronze cymbals."[45] Hephestion, master of meter, cites this passage without referring to the Hellenistic poet.[46] Modern critics, and especially Wilamowitz,[47] whose authority, even if ill-founded, nevertheless weighs heavily, believe these verses to be either by Callimachus or by Euphorion of Chersonesus, because of the scansion. Otto Weinreich, followed by Rudolf Pfeiffer, voiced serious reserves about the matter. Innumerable poems have disappeared between Callimachus and Catullus that might have had the same scansion and theoretically could have contained these two verses. Besides, it is not at all obvious that Catullus was specifically imitating this passage. The *galles* in the feminine was ostensibly a commonplace, so it is wiser not to attribute paternity to Callimachus.[48]

This all helps establish that the most ancient Greek evidence of the term we can truly date goes back to the second and first centuries B.C.E. We can find examples in Polybius and in the inscription from Eresos on Lesbos mentioned in Chapter 2.[49] This is significant. It allows us to advance the likely hypothesis that *gallos* in Greek is in reality a term borrowed from Latin after the arrival of the Galatians in the eastern Mediterranean. This occurred after the introduction of the cult of the Mother in Rome, which called attention to this type of character. Furthermore, in classical Greek, other terms are used to designate the priests of the Phrygian goddess.[50] As for Latin, it chose a word for the eunuch priests of the goddess from its own vocabulary. Everything thus indicates that the Romans did not need such a word before 205 B.C.E. The word selected simultaneously applied to both the Gauls and the rooster (cock).[51] For the Romans, the *galli* were actually the eastern Gauls, Galatians, whose sexuality was an object of mockery. Generally speaking, the Gauls were considered by Roman historians to have demonstrated ambiguous sexual behavior. They were also attributed military behavior evoking that of the *curetes* or *corybantes*. They would beat their weapons to hold back the enemy's shields, according to a custom of their ancestors, while singing, screaming, and dancing.[52] Thus, their gestures were much like those of the *galles* described in the feminine by Pseudo-Callimachus.

Should this lead us to suppose that the Mother of the gods was herself considered to be a Gaul? Of course not. We should, however, recognize that her cult, from the Roman point of view, was characterized by deep ambivalence. It is because of this irreducible and scandalous backdrop, confined to the realm of foreign practices and not admitted into the aristocratic religion of Rome, that the image of the Phrygian adulators of the Mater Magna can sometimes be connected to the Gauls.

The Gauls and the Mother

If we now change perspectives and place ourselves on the Galatian side, what can we observe? The response is apparently simple: we are dealing with Celts who encounter an old local figure in Phrygia, the Mother of the gods. The ancestors of the Celts had, by the way, already frequented or brushed elbows with this goddess in another form in the region of Marseille. Perhaps they were prepared by this ancient contact to give themselves up to the work of recognition and interpretation. Transformed into *galles* by the irony of Hellenistic civilization, the Gauls seemed predestined to maintain close religious relationships with the divinity of these eunuch priests. They must not have found the Anatolian Mother of the gods to be a perfect stranger, but rather a strangely familiar divinity. It is not even necessary to explain this by way of a detour to Marseille or by referring to the Roman imagination. It is enough to observe the importance of two well-known historical and religious facts that are directly perceptible through sources of Celtic origin.

First of all, the cult of the Mothers is well documented in territories connected to the Gauls, the Bretons, and the Irish. In the same places, there are cults linked to stones and rocks. The encounter between a Hellenistic discourse — characterized by a whole rhetoric of otherness[53] — and the reception by the Celts themselves of cultural and religious realities that they encountered in Asia Minor would alone merit an entire study unto itself.[54] I shall therefore content myself here with sketching out the framework within which this interpretative work, readjustment, and "syncretism" doubtlessly operated.[55] A Celtic reality thus corresponded to the Greco-Roman imaginary world of the Gaul on the political and literary level, since the Gauls claimed that in terms of military and ritual practices, they were indeed different.

Many features of the western Celtic world characterize behaviors and sensibilities similar to those the Greek and Roman authors attribute to Phrygian religious cults. In *Germania*, Tacitus speaks of the Estae on the Baltic coast, a population that must have been Celtic because they spoke a language like the Bretons. He attributes a cult of the Mother of the gods (Mater deum) to them, whose rituals were characterized by images of a boar protecting warriors in combat.[56] The link between the boar and the Mother can be compared with the one between Atys's destiny and this animal in Herodotus and Hermesianax. In the land of the Voconces, a rock fallen from the sky, which was seen by Pliny the Elder, became a cult object.[57] In 61 c.e. the famous Boudicca (Boadicea), the wife of the king of Brittany, Prasutagos, became the chief of the army, a kind of Amazon queen, and called the Bretons into battle against the Romans. Scenes of sheer horror are described, whose detailed cruelty can be compared to the account Arnobius gave of the fight between Agdistis and the Mother in Pessinos on the occasion of Attis's marriage. Women are hanged, their breasts cut off and stuck in their mouths. On this occasion, the Celts celebrated and made sacrifices in a forest during a ceremony dedicated to their most important divinity, called Andraste, whom a medieval copyist may have been tempted to transform into the Greek Adraste, another figure of the Mother.[58] As for Dio Cassius, he informs us that she was the equivalent of Victory, the divinity who received the Mater Magna on the Palatine.[59] In all likelihood, we are dealing with a reading of Celtic civilization by the Greco-Roman tradition, through clichés close to the ones at work when this same tradition considers the foreign and scandalous practices from the universe of the *galli*, up to and including in Rome. Although this appears to be something of an amalgam, it is largely supported by facts and observations of authentic practices.

From this point of view, we must first and foremost obviously consider the cult of the Celtic Mothers — Matres, Matrae, or Matronae. We must also consider the numerous votive reliefs that are evidence of their importance in Gaul, in Great Britain, in the Rhineland, and Transalpine Gaul.[60] Sometimes, these female figures are represented in the form of a single figure. More often, they are grouped in triads or dyads, side by side, seated in little kiosks of the *naiskos* type. Although iconographically very close to the Hellenic Mother of the gods, they do not share her attributes (phiale, tympanum, and lion). The Celtic Mothers support baskets of fruit on their laps, a cornucopia of abundance, or a swaddled nursing baby. They can sometimes appear with the features that identify them more specifically with the *Mētēr oreia*, a "Mountain Mother" who is at the same time the Mother of the gods. Thus in Ireland, Anu and Ana, two hills in Munster shaped like two breasts, twin hills in the area of Killarney, stand as an epiphany to the ancient Mother of the gods of the north, a bust fixed in the landscape.[61] Another famous name in Ireland for the Mother of the gods is Danu or Dana, part of the original pantheon of the Tuatha Dé Danann. The triple Bridget, patron of poets, forgers, and physicians, also has her place in the long list of Celtic Mothers.

The supernatural rock or stone is another symbolic element to which the Celts were certainly able to attach aspects of their own religious and political culture to Phrygian elements. The documentation on Celtic stones is conveniently found assembled in two studies extending a celebrated inquiry in 1913 by Wilhelm Heinrich Roscher on the symbolism of the "navel of the earth."[62] Roscher did not deal with the Celtic world in this text, and J. Loth attempted to fill this void in an article which appeared in 1915.[63] Roscher incorporated Loth's findings into a new study in 1918.[64] Finally, Jan de Vries, inspired, like Loth, by Roscher's 1913 publication (he seems not to have known the 1918 one), published a short study on the royal Irish stone in 1960.[65]

It emerges from these studies, once they have been rid of outdated theories they contain, that the places of Celtic tribal reunion often corresponded to sanctuaries situated at the intersection of their borders, generally in sacred forests called *nemeton*.[66] Of course, this brings to mind the country of the Carnutes (also called Carnuti or Carnutae) to which Caesar alludes.[67] In addition, although none of the three authors mentioned speak of it, one also thinks of the *drynemeton* of the Galatians, where the Council of the Three Hundred met, accompanied by the dozen tetrarchs who wielded power over the three tribes (Trocmae, Tolistobogiae, and Tectosagae).[68]

In the Irish territory, a stone with fantastic properties that becomes the subject of legends often marks such places connected to the constitution of power. Thus, the royal Lia Faïl stone on the Tara hillside (formerly Temaïr), also called the *fo-ail*, or "stone which is under the king," was supposed to have cried out if someone destined to become a sovereign stepped on it.[69] According to the summary given by Jan de Vries, this is the legend of Conn Cétchathach, a great Irish king of the second century C.E.:

> One morning on the Tara hill, Conn Cétchathach stepped on a stone that cried out so loud that it was heard throughout the island. At the same instant, a thick fog surrounded him and a fairy prince emerged from it to predict the future of Ireland.

His successor, Connaïre Mor, was elected after an intertribal ritual and meeting at the same place:

> The men of Leinster and the family of Conn Cétchathach met at Temaïr to elect a king. There was a chariot there to which horses of the same color that had never been harnessed were hitched. The only one who could mount this chariot was the one destined to become the king of Ireland. The horses would buck at the sight of

anyone else.[70] On the chariot, there was a garment too large for anyone not destined for the throne. There were also two rocks, Bloc and Blugne, so close to each other that one could barely put a hand between them. Yet these rocks would separate to allow the chariot to pass when the legitimate king was seated in it. This was also where a rock called Fal was to be found, raised up like a pillar, whose name means "the *verpa* of the rock." It would only bellow at the chariot of a legitimate king. But when Conaïre Mor was presented to be elected, the chariot accepted him, the cloak fit him, the two rocks separated, and the Fal bellowed. "Fal has accepted him," the men cried out.[71]

It is true that the Celtic traditions concerning royal rocks do not have a direct or explicit relationship with a divine Mother. The stone itself is certainly supernatural, but not an effigy of a goddess. Nonetheless, along with the cult of the Mothers, these legends constituted fertile ground for the assimilation by the Galatians of a Phrygian tradition joining the themes of the stone fallen from the sky and the foundation around the sanctuary of Agdistis of a priestly state that was both a market and a place of pilgrimage.

Moreover, the encounter between the Galatians of the third century B.C.E. and Phrygian culture would have been prepared, or, we could say, preprogrammed on the linguistic level, if we are to believe Bernard Sergent's bold suggestions.[72] Based on a lexical analysis of Anatolian theonyms, toponyms, ethnonyms, and anthroponyms of the Greek and Roman periods, and supported by mythological evidence, Sergent argues that a Celtic presence dating back to the eighth century B.C.E. explains the numerous traces of Celtic vocabulary, in generally conservative contexts, found in northwestern Anatolia. The two key pieces of evidence in Sergent's theory are the name of the mountain Arganthoneion — near Kios — undoubtedly a Celtic name, and the name of the unfortunate Bormos whose death is mourned in Mariandynian ritual. However, it is necessary to observe that these two names do not appear before the Hellenistic period.[73] Rather than it being evidence of the first wave of Celtic immigrants, should we not then take Sergent's rich documentation for ample proof of the immense cultural influence of the Galatian presence in the third century B.C.E. in regions that mostly remained marginal? Such a presence would likely have influenced the naming of places and gods.

In any case, let us note that when they established themselves in the region of Pessinos, the Gauls encountered, if not Celtic linguistic elements already in place, then at least a number of key Phrygian religious and symbolic elements, which they could have interpreted in their own way and transferred into their own religious system. This must have facilitated the surprising integration of the Gauls, at least one of whom bore the title of Attis, at the heart of the priestly legislature of Pessinos.

The presence of the Gauls at the peak of the Pessinontian hierarchy is confirmed by correspondence between the Attises of Pessinos and Eumenes II and Attalus II of Pergamon.[74] ("Attis" is obviously used here as the name of a function, like "father" or "pope.") In the second of these letters, King Eumenes mentions the completely Gaulish name (Aioiorix) of the brother of the Attis in power. This is startling proof of rapid integration. By this period (163–159 B.C.E.), the Galatians were thus evidently integrated into religious and political life in Pessinos and were completely familiar with the rites of the Mother.

Rome and Pessinos

Throughout Roman history, Pessinos is mentioned as an important site of the cult of the Mother in Asia Minor. In Augustus's time (that is, from the time of Dionysios and Livy), it was still a marketplace, one of the largest in the region, and was set up around the venerated sanctuary of the Mother of the gods, Agdistis.[75] Travelers went there to see the tomb of Attis.[76] Strabo informs us that "the kings of Attalos's dynasty had decorated the sanctuary in a manner befitting its sacredness by erecting a temple and portico in white marble." He also adds that the Romans were the ones to ensure the sanctuary's celebrity.[77] Cicero recalled that "during the most important and dangerous wars, [Roman] generals made vows to this goddess and fulfilled them in Pessinos itself at the same main altar and in that very place."[78] The emperor Julian, also the author of a *Discourse on the Mother of the Gods*, followed this custom himself. During his voyage from Constantinople to Antioch in June 362 B.C.E., he made a detour, or rather a pilgrimage, to Pessinos.[79]

This Roman fidelity to Pessinos is not a late invention. In fact, it appears to be part of a reciprocal fidelity. In 190 B.C.E., that is, fourteen years after the Mother's introduction into Rome, but only one year after the dedication of her sanctuary on the Palatine, Livius Salinator was operating in the region of the Hellespont and preparing to besiege Sestos on the European coast: "When the soldiers were already approaching the walls, some fanatical *Galli* with their ritual dress first met them before the gate; they said that by the order of the Mother of the Gods they, the servants of the goddess, were coming to implore the Romans to spare the walls and the city. None of them was injured. Presently the whole senate with the magistrates came to surrender the city. Then the fleet crossed to Abydus."[80]

The mediation of the *galli* and the reference to the Mother of the gods, in a context of a town under siege, played a significant role in favor of the walls of the city. We recognize an allusion here, certainly an intentional one, coming from the *galli* of Sestos, to the important function, recognized in Rome, of this crenelated divinity.

In 189 B.C.E., Roman armies were engaged for the first time in Asia Minor. The consul L. Manlius Vulso undertook an expedition against the Gauls that was intended to definitively end their incursions against Pergamon, where Eumenes reigned: "Advancing across the country, the consul had a bridge built across the river Sangarios, whose bed at this spot is extremely steep and difficult to cross. While he was camping not far from the river, the *galli*, who wore medallions on their chests and sacred images,[81] introduced themselves to him on behalf of Attis and Battakes, priests of the Mother of the gods in Pessinos. They announced to him that the goddess promised him victory and power. Vulso reserved a friendly welcome for them."[82]

A little before 102, a priest-magistrate from Pessinos, likewise called Battakes, came to Rome. We are told that he did so on the orders of the goddess, both to purify the temple of the Mother in Pessinos, which he claimed had been contaminated, and to promise victory to the Romans. The Romans' enemies were no longer the Gauls there, but comparable foes, the Cimbri and the Teutons.[83] Although this episode is somewhat fantastically colored, it shows us that, if the Palatine sanctuary had been in contact with the one in Pessinos, this solidarity was nevertheless felt to be ambiguous. The Battakes, as Diodoros reports, had clothing and special ornaments that were very different from Roman ones. He wore an immense crown and a robe embroidered with gold, like a king. He gave speeches to the people on the Forum and inspired the crowd with superstitious fear. He was received and lodged at the state's expense, but it wished to prevent him from wearing the crown. He was questioned regarding the purification, and his fanatical answers unleashed the anger of a tribune, which led the people to insult him and drive him away. The Battakes hid at home. As for the tribune, he came down with a fever and died within three days, which the mob considered divine punishment of one who had insulted the priest and the goddess. It was then that the Battakes received permission to wear the sacred robe. The people honored him with magnificent presents, and when he left, a good many men and women accompanied him out of Rome.

The Roman visit of the priestly emissary from Pessinos is a story structured like a true legend. The great priest from Anatolia humiliated by a local magistrate, the divine punishment that follows, the recognition of the powers of the goddess by the people, and the change in attitude with regard to the priest all have mythic attributes. Appropriately, H. S. Versnel supposed this account to be related to a Hellenistic tradition concerning the introduction of the Mother of the gods in Athens.[84] As inscribed in Roman history, the mission of the Battakes is undoubtedly presented as a transformation, in the sense in which Claude Lévi-Strauss would mean that. It did not necessarily derive from the Hellenistic myth about the arrival in Athens, shortly before the foundation of the *mētrōon*, of an Anatolian beggar priest of the Mother, a *mētragurtēs* whose "passion" underlay the cult of the goddess in the Athenian Agora.[85] This story, which postulated the explicitly oriental origin of the cult of the Mother in Athens, looks like religious propaganda, leading one to believe that it comes from a marginal religious association in terms of Athenian society. The version reported by the Byzantine lexicon *Suda* can serve as a reference. A *mētragurtēs*, an itinerant priest of the Mother, comes to Attica. He initiates (*emuei*) the women (*tas gunaikas*) to the Mother of the gods. Athenian men kill him and throw him head first into the *barathron*, a pit into which criminals were flung. An epidemic (*loimos*) breaks out, and the Athenians consult the oracle, who entreats them to pacify the murder victim. This is why they build a *bouleuterion*, into which they transport the body of the *mētragurtēs*. Having surrounded this *bouleuterion* with an enclosure, they dedicate it to the Mother of the gods and also erect a statue of the *mētragurtēs*. They used the *mētrōon* as an archive (*archeion*) and a depository for the laws (*nomophulakeion*), after having filled in the *barathron*.

The scholiast on Aristophanes adds some details: the *barathron* was a cleft in the earth, a *chasma*, a kind of dark well, with hooks turned toward the top and bottom.[86] The Phrygian *mētragurtēs* who came to initiate the women angered the Athenians because he claimed that the Mother had come to look for her daughter, Korē. Enraged by his murder, the goddess rendered the country sterile. An oracle informed the Athenians of the cause of the drought. They filled in the *chasma* and curried favor with the goddess by offering sacrifices. The emperor Julian depicts the Phrygian, whom he calls Gallos, as a religious innovator in the cult of the goddess, interchangeably referred to as Deo, Rhea, or Demeter.[87]

A mother searching for her daughter, the goddess mourns her missionary priest, devastated by his murder. The Greek story forgets Korē and only retains the Mother, who has the aspect of an Erinye. The connection with typically

Athenian traditions—especially those that we have encountered in Euripides' *Helen*—is obvious. Yet these traditions are modified by the male Phrygian priest, a displacement toward the masculine that, without naming it, reveals the pole of attraction of this exotic legend integrating the story of the *gallus* Attis (unmentionable in public) into the classical Athenian context.

Versnel suggests that the Roman story might actually be more ancient than the Greek one. His theory is that the Greek tradition would have been reelaborated according to a later paradigm at the beginning of the first century B.C.E. It would be at this point that the figure of the *gallus* was introduced. Nevertheless, it is difficult to understand how the historical Roman legend of the Battakes reaching Rome during the period of Marius and Sulla could constitute such a paradigm. An inverse hypothesis can also be envisioned. The Greek story of the *mētragurtēs* would be the more ancient story, the origin and the model for the Roman legend of the Battakes, a historicized myth. This is possible if we date the first story from the end of the fourth century B.C.E., as Giovanni Cerri suggests.[88] Unfortunately, this earlier date relies on arguments that are all too fragile.[89] We must therefore recognize that these legends are two products, one Roman and one Greek, with the same narrative structure in place by the end of the Roman Republic. We do not need to suppose any direct influence of one on the other. Both emerged from the same religious mold, an indissoluble mixture of Roman, Greek, and Anatolian traditions.

CHAPTER SIX

Attis in the Imperial Period

Transformations of the Liturgy

In the middle of the fifth century, the Roman calendar officially became Christian. In 448 C.E., the day of Christ's death (*Christus passus hoc die*) was recorded as having been March 25. The day of Christ's Resurrection (*resurrectio*), March 27, was specified as the day the "ancients called the *lavatio*" (*lavationem veteres nominabant*), thereby recalling, perhaps because it was necessary to do so, the memory of the great public pagan celebrations.[1] Some celebrations apparently survived in a slightly less sacred version. The Megalesia simply became "circus games" (*ludi circenses*), taking place between April 4 and 10.[2]

The pagan celebration of the Megalesia had still been very much alive in Roman memory a century earlier, as shown (for 354 C.E.) by Philoscalus's calendar,[3] which is our main evidence for what is often called, by analogy with the Holy Week of Easter, the "holy week of Attis." For the month of March, Philocalus provides the following list of events:

March 15   *Canna intrat* [entrance of the reeds]
March 22   *Arbor intrat* [entrance of the tree]

March 24   *Sanguem* [blood]
March 25   *Hilaria* [day of joy]
March 26   *Requ[i]etio* [rest]
March 27   *Lavatio* [bathing][4]

From this we can deduce, by integrating other information passed down through literature and iconography, that the fourth century continued the ancient ritual of the *lavatio*, inherited, like the Megalesia, from the Republican period. In addition, in the fourth century, these holidays existed in a form synthesizing elements of a long liturgy that was an integral part of the drama uniting and separating the Mother of the gods and Attis. Philocalus's calendar, given its post-Constantine date, provides precious evidence of the ultimate development of these liturgical practices under the empire. In its final form, the various episodes in the cult drama took place during the month of March, from the ritual "entrance of the reeds," or *canna intrat*, on March 15, up to the *lavatio*, its conclusion on March 27.[5] The "entrance of the reeds" (*canna intrat*) was marked by the procession of the college of *cannophoroi* (or reed-bearers), an allusion to the Mother's discovery of the infant Attis abandoned on the banks of the Gallos River.[6] On March 22, the "entrance of the tree" (*arbor intrat*) was performed by the group of *dendrophoroi*. This event can be understood in its relationship to the Pessinontian myth and relevant iconography showing that Attis's death occurred under a pine tree. The day of blood (*sanguem*, March 24) was marked by the ritual castration of the *galli*. The connotation of the *hilaria* on March 25 was laughter and rediscovered life, even resurrection. The *requietio* has been interpreted as a day of rest, necessary after the bloody and hysterical effervescence of the two preceding days.[7] Finally, the *lavatio* maintained the function it had had at the end of the Republic. Through the ritual bath in the Almo River, it cleansed the goddess of all impurities in order to reestablish the balance of her divine actions, which had been perturbed by her period of mourning. The entire ritual cycle thus ensured the fecundity of the earth and the planted fields, at the same time as it protected the health of the emperor and political communities.[8]

Pieter Lambrechts and Duncan Fishwick, whose work I am using here, have convincingly reconstructed the stages of the development of this group of liturgical practices.[9] Claudius, who reigned from 41 to 54 C.E., officially made these March ceremonies public events. Originally, there were only three of the events named in Philocalus's calendar. There was the *dendrophoria* on March 22, a ritual celebrated by the *dendrophoroi*, a college we know was instituted in the first century by this same emperor.[10] The "day of blood" (*dies sanguinis*) also took place on March 24 and the *lavatio* on March 27. Once again, given the state of things up until the second century, it was mainly a mourning ritual. It started with a commemoration of the death of Attis (the procession with the pine tree) that culminated in the *galli*'s self-flagellation and castration (on the day of blood) and concluded with the *lavatio* (the ritual bath). This cycle was already known to Ovid as the purification of the goddess responsible both for bloodshed and the demise of her mutilated young lover.[11] What is new under Claudius, with regard to what we observed at the end of the first century B.C.E. in Dionysius of Halicarnassus and in Ovid, is the emergence of the official view under the auspices of the city. The whole ritual that the *galli* already practiced under the Republic was, in a much more circumspect manner, protected by the sanctuary walls up on the Palatine Hill.

During the second half of the second century, most likely at the end of the reign of Antoninus Pius (137–61 C.E.), this scenario introduced by Claudius's reforms was once again modified.[12] The first epigraphical evidence mentioning the college of *cannophoroi* suggests that the inaugural ceremony of March 15 (the *canna intrat*) described in Philocalus's calendar was instituted at the same time. With this new prelude to the festivities, the story of the birth of Attis, and not only his love life and death, was connected to the cycle of spring festivals. At the same time, a new kind of high priest appears in the form of the *archigallus* and a new ritual bull-killing practice becomes known as the *taurobolium*. The three elements that emerge a century after Claudius (the *archigallate*, the *taurobolium*, and the ritual practiced by the *cannophoroi*) do not necessarily appear together, nor are they necessarily interconnected.

Thus, the *archigallus*, a Roman citizen and not a lowly one at that,[13] is often linked to the practice of the *taurobolium*, a ritual that could take place at any time during the year. Yet he has no known, recognized, regular role in the organization of the March ritual, which remains completely independent. The *taurobolium* was an aristocratic ritual whose purpose was to guarantee the health and well-being of the imperial house and the city. It can be considered as both a political and mystical alternative for citizens who could not participate in the castration reserved for the *galli*. Thus, it constitutes an element, among others, of a deep reform at the end of the second century that aimed at integrating more citizens into the so-called Phrygian practices. In the framework of the March ceremonies, this also explains the creation of a new college of citizens, the *cannophoroi*, joining the *dendrophoroi* (or tree-bearers) already introduced under

Claudius. The March rituals, during which the most aristocratic religious associations gathered side by side with the *galli*, became almost as important as the ritual of the Megalesia in April, which continued to be practiced according to the ancient traditions.

The March rituals, as described in Philocalus's calendar, were not completely and definitively defined within the liturgy until the third or fourth century. The last festivity to be included was the all-important day of *hilaria*. A festival of rejoicing and gaiety, literally a festival of laughter, it indicated, from the fourth century on, for some thinkers (but not necessarily for everyone), Attis's return to life.[14] "They claim that he has returned to life," *revixisse iactarunt*, such are the terms used by Firmicus Maternus, who wrote in approximately 346, that is eight years after Philocalus's calendar.[15]

The fourth-century Neoplatonist Sallustius, whose exegesis closely follows the emperor Julian's, interpreted the *hilariae* as an "ascent" (*epanodos*) toward the gods.[16] A testament of sorts written in the eastern part of the empire a bit before Justinian's edict (i.e., around 550 c.e.) suggests what this would have signified for a Neoplatonist. In his *Vita Isidori*, Damascius mentions a personal experience that took place in Hierapolis in Phrygia, not far from Aphrodisias. There, under Apollo's temple, there was an underground passage that emitted deadly fumes. Even birds that flew over this chasm were said to die. Only "initiates" (*tetelesmenoi*) could safely descend into it. Overcome by curiosity — or by confidence: *hupo prothumias eknikethentes* — Damaskios attempted the experiment successfully, along with the philosopher Doros. As soon as he returned, he fell asleep. In his dream, he became Attis and the *hilariae* of the Mother of the gods were performed for him. When he awoke, the dream was interpreted as being connected with the expedition the day before. Damaskios says that it clearly signified for both Doros and himself "the fact of having been saved from Hades."[17] The descent into the abyss was actually a trial, from which they return armed with the assurance of initiates. In light of this adventure from the beginning of the sixth century, whose protagonists remained faithful to the tradition of the old religion,[18] the *hilariae* therefore truly appear as Attis's victory over death.

Christian Readings

Let us recall that in the version of the myth recorded by Arnobius around 300 c.e.,[19] Attis was not seen as having been resurrected. A veritable cult grew up around Attis, who was thought to be a god, not simply just a priest or a lover —

"Cybele's Attis," or the "Phrygian child," "Sangarius's son," the "Little Herdsman," or the "Shepherd." The cult did not develop in the Roman world[20] until the middle of the second century, or perhaps even later, during the third or fourth centuries.[21] Attis shared the divine characteristics of the Mother of the gods as soon as he had become *deus magnus*, and even *omnipotens*. Sometimes, as a result of a parallel evolution, he was considered to be the son of the goddess.[22]

In its relationship to the myth, the March ritual goes through three stages. In the beginning, it first centers on the love relationship and the bloody end of the Mother's young lover; afterward, it is transformed by the introduction of a story referring to birth and childhood; and finally, it takes on the form of an orientation toward the resurrection theme. As of the second half of the second century, the birth and childhood theme, quickly followed by that of resurrection, was also preceded by the image of a miraculous and virginal conception. In order to comprehend the context in which these metamorphoses operated, such as they were manifested in Christian and other sources directly or indirectly affected by the restrictive presence of Christianity,[23] it is necessary to examine the writings of the Fathers of the Church. This documentation contains numerous allusions to and sometimes accurate analyses of the cult of the Mother and Attis.

During his travels to Ephesus, the Apostle Paul encountered merchants selling images of the Great Artemis strongly resembling the small *naiskoi* that were part of metroac piety. If one prudently abstracts this paradigm, the most ancient Christian criticism aimed at the cult of the Mother of the gods would be the first part of Justin's *Apology*, in a text dedicated to the emperor Antoninus Pius. While distancing himself from those he considered "so-called" Christians (spiritual heirs of Simon Magus and Gnostics in the movement contemporary with Marcion, whose morality he could not guarantee), Justin refuted accusations made against the true followers of Christ. He especially refuted accusations of their supposed sexual promiscuity and their practice of ritual murder, including cannibalism. Justin underscored that it was, on the contrary, the polytheistic subjects of the emperor who engaged in such practices. He exemplified this by citing the frequent abandonment of children, who were then driven to prostitution.[24] Again in terms of sexual mores, he also emphasized the paradox of attributing mysteries to the Mother of the gods. Although her name should indicate her august divinity and supposed mysteries, these were in fact linked to the practice of sodomy, of which the self-castrated eunuchs were guilty. Justin attacked the *galli's* practices, which were all the more shocking in his eyes because they were openly practiced, and apparently widely accepted. Justin ironically claimed that the attribute of the serpent, a great symbol and mystery, of course, but one that also referred back to the Fall [of Man], accompanied (as it should) each of the false divinities of the official religion.[25]

What he was driving at was not, all in all, very original. It was the very same point that aroused the satirists' interest and the pagans' morality. Juvenal and Martial also poked fun at the *galli*'s behavior.[26] Seneca dedicated a few pages to the subject, which mix up the rites of the Mother of the gods with those of Ma-Bellone, and the passage later gratified Saint Augustine:

> One cuts off his virile organs, another slashes his arms. How can they fear the gods in their wrath, who thus gain their favor when they are to be propitiated? Rather, gods who would demand this should not be served in any manner at all. So great is the madness of their disturbed and unseated minds that the gods are given satisfaction in ways beyond the ragings of even the vilest men in tales of legendary cruelty. Tyrants have lacerated the limbs of some; they never ordered anyone to lacerate his own. On the whims of kings some have been castrated, but no one ever, at the command of his lord, unmanned himself by his own hands. They slay themselves in their sanctuaries; they beseech the gods with their wounds and with their blood. If one has the chance to look closely at what they do and what they undergo, he will find these things to be so unseemly for decent people, so unworthy of freemen, so unlike the actions of the sane, that no one would doubt that they are mad, were they but mad with the minority; now, however, the crowding number of the insane serves as proof of their sanity.[27]

Barely a generation after Justin Martyr, Tertullian and Minucius Felix, who follows Tertullian like his shadow,[28] criticized more specific aspects of these practices. Their criticism referred to the whole "Phrygian" liturgy in March and to the then recent institution of the *archigallate*. Tertullian mocks the so-called prophetic talents of the *archigallus* by reporting that a few days after Marcus Aurelius's death (which no one yet knew of, because it occurred when he was away from Rome on March 17, 180 C.E.), this supposedly clairvoyant great priest proceeded as if nothing were the matter. Although the emperor was already dead on the day of blood, the priest performed purifications and all the regular prayers to ensure his good health. Elsewhere Tertullian criticizes those who allegorically connect the blood ritual and the *lavatio* to the destiny of Mother Earth, tilled, harvested, and watered. This criticism directly attacks an ancient exegetical tradition found in both Lucretius and Varro.[29] It is important to note the fact that Christian intellectuals' criticism at the cusp between the second and third centuries mainly focused on the *galli's* practice of castration and their ambiguous ministry.[30] The particular attention given to this issue can be explained by the obvious and fascinating proximity between these practices and otherwise very Christian preoccupations. Far from being more foreign to the preoccupations of a Father of the Church than to an ancient Roman, castration was both a potential — and sometimes actually chosen — solution for a penitent Christian and an operation regularly practiced by physicians of the period.[31] The suspicions about Origen constitute the best-known illustration of this.[32] Peter Brown also mentions a young Christian in Alexandria in the second century whose castration put an end to rumors about his behavior toward women for whom he acted as spiritual guide.[33] The same reason would be invoked for Origen's possible self-mutilation.

Strangely enough, all this is very similar to the famous story of Combabos in Lucian's treatise *De Dea Syria*. Combabos, whose name evokes the *gallos — kubebos* — castrated himself to repel the advances of Queen Stratoniki, whom he had guarded during a pilgrimage before becoming the founding hero of the cult of Hera in Hierapolis in Syria, practiced by *galli*.[34]

What Lucian reports in the form of a religious myth is not very different from what we can read in another equally edifying story in the Acts of John. Blinded by his desire for a married woman, a young man from around Ephesus kills his father, who is opposed to his plans. After John miraculously resurrects his father, the "murderer" converts to Christianity, is overwhelmed by guilt, and castrates himself. He then joins the apostle in his evangelical work. The apostle admonishes him as follows:

> Young man, the one who gave you the idea to kill your father and become the lover of another man's wife is the same one who portrayed your cutting off your member as a just act. Alas, you should have eliminated, not your bodily parts, but rather the thought that through their intermediary showed itself to be harmful. For the organs are not what does harm to man, but rather the invisible sources according to which all shameful impulses get started and manifest themselves.[35]

Such adventures are not always reserved for fictional tales. During the same era, the Montanists were spreading their apocalyptic and ascetic doctrine throughout Phrygia, land of the Mother of the gods and the *galli*, not far from where the apostle John was preaching. Tertullian was one of those who adopted Montanism, proof of its diffusion as far away as North Africa. Although Tertullian did condemn physical castration, we must emphasize that Montanus — the founder of a movement synonymous with the presence of two prophetesses,

Maximilla and Priscilla — was qualified by St. Jerome as *abscisus et semivir.*[36] The Church was confronted with this problem of eunuchism and hesitated before taking sides. This was chiefly because Jesus had undeniably identified three categories of eunuchs: (1) those who are born eunuchs, (2) those who have been (forcibly) made eunuchs, and (3) those who have chosen to castrate themselves for the sake of the Kingdom of Heaven (Matt. 19:12). It was not until the Council of Nicea in 325 that organized Christianity formally condemned voluntary physical castration, while nonetheless extolling what is conventionally considered its sublimated, psychic or spiritual, form: celibacy or abstinence.[37]

Thus, the Christian intellectual at the end of the second century regarded the *gallus* dedicated to the Mother of the gods very differently than did the average citizen of the Roman empire. For the average citizen, the loss of virility could only have been considered a forbidding threat, something unthinkable as a choice. The resulting effeminacy would be equated, in this traditionally male-oriented view, with the loss of a jealously guarded superiority. The philosophical education of the Roman elites of the second century encouraged mastery of the body. Sex was not to be condemned, but rather managed. Just like morality and diet, the idea was to avoid dangerous excesses.[38] This, at least, was the theory. In practice, of course, things were a bit more complicated.

Under the emperor Hadrian, Roman law banned castration altogether. Up until then, it had only been condemnable if suffered as a wrongfully imposed act. The new law specifically banned self-castration.[39] The Roman world was fascinated by castration, as evidenced by the integration of colleges of citizens into the Phrygian ritual and the institution of the *archigallate.* The state attempted to control forms of religious fervor, up until then considered completely foreign, that were starting to become contagious.[40] It so happened that these expressions of sensibility interfered with the spiritual interests of Christianity, which also had to manage the delicate relationship between a concern for respecting Roman society's norms and appetites for excesses of asceticism. Rather than a single opposition between two religious worlds foreign to one another, we are dealing here with the emergence of a plurality of attitudes dictated by commonly held preoccupations in the same world, which went beyond cultural boundaries. Given coexistence, encounters, and interactions in the immense stew that constituted the empire, there was a plurality of feelings concerning the same object. Michel Foucault's later works have long called our attention to this type of phenomenon, which has become the subject of increasingly more focused historical examinations.[41]

At the same time that the "Phrygian" practice of the cult of the Mother was being made official in Rome, Christianity was reflecting on issues such as abstinence and chastity, neither of which exclude a priori any experimental hypotheses.[42] We would be wrong to stop here and simply state the existence and the analysis of a phenomenon that was the result, not of syncretism, but rather of an extremely complex mechanism of exchanges. While it integrated Attis into the universe of citizens, first through the college of the *dendrophoroi* and then through the *cannophoroi*, Rome condemned the self-castration of these same citizens and invented a new ritual procedure, the *taurobolium*, which can be viewed as a kind of honorable alternative to the *galli's* ritual practices. This group of initiatives was an extension of the old Republican censure of the foreign rites of the Mater Magna. It was an amended revision of the ambivalence already observed during the Republican era in the relationship between the *galli's* exotic practices and the aristocratic rituals during the Megalesian games.

Nevertheless, this transformation at the same time implies a reference to models not part of the Greco-Anatolian tradition. Attis's childhoods — the myth of his birth and abandonment presupposed by the ministry exercised by the *cannophoroi* — were first discussed in Pausanias's book 7, written in 170 c.e. This account introduces a surprising idea, which so closely resembles the notion of an "immaculate conception" that it might be confused with it: Attis's mother is impregnated by a fruit slipped into her *kolpos*, a word the meaning of which is ambiguous — it could designate a fold in a piece of clothing, or in the body, such as in one's bosom or lap, or even, in medical terminology, the female genitals and their folds.[43]

As we shall see, the ritual of the *taurobolium* stubbornly refuses to let itself be explained by Greco-Anatolian antecedents and ends up being assimilated to a baptism by some Christians. As for the *archigallus*, he is the portrait of the great Near Eastern priest, a dignified homologue of the Christian pope. Is it therefore possible that Christianity, as early as Antoninus Pius and Marcus Aurelius, influenced the development and reelaboration of metroac religion as a whole?

This was the opinion of some Christians during ancient times, and they were not completely wrong. One thing bears repeating, however, and that is that if there were influences and attractions, whatever they may have been, that certainly played a role, it was something that worked in both directions and was made possible by the existence of common interests. We should therefore think of mutual "interferences" rather than of imitation. These interferences might be debated and identified, but they had their effects in a pluralistic and conflictual environment characterized more by controversy than by assimilation.

The Mutilated Body

Just as Rome could not assimilate the Phrygian rite unaltered, Christianity could not allow itself to be reduced, in its doctrine on chastity, to what is proclaimed in the myth of Attis and the Mother. Christian writers are especially vehement on this point. Although they roundly condemn the scandalously erotic side of the relationship between the goddess and her first priest, there is, however, still quite a bit of ambiguity. In writing about the bloody spectacles he frequently attended in his African youth, Tertullian inaugurates what was to become a tradition. He evokes the hyperrealistic performance of the myth of Attis, and especially the episode where Cybele is rebuffed by her little shepherd and sobs. This scene culminates with the on-stage castration of the actor (a prisoner condemned to death) playing the role of the god from Pessinos.[44]

In his *Octavius*, Minucius Felix connects the myth known at least since Ovid — or rather, one of its versions — with a scene worthy of vaudeville: "I am ashamed even to mention the rites of Cybele of Dindymos. She, being the mother of numerous gods,[45] was old and ugly, and couldn't entice her adulterous lover to lewdness. And so she mutilated him, no doubt so that she could make a eunuch of a god. It is by reason of this fable that the *galli* go so far as to sacrifice their virility to the goddess. But this is no longer a cult — these are tortures."[46]

Yet these are tortures inflicted by the libido, and that is precisely what enrages Minucius Felix. Attis's mutilation is a self-mutilation that does not effect an end to desire. This is what the Christian reading insinuates by insisting on the theme of the lovers' spite and vengeance. The result is explicit in the Hellenistic or Roman story constituting the model for this parody, where, on the contrary, self-castration ensures the permanence of an erotico-religious relationship between the goddess and her lover after his death. This relationship constitutes the essence of the *galli*'s priesthood. The meaning of Attis's castration for a Christian thinker in this context is therefore quite obvious. The myth of Attis and the Mother is given as an explanation of the *galli*'s priesthood in erotic terms, at the antipodes of any idea of chastity or renunciation. The framework is that of a relationship uniting the faithful with a divinity who is the Mother. In Christian eyes, Montanist or otherwise, the priesthood of the *galli* had to have appeared as a sort of diabolical imitation of the sacred chastity to which it aspired, whether hypocritically or not.[47] Christian continence would theoretically only function to allow the Spirit to accomplish its saintly work. In some way, it would be able to content itself with freeing up the space necessary for grace, since it has no positive function in itself. This is, at least, what we find, inter alia, in Tertullian.[48] We

shall see that another kind of discourse, linking chastity to explicitly erotic metamorphoses, is also simultaneously present. Peter Brown shows, however, that
what defines Christian specificity in the context of the second-century thinkers,
and constitutes a radical new thing in terms of the surrounding environment, is
the emphasis on sexuality, as opposed to mortality. Thus, sex became the main
focus of reflections concerning the fragility of the human condition.[49] In the
classical world, sexual reproduction was the sine qua non of survival in terms of
the social, communitarian perspective. With the concern for individual health
and salvation beyond this world, it becomes impossible to consider sexual reproduction as a response to or a result of death. On the contrary, the existence of
sexual reproduction becomes the main cause of death. Desire then becomes
something to combat. The myth of Attis also negates sexual reproduction in
every possible way. Yet it does so, in its not yet Christianized versions, without
giving up desire. To understand how sexuality ends up becoming the cause of
death in this myth (which is explicitly the case in Julian's version and already
transparent in Arnobius's), we must hypothesize some complicity with Christian
thought.

The "Son" and the Mother

While keeping in mind the essential and consistent features of the Hellenistic
version of the story in which Attis is not portrayed as the son of the Mother of the
gods, it is now time to investigate the paradoxes present at the heart of the version
reported by Pausanias and Arnobius. We know that in Minucius Felix's time,
there was a story circulating outside of Christianity and related to the Pessinontian ritual where Attis appears to be born as a result of a kind of immaculate
conception. As the child of a princess fertilized by the fruit of a tree, he is
connected to Agdistis, whose blood and semen caused the tree to grow. Attis is
thus presented as having been indirectly engendered by Agdistis, a being created
through Zeus's desire for the Mother.

For Freudian psychoanalysis, the castration complex is connected to the formation of the superego. "In the 'threat of castration' that seals the prohibition
against incest, the function of the law as it is instituted in the human order takes
root."[50] To oversimplify, we can say that the Father (the state) tells the Son: "You
shall not sleep with your Mother," which when extrapolated becomes: "You shall
be a eunuch for (or of) the Mother."

We need not dig deeply to discover a process of this type at work in the Attis myth. It is enough to read it. What does Attis do? His madness leads him to follow the paternal injunction to the letter of the "Freudian version," which sends him back to the Mother at the same time as he seems to escape her. He is ultimately obliged (by the Mother) to choose the only way for a son to stay (despite everything) with his Mother. Pausanias — and Ovid before him — reported the development of the myth as follows: A wedding is prepared that aims at tearing Attis out of his savagery and barely disguised incestuous ways. Because of his relationship with his Mother, Attis cannot go through with this marriage, which has been organized by a paternal, civic figure (the king). The link uniting him to the Mother appears stronger than the social sanctions involved. Motivated by the madness the Mother dictates to him, his only solution is to castrate himself, which will lead to his death. However, beyond this outcome and under the influence of the Mother's remorse (since the Mother does regret the consequences of her anger), this solution also constitutes the foundation of a religious practice that was both scandalous and necessary for the city.

Once it has become a religious act, castration signifies that the state cannot be satisfied with repressing the Mother without displacing her. To endure, it needs to organize a space for this unspeakable thing within the recognized bounds of a ritual practice. From myth to ritual, from sin to the act that negates it while commemorating it, there is a recognition of the Mother as a formidable figure. Zeus, in the Greek myth, masters neither the Mother's strength nor her sexuality.

Considered from the Christian viewpoint, such a scenario can only mean the possibility of a reversal of meaning, the risk of overemphasis and an inadequate interpretation of the role of the Mother, as the Virgin Mary, in her relationship to the ideal of sexual renunciation. To equate the Christian with Attis would be to make Mary into a divine figure as important as God or Christ, and to whom the believer would express his desires. This is the main reason why the Christian Fathers from the end of the second century on show such profound disgust for and anger about the *galli* and their myth. They were not disgusted by castration per se. Rather, they greatly feared that the Phrygian rite would reveal — albeit through a diabolical imitation — a desire condemned by dominant theology.

Further on, we shall review additional arguments. In particular, we shall need to investigate the surprising repression of the loving figure of the Mother for these same early Christian authors. In the minds of theologians and intellectuals, this repression contrasts greatly with the images of the Mother of God that bear witness (as early as Roman catacomb images from the first half of the third century) to a much more spontaneous piety.

Attis and the Gnostics

The revamping of the rituals of Attis and the Mother and the rewriting of their myth that took place between the second and fourth centuries can therefore be envisioned as a process taking place within a great philosophical debate between Christians and pagans. Certainly, it takes place as a confrontation, but it does so in a common space. Perhaps the most extraordinary evidence of this sharing — in every sense of the term — can be found in the *Refutation of All Heresies* by the most important Christian author of the third century, Pope Callistus I's rival, the unfortunate St. Hippolytus (who died an exile in Sardinia under the emperor Maximinus in 235 C.E.). Perhaps because it was written in Greek, or perhaps because of doctrinal reasons or religious politics, this work by St. Hippolytus was not known in the western part of the Christian Mediterranean. Book 5, which is of particular interest to us here, was found only in the nineteenth century, at Mount Athos, along with six other books.[51] For us, the *Refutation of All Heresies* is a privileged source, revealing what could have most likely developed at the end of the second century in terms of applied comparativism. In his itinerary of errors, Hippolytus's outraged gaze fell on the Naassenes, a Gnostic sect who acquired their name from a curious etymology, he says, combining the Hebrew *naas* (serpent) and the Greek *naos* (temple). These Naassenes worshiped the serpent (*naas*) as a symbol subsuming the infinite diversity of the gods that populated the sanctuaries (*naoi*) of different nations. They believed that these gods were the allegorical equivalents of the incarnated Christian God. Among these gods, they particularly focused on the divinities encountered in the mysteries of the Assyrians, Egyptians, Phrygians, and Samothracians. The knowledge they had of them — which was distinctly literary and replete with quotations from Homer, Archilochos, and Herodotus, among others — perhaps derived from an erudite anthology compiled in the first century C.E.[52] The fact that the Naassenes privileged Attis, the Mother of the gods, and the ritual of the *galli* demonstrates their clear interest in the metroac ritual celebrated in March, which was evidently known to them in an Anatolian version. One of the names under which they identified Attis was Papas, which directly relates to the well-documented cults in Phrygian epigraphy during the first centuries of the empire.[53] Hippolytus presents the Naassenes as a relatively obscure contemporary sect — which places them in the first third of the third century — without situating them geographically.

Before approaching the reading of the passages directly concerning Attis and the *galli*, we need to look at the broad outline of the Naassene system according to Hippolytus. The key factor was the relationship linking two entities: celestial and bisexual Man, Adamas, and the Son of Man, Jesus. Man was triple, like the triple-bodied Geryon, composed of the intelligible (*noeron*), the psychic (*psuchikon*) and the earthly (*choikon*). To know this Man was to know God. This was the sense of the Gnosis. Descended from the celestial region, three men made up Man and were found together in Jesus, son of Mary. Each addressed himself to his own from his own being. The intelligible addressed the assembly, the Church of angelical beings, the chosen people; the psychic addressed the assembly of psychics, the missionaries (those with a calling); and the earthly addressed those of the land, the captives. The words of Jesus probably had three hierarchically ordered interpretations. We do not know whether it was theoretically or practically, but they corresponded to distinct groups of faithful within the same Church. The Naassenes attributed this teaching to the Lord's brother James, who had passed it along to Miriam.[54]

The three elements constituting primordial Man are the "Nous" (or intellect), "Chaos," and the "Psyche" (or soul). At the conclusion of his analysis of the beliefs of this sect, Hippolytus gives us the Naassene Psalm, where these three aspects are described. This hymn gives us insight into the manner in which the doctrine was formulated independently of comparativist commentaries drawing parallels between the myths and rituals of different "nations":

The universal law of the All was the First-born Mind;
the second one after the First-born was the outpoured
Chaos, while the Soul got the third rank, with the duty to fulfill the law.
For that reason she put on the form of a hind
and started toiling as a captive, being a game for Death.
Sometimes she would live in a royal palace and look at the light,
but sometimes she is being thrown in a den, and there she weeps.
{Sometimes she rejoices, sometimes she weeps aloud;
sometimes she is a judge, sometimes she is being judged;
sometimes she dies, sometimes she is being born.}
Finally, she — wretched in her sorrows —
in her wanderings entered the exitless Labyrinth.
Then Jesus said: "Look, Father:
this prey to evils is wandering away to earth,
far from Thy spirit (*or* breath)!

And she seeks to escape the bitter Chaos,
but knows not how to win through.

For that reason send Me, Father!
Bearing the seals I will descend;
I will pass through all the Aeons;
I will reveal all the mysteries
and show the forms of the gods.
I will transmit the secrets of the holy way,
calling them Gnosis (Knowledge).[55]

In this doctrine, the promise of salvation runs alongside other Gnostic currents, from Hermeticism to Neoplatonism. The incarnation of Jesus has its raison d'être in its indication of the upward path, that is, the path the soul must take to rise up toward the intelligible in a well-known movement corresponding to the Platonic *anagogē*. The Fall, which presupposed the necessity of such an exercise, was therefore a theme the Naassenes reflected on intensely. They developed it in a myth of dualist inspiration, borrowed from those they called the "Chaldeans." The first man on earth was Adam, an image below of the Man above, Adamas, or God. At first inanimate, he remained immobile like a statue until Psyche intervened. The soul's action results in the celestial Man knowing suffering through the torments inflicted on Adam, his earthly image reduced to slavery. The soul is the principle of movement in perpetual transformation. It is also the principle of desire. It is the cause of the production of things, and therefore also the cause of unhappiness. The soul animates everything, even stones, which the Naassenes believed would grow.[56]

To explain the descent of the soul, its union with matter, and the conditions for its ascension, the Naassenes used mythological exegesis, calling on barbarian and Greek mysteries, discourses that they make into allegories. Hippolytus claims that the Naassenes borrowed their doctrine from philosophies foreign to Christianity.[57] Nevertheless, we get the impression by reading his report that references to the Assyrians, Egyptians, Phrygians, Greeks, and Thracians were presented more as erudite commentary. Their function was to show that their Gnosis, which claimed to be Christian, knew the truth about the gods of the empire. The fact that the true nature of these gods had been revealed by Jesus himself, according to the hymn quoted above,[58] indicates in any case that this commentary figured in one or more texts used by the sect. Perhaps one of these was the *Gospel According to the Egyptians*, to which reference is made.[59]

Diverse myths are brought together to explain the tribulations of the soul, from its fall to its ascent: the Assyrian Adonis and Endymion, the Egyptian Osiris, Adamna and the Hermonian Corybas in Samothrace. Many references to Attis occur in this context.[60]

The desire to make Adonis, the soul, a victim of Aphrodite corresponds to the Fall into reproduction. The desire attracting Persephone to him corresponds to death. Thus, death is conceived of as the negation of reproduction. When Selene falls in love with Endymion's beauty, we can see that a process of returning upward has begun. In fact, this means that the soul's desire comes from a superior world. Ascent and reintegration are realized in the episode where the Mother of the gods castrates Attis while still loving him. This last, paradoxical proposition designates the fortunate female nature of superior, hypercosmic, and eternal things, which supports the male power of the soul.[61] The heavenly union of Attis and the Mother erases the gender distinction and causes it to lose all significance. Primordial Man is, we recall, both male and female (*arsenothelus*). Castration frees Attis, again the soul, from the earthly zones, the inferior areas of creation. It brings him up higher to an eternal substance where there are no longer male and female but rather a new creation, a new male-and-female man. This myth was the basis of the Naassene distaste for and ban on sexual union.[62] Hippolytus wrote that the only thing the Naassenes did not do to completely participate in the mysteries of the Mother was to become eunuchs, that is, to become *galli* themselves.[63] They affirmed that the myth of Attis had to be understood in terms of his relationship to the Mother, interrupted by his marriage and reinstated through his castration. According to the Naassenes, the following affirmation by Paul the Apostle in the Epistle to the Romans would hold true:

For since the creation of the world His invisible *attributes* are clearly seen, being understood by the things that are made, *even* His eternal power and Godhead, so that they are without excuse.

Because, although they knew God, they did not glorify *Him* as God, nor were thankful, but became futile in their thoughts, and their foolish hearts were darkened.

Professing to be wise, they became fools,

And changed the glory of the incorruptible God into an image made like corruptible man — and birds and four-footed beasts and creeping things.

Therefore God also gave them up to uncleanness, in the lusts of their hearts, to dishonor their bodies among themselves,

Who exchanged the truth of God for the lie, and worshiped and served the creature rather than the Creator, who is blessed forever. Amen.

For this reason God gave them up to vile passions. For even their women exchanged the natural use for what is against nature.

Likewise also the men, leaving the natural use of the woman, burned in their lust for one another, men with men committing what is shameful, and receiving in themselves the penalty of their error which was due.[64]

The Phrygians to whom the Naassenes were referring called Attis Papas. They interpreted this name as a derivative of the verb *pauein* ("put a term to, end") "because he has put an end [through his castration] to everything that, before his appearance, was moved in a disordered and dissonant fashion."[65] They also called Attis the "corpse," because he was buried in his body as in a tomb, and a "god," because of his transformation. He appears as the "goat herder" or "shepherd" (*aipolos*), sometimes "sterile" (*akarpos*), sometimes "full of fruit" (*polukarpos*).[66] He is sterile when he is carnal and fulfills "the desires of the flesh," and full of fruit when he renounces sex.[67] The shepherd — a good thing for the "psychics," those who have been called to their mission on earth, but a bad thing for the chosen ones — can be understood as the one who inspires constant movement in the world. His name is *aipolos* and that can be linked to *aei-polos*, "the one who is constantly moving." Thus, we can see how Attis is both a human and a cosmic character, with themes that suggest the incarnation and resurrection of Christ to the Naassenes. First, Attis is the corpse and then he is a god in this soteriologic discourse emphasizing the virtues of sexual abstinence while negating castration. The "verdant harvested ear," a traditional, and even commonplace, metaphor for the *galli*'s mutilation, was explained by the Naassenes through reference to what could not be spoken, that is to say, a mystery analogous to that revealed by the hierophant when he showed an ear of wheat to the initiates on the holiest of nights at Eleusis.[68] Like traditional shepherds, the child Attis plays the syrinx. The Naassenes understand this to be an expression of the spirit of God, that is, the breath (the *pneuma*) filled with harmony at the origin of the *psyche* and the incarnation of the Son of Man.[69] Hippolytus recounts the contents of a well-known poem that one could hear recited in public at the theater, noting ironically that it was no mystery that the Naassenes were crazy enough to associate what they heard with themselves and were sure to understand everything as a description of their own esoteric system.

Whether you descend from Cronos or Zeus, happy one,
Or even from Rhea, salutations, great god,

Attis, plaintive music of Rhea.

The Assyrians call you Adonis, the thrice regretted,

All of Egypt calls you Osiris,

Greek wisdom names you the heavenly horn of the moon god,

The Samothracians call you saintly Adamna,

The Hemonians Corybas,

And the Phrygians sometimes Papas,

Sometimes corpse, sometimes god, or the sterile one,

Or the shepherd, or the cut green ear,

Or male player of the syrinx,

Who gave birth to the fruit-laden almond tree.[70]

Hippolytus goes on to note that the Naassenes discovered this polymorphous Attis in yet another hymn, which they immediately adopted:

I am going to sing the psalm of Attis, son of Rhea,

Without the accompaniment of vibrating bells

And without the moaning flute

Of the Idaean Curetes.

It is with the Apollonian muse of the phorminx

That I shall blend my hymn: *euoi*,

Euan, as Pan, as Bacchus,

As the shepherd of bright stars.[71]

The most interesting evidence of all is a fragment of the myth of the birth of Attis as retold by the Naassenes. Instead of being born, as in Pausanias's version, from the daughter of the river fertilized by the fruit of the tree, Attis is presented as having been born directly from the tree, without any female mediation. The almond tree thereby becomes a symbol of the First Father.[72] In this Christian version, which we can qualify as extreme, if not fundamentalist, Attis simply has no mother at all: "The Phrygians say further that the Father of everything is an almond tree [*amygdalos*]; not [an actual] tree, they say, but the preexisting almond tree that, containing in itself the mature fruit, begins in some way to palpitate and burgeon in its depths to tear off its envelope [literally, its *kolpos*] and engender its own child, the invisible, the unnamable, the secret."[73]

The tearing results from an etymological play on words between *amygdalos* (the almond tree), and *amuxai*, "to tear." Hippolytus must have been delighted to add *amuchai*, a medical term designating the pocket of an abscess, lanced by a surgeon. As for the envelope that is torn, as we have seen, the meaning of the word *kolpos* is ambiguous. [74]

From Arnobius to Julian

Around the year 300, almost a century after Hippolytus's sarcasms regarding the Naassene exegesis of the myth of Attis, Arnobius comments on this same myth. It is no longer a twisted version of this story. Arnobius allows us to appreciate how the Gnostic reading was an attempt at inverting the traditional ancient tale.[75] Arnobius rightfully discovers that the Pessinontian myth on which the *galli*'s practices were based was not, as the Naassenes tried to make it out to be, a negation of maternity and nostalgia for an ancient, primordial androgyny leading to the figure of the Father. On the contrary, it was just the opposite: a systematic and equally shocking negation of the traditional customs of the male sex. Although Jupiter does not manage to unite with the Mother, this does not prevent Agdistis from being born. Agdistis is castrated, but this does not prevent the birth of Attis. The rock Agdus, then the daughter of the Sangarius (Nana) are very much mothers who do without husbands. When the fathers appear, they are presented as failures in terms of the marriages involved. Midas prepares a wedding ceremony for his daughter, but this is interrupted by the sudden appearance of goddesses, and Gallus castrates himself, while his daughter lops off her own breasts. Arnobius underscores that there is a story line "in this myth totally hostile to the male sex," which is to say above and beyond the image of castration: hostile to male roles altogether. Even the animal that nourishes and cares for the abandoned Attis loses its virility; it is a billy goat that gives milk.[76] Furthermore, Agdistis's monstrous behavior shows how male homosexuality runs parallel to Arnobius's expressed suspicion about the real intentions of the Mater Magna. According to Arnobius, she should behave like a grandmother, but the theater reveals on stage the infamous nature of her desire.[77]

This last aspect is particularly significant. It shows that the duality of the goddesses in the Pessinontian myth reported by Arnobius's sources — one maternal and the other a lover, but in a male homosexual way — does not correspond to the theatrical representation, where it was customary to portray a single goddess intent on pursuing Attis with her wily attentions. It is possible, then, that there was a transformation of the myth sometime between Pausanias, who only shows Attis with a single goddess, and Arnobius. This modification might have been introduced in a philosophical context outside of Christianity in order to emphasize the erotic difference between the condemned foreign practice of the *galli* (Agdistis's role) and the desirable expression of chastity in the form of the Roman Mater Magna. We begin to perceive a new metamorphosis of the constitutional ambivalence of the Mother of the gods. First observed on the political level, in Athens and in Republican Rome, the duality of Attis as an object of love indicates a progressive slide in the direction of the chastity theme, a displacement that was probably not the work of Christian ideologists alone.

If we take these Christian writers literally, up to the fourth century, Roman tradition remained strictly faithful to the classical version. This assurance is not entirely genuine, since it comes from authors who had no reason to recognize the similarity between their adversaries' concerns and their own. Lactantius, a Christian writer who had been one of Arnobius's students, denounced the scandal of self-castration because it created beings that were "neither men nor women" during the public municipal festivals (*sacra publica*).[78] According to Lactantius and what is generally known of it, the act of castration was first committed by the Mother of the gods. She became so enraged when she surprised her beautiful adolescent lover in the arms of another that she made him into a half-man (*semivir*) by cutting off his genitals.[79] In fact, it was not until Julian, "the Puritan pagan," according to Glen Bowersock's epithet,[80] that we explicitly encounter an interpretation recalling the Naassenes' laborious analyses, in this preoccupation with ridding the Mother of any and all erotic motivation. It is not necessary to think that, on this point, Julian had been affected by Christian influences. His inspiration in his *Discourse on the Mother of the Gods* is perfectly Neoplatonist, even if it pretends to ignore another Neoplatonist interpretation: Porphyry's, which although also chaste and allegorical, contradicts Julian's.[81] Not long before Julian wrote, around 346, Firmicus Maternus composed his essay on *The Error of Pagan Religions*,[82] one of the most comical versions of the love story between the Mother and Attis. This apologist constructs an interpretation linking the March ritual to a new fact explicitly alluded to, the resurrection of Attis. The story no longer ends, as it does traditionally, with the ritual of the *galli* established after the death of Attis. The mission of the cult was to console a capricious and guilty lady in mourning: "to calm this irritated woman or to find her relief from her remorse." To do this, the Phrygians living in Pessinos dedicated themselves to her in an annual mourning ritual celebrating the loves of this unfortunate queen, where they proclaimed "the resurrection of the one buried not long before." Without any irony or sarcasm intended, this resurrection version evokes a Hellenistic euhemerist scenario long associated with other divinities—for example, in sources known to Diodoros Siculos. Yet such a scenario is quite new for Attis. It is applied here specifically in connection with the Philocalus calendar dating from 354. In Julian's exegesis and in that of Firmicus Maternus, and in Porphyry as well, specific reference is made to the stages in this same liturgy. Yet the essentials of the scenario, it must be recognized, already figured, and in a positive light, in the Gnostic Christian exegesis of the Naassenes more than a century earlier, which is closer to Julian's than to that of Firmicus Maternus. In Julian, Attis's marriage to the nymph signifies death. His castration and ascent toward the Mother mark his return to life. Likewise, the Naassenes depicted Attis as sterile and dead in his earthly existence and fertile and godlike once he renounced sex. This type of paradox is strangely familiar to us, leading us to other paradoxes, destined to express the mysteries of the Incarnation, the cross, and the virginity of the Mother of Jesus.

The *Taurobolium* and Deo's Mysteries

Returning more or less to our point of departure, let us now reconsider anew this elaboration at the end of the second century C.E. of the constituent elements of a new ritual, the "sacred week of Attis," simultaneously with the broad structure of the Christian polemic against that ritual. Even if it means quickly going over much ground that others have patiently explored elsewhere, it is necessary to pause here and consider two phenomena that emerged independently of each other during this period, both of them closely connected to a new attitude toward the Mother and her cult, although unconnected to the March ritual as a whole. Analyses of the relationship between these two relatively obscure subjects are frequently contradictory. The first issue concerns the word *taurobolium*, to which I have already alluded. The second issue, which I have yet to discuss, is often treated as a peripheral matter with regard to the first. It only makes sense in terms of the *taurobolium* and concerns the emergence of a myth relating to an initiation ritual that was part of mysteries independent of the March ceremonies but similarly part and parcel of the realm of the Mother of the gods.[83]

Like the word *criobolium*, which frequently accompanies it within the same ritual context, the word *taurobolium* originally designated a particular kind of sacrifice first evidenced in Asia Minor and, in particular, in Pergamon and Ilium.[84] The meaning of these words is clear. Their formation designates an act assimilating sacrifice to a real or simulated hunt.[85] And such is very much the meaning, imposed by the context, in the four most ancient occurrences of it. This evidence mentioning either a *taurobolium* or a *criobolium* is epigraphic and does not concern the cult of the Mother of the gods.[86] In the most ancient inscription from Pergamon ca. 135 C.E., there is simply a mention of competitive games (*ta kriobolia*) practiced as a hunt by the Ephebians, who sacrificed the animal, a ram (*krios*), after a show that was a kind of religious ceremony. Here we have a ritual including competitive trials closely resembling bullfighting and the corridas well attested to in ancient Asia Minor, where they ended up being introduced into the circus games performed by gladiators.[87] In Ilium during the first century B.C.E., the *taurobolia* were performed in honor of Athena during the Panathenaia.[88] In Pinara, also in Asia Minor, during the same period, many *taurobolia* took place, along with hunts, banquets, and prizes generously distributed by a Maecenas, whose benevolence is detailed in an inscription.[89]

For the word *taurobolium* used in the singular, however, we must look to Italy in the second century, where the term referred to a different type of sacrifice. The first occurrence of this type of ritual was on territory neighboring that of the Phrygian Mother. It took place in Puteoli (now Pozzuoli), on the coast of Campania, north of Naples, and is attested to by a votive inscription that speaks of "Heavenly Venus's *taurobolium.*" The goddess to whom this ceremony was dedicated was the equivalent of the Ouranian Aphrodite, most likely the Syrian goddess. According to the inscription, the event took place on October 7, 134, and was conducted by the priest Titus Claudius Felix at the request of Herennia Fortunata, as ordered by the goddess.[90]

From 160 until the end of the fourth century, all evidence of *taurobolia* or *criobolia* relates to the cult of the Mater Magna and Attis.[91] We can therefore date the beginning, or at least the definitive organization of this new rite, to the reign of Antoninus Pius. It then spread from Italy, especially from Rome and Ostia, to Gaul, Spain, and Germany, as well as to North Africa and eastern Europe (to Dalmatia and, finally, to Athens). The *taurobolium* was performed by private individuals and sanctioned by the *archigallus.*[92] Its objective was to preserve the emperor's good health.[93] After studying the epigraphical formulae designating the ritual, Jeremy Rutter and Robert Duthoy, each in his own way, noted that an evolution had taken place. While the *taurobolium* continued to function to preserve the emperor's well-being, it was gradually assimilated into an individual's personal initiation rite, the equivalent of a mystic resurrection. Rutter suggests that in its final form, the *taurobolium* was assimilated to baptism and became an anti-Christian weapon invented by the pagans.[94] In the fourth century, the individual who completed the ritual was frequently called a *tauroboliatus.*[95]

In addition, the expression *in aeternum renatus* appears on a taurobolic altar in Rome from the same period. Historians who have studied the *taurobolium* have sometimes wanted to distinguish between what belonged to the initiation rites of a private cult as opposed to what would have been part of an official practice aimed at preserving the emperor. However, it is not wise to make such a distinction. We know from the earliest accounts that: (1) the *taurobolium* always remained a relatively aristocratic ritual, performed for the well-being of the emperor or the city; (2) it was not inscribed as a calendar holiday; and (3) it took place on various dates at the expense of the individuals involved,[96] either upper-class citizens or aristocrats,[97] who were acting on divine orders.[98] Accordingly, it would be fruitless to search for a later development that might have transformed the *taurobolium* into an initiation ritual. From the start, it was a private initiation ritual, not a public one, but this did not mean that it did not have a political purpose. Thus, it rightfully figures in the list of initiation practices in the very aristocratic milieu of Vettius Praetextatus and his friends at the end of the fourth century. Praetextatus (d. 384), prefect of the city of Rome and the leader of the opposition to Christianity in the Senate, underwent a *taurobolium* and was "initiated into the bull mysteries of Dindye and Attis." His wife, Pauline, was also initiated.[99] Between 370 and 390, a series of epigraphic dedications coming from the Phrygianum, the sanctuary of the Mater Magna near the Vatican,[100] gives the names of twenty-three people (nineteen men and four women): pontiffs, priests of Vesta, augurs, quindecemvirs, septemvirs, priests of Mithra, of Sol, of Hecate, Liber, and Isis. Fifteen of these are listed as *tauroboliati*. Herbert Bloch analyzed this group of monuments as the expression of religious propaganda posted for all to see. Furthermore, the influence of this milieu can be observed not only in Ostia but as far away as Greece.[101]

Praetextatus was the proconsul of Achaea from 362 to 364 and no doubt took advantage of his stay there, as did his wife, to have himself initiated into the various mysteries of Iacchus and Kōrē in Eleusis; of Dionysus in Lerna, and of Hecate on Aegina.[102] Perhaps he even encountered Attis and the Mother of the gods on Greek soil. Fifteen or so years later, under the mandate of another proconsul, Phosphorius, who was probably from the same milieu, a certain Archelaos was initiated by a *taurobolium* into various mysteries. In the Argolid, he became an initiate of the mysteries of Dionysus of Lerna and in Phyle, in Attica, of those of Attis and Rhea.[103] The appetite for mystical experiences in this social circle was closely connected to political ambitions. This is clear when we note the protagonists' occupations — prefects, vicars, proconsuls, and so on — and their common aversion to Christianity, which was nevertheless about to triumph over them.

What remains to be seen is what the taurobolic or criobolic sacrifice specifically entailed in this context. The only description we have of this ritual was written around the year 400 by Prudentius, whose viewpoint was that of a Christian looking back in time long after this ritual practice had apparently died out altogether, so I shall set it aside and begin with other sources.

In fact, we have indications of this ritual prior to Prudentius's account. We know, for example, that there is mention of it in epigraphic evidence before 250 where the sacrificed victim was castrated during the ritual. After having been cut off, its sanctified (*consecratae*) genitals (*vires*) were [ritually] handled and then transferred from the place of the ritual — the Vatican, in Rome — to their burial place, after being cremated.[104] A receptacle called a *cernus* (in Greek, *kernos*) is mentioned on several occasions as having played a significant role in this ritual. Robert Duthoy sees no connection between this receptacle, used in other mysteries, and the *vires*.[105] It is true that the two elements never come together in the inscriptions. But the function of the inscriptions was not to describe the ritual. An allusion sufficed to place the occasion of the dedication. We find the phrase *cernophora matris deum* in two separate inscriptions that designate at least an occasionally priestly role for the "carrier of the *kernos*."[106] Moreover, in Nikander, the term *kernophoros* in the feminine refers to one of Rhea's priestesses.[107] Duthoy correctly notes that the use of *kernos* in the cult of the Mother is attested to at the beginning of the third century B.C.E. by Alexander the Aetolian, who mentions a *kernas* among the goddess's priests, apparently another *kernos* carrier.[108]

In an explicitly mystic context centered on the Mother, Clement of Alexandria uses the same ritual utensil. Duthoy and Rutter both refuse to draw any conclusions from these converging indications. However, Duthoy's inventory of verbs designating ritual action is very useful.[109] Besides *facere* and *celebrare*, we find the verb "accomplish" (perform, undergo, complete) connected to the ritual of the *taurobolium;* the verb *movere*, implying movements or displacements; and a whole series of words including *suscipere, accipere, percipere*, and *tradere* — three manners of receiving, and only one of transmitting. What is transmitted and received appears to be the *taurobolium* itself. Here the transmission and reception of the ritual is the mystery, even if the *kernos*, the main element, can sometimes also designate the whole ritual, in that one receives the *kernos* just as one receives the *taurobolium*.[110] Through this vocabulary, we can perceive the nature of the initiation rite, whose objective is to "taurobolize" the dedicant. In other words, the purpose of this ritual was to transform him or her in one way or another.[111] This mystic quality becomes more and more explicit in the fourth-century inscriptions. The terms *teletē* (initiation) and *mustipolos* (guide of the initiates); the dedication, in Greek, of a "symbol of the pure mysteries" in Rome; and mention in Attica of "secret passwords" leave us in little doubt.[112] There is no need to imagine a radical evolution at this level between the second and the fourth centuries. Clement of Alexandria, writing at the beginning of the third century, very shortly after the ritual came together under Antoninus Pius, is quite clear on the subject.

We find the pertinent information in book 2 of the *Protrepticus,* Clement of Alexandria's famous essay on the mysteries. The passage is prefaced by an allusion to Dionysus celebrated by the *orgia,* the bacchants' rituals. According to Clement, who enjoys the play on words, these bacchantes, with their cries of "Evoe!" call on Eve, the origin of sin. Deo and Korē, the two goddesses of Eleusis and patronesses of the mysteries (*musteria*) follow these initiates of the serpent. Clement's preamble raises the question of the "etymology" of the words *orgia* and *musteria. Orgia* ("ritual") would derive from *orgē* ("anger") and refer to the story of Deo's anger at Zeus. According to Clement, *ta musteria* (the ceremony of the mysteries) comes from *musos* ("stain") and refers to the sin committed against Dionysus.[113] Clement does not at first say what specific incidents of anger and sin are actually involved. This preliminary imprecision allows him to hide the classical myth and substitute a new version, which I am tempted to call Orphic. The classical Eleusinian myth of Demeter's sadness and anger when she is deprived of her daughter Persephone is displaced in its subsequent development by the anger of a divinity named Deo, the sexual victim of Zeus's violence. The Eleusinian myth in reference to which the version reported by Clement is developed is not forgotten but is greatly modified. Deo represents both Demeter, as Persephone's mother, and Rhea, as the Mother of the gods. A similar modification occurs with Dionysus. The stain can be understood as belonging to Pentheus or one of the other classical adversaries of the Maenads and goes on to mark the Orphic Titans, the assassins of the infant Dionysus. Clement refers to a mythological corpus outside of the tradition of Homer and Euripides. He attempts to join everything together by radically transforming Demeter's doings and Dionysos's passion. The main episodes of this group of stories, which Arnobius has passed down to us in a more precise and highly developed fashion, and in a specifically Phrygian[114] version, are as follows: Zeus copulates with Deo in the form of a bull; Deo—both Rhea and Demeter, mother and wife of Zeus—in her furious anger transforms herself into the forbidding Brimo; Zeus pretends to castrate himself to appease her and throws the testicles (which he has actually torn off a ram) at

Deo's breast.[115] Clement explains that this is why the initiates, not of the Eleusinian mysteries, but those of the Phrygian mysteries (as per Firmicus Maternus)
pronounce the following symbolic statements: "I have eaten in the drum; I have
drunk from the cymbal; I have carried the *kernos;* I have slipped under the veil."[116]
Firmicus gives the following variation on the above: "I have eaten of what was in
the drum [*tumpanon*], I have drunk of what was in the cymbal, and I have thoroughly learned the mysteries of the religion"; in Greek: "I have eaten by taking
from the tympanon, I have drunk at the cymbal, I have become an initiate of
Attis."[117] It is possible that the expression "I have eaten of what was in the drum,"
refers to a practice of ritual mendicancy like that of the *galli,* who collected food
in their tambourines.[118]

Clement's story continues with the birth of Pherephatta, born from the union
between Zeus and Deo-Brimo. Zeus couples with his daughter Pherephatta in
the form of a serpent. The child born of this new incest appears as a bull. This last
trait seems to announce Dionysos and the Orphic tale of his dismemberment, as
discussed in the continuation of Clement's report.[119] Deo is the name of the
divinity whose anger first starts this drama. Clement specifies that she is confused
with both Demeter and Rhea (the Mother of the gods). This genealogical confusion goes back beyond the immediate source of Clement and Arnobius to an old
Greek reflection on the divine equivalencies already evidenced in the context of a
philosophical allegory in the Derveni papyrus. Deo's anger and her pacification
through trickery, a simulation of castration to which the mysteries called Phrygian by Arnobius relate, are part of this demonstration of the Mother's change in
attitude. The Mother of the gods also forgets about her anger in the chorus in
Euripides' *Helen.* She too was a goddess close to Demeter, but whose attributes
and land were Rhea's. What we find in Clement in reference to these "Phrygian
mysteries" thus indirectly refers to an old heritage. This is a story influenced by a
philosophy close to Orphism and whose aim was to bring the Mater Magna back
to prestigious, ancient Greek sources, filtered through a philosophy of the mysteries. So many speculations of this type, linked to the introduction of new forms of
initiation, could have enjoyed a certain success during Clement's era. We have
seen another indication of this in Pausanias's stories, a bit earlier on, where he
tells us of Demeter Erinye of Arcadia, a character similar to Brimo, who is
enraged at having been raped by Zeus's brother, the equine Poseidon, in the
form of a mare. The goddess gives birth to an infernal daughter, Despoina, a
"Young Miss" whose name must not be spoken. Clearly, she parallels Clement's
Pherephatta.[120]

The specifics on the Phrygian ritual connected to the myth reported by Clement are unfortunately quite slim. They are limited to a citation of a formula evoking two musical instruments of the cult of the Mother of the gods, the tympanon and the cymbals, and the name of a sacred receptacle, the *kernos*. A ritual meal is mentioned during which all these objects served as receptacles for food and drink.[121] Finally, there is the issue of a movement or passage, a kind of diving under a veil.[122] We are not able to draw any conclusion from these elements regarding the exact procedures of the ritual. Nonetheless, I suspect that the Christian authors who reported it regarded this ritual as a satanic parody of the Eucharist. On the other hand, three of the aspects mentioned as symbols with respect to an initiation — the tympanum, the cymbals, and the *kernos* — all explicitly appear in the context of the taurobolic inscriptions. These inscriptions commemorated a ritual also addressed to a divinity called Deo, who appears a short time before Clement of Alexandria, in a milieu entirely open to the appeal of Hellenistic mysteries.[123] A pure coincidence? I don't think so, because one of the rare, specific bits of information we have on the *taurobolium* is that the testicles of a ram or bull were handled with great care. They were treated as ritual objects, up to and including a funeral service performed for them. So, it is very much Zeus's manipulation of these same organs that constituted the core of the myths introducing the formula of the mysteries in Clement.

In his 1929 study concerning the influence of Phrygian rituals on the genesis of Montanism, Wilhelm Schepelern already drew the obligatory conclusion from this group of facts.[124] In the story reported by Clement, Zeus wants to be pardoned for his sexual violence and throws a ram's testicles at Deo's breast, as if he had castrated himself. By connecting this proposition to the inscriptions encountered on the taurobolic or criobolic monuments mentioning the cutting off, handling, and burial of the *vires* of the animal, Schepelern observed that the Deo myth reveals the essential function of the *taurobolium*. It was a rite of substitution that permitted Roman citizens to have themselves initiated into the Phrygian rites of the Mother, while avoiding castration.

Although historians generally have maintained the final conclusion of this demonstration, they have often neglected to maintain its premises, which include recourse to Clement's testimony. Rutter and Duthoy revisit this subject, as do Lambrechts and Vermaseren, but without reference to Schepelern's argument. The substitution thesis is not, however, accepted by Garth Thomas, who does not understand how a rite of human castration could be replaced by offering a bull's testicles, since these would be of no interest to the women who organized the *taurobolia*.[125] Instead, we see how the castration displaced to a sacrificial animal, and the mystery's focus on a divinity close to Demeter, might have made this aspect of the "Phrygian" cult reserved for the *galli* something women could participate in as a socially valuable mystery (a *teletē*). Our sources show how the *taurobolium* emerged at the same time as the college of *cannophoroi* and the institution of the *archigallate*. Roman society as a whole (through both religious associations and private initiatives) was concerned with integrating a ritual practice thus far officially divided into two sharply contrasted versions: the Roman version, with the Megalesia, and the Phrygian version, elaborated in the Palatine enclosure. The female cult practice of the Mater Magna, a matronly divinity introduced by Claudia Quinta, had a Phrygian clergy directed by both a priest and a priestess. The numerous ex-votos discovered in the goddess's sanctuary demonstrate why this cult could no longer remain limited to expressing individual piety.[126] While becoming an explicitly Hellenized initiation ritual, like one of the other Greek mysteries, it became a cult open to women as well as men. Thus, the *taurobolium* could claim its political and elitist role and even take on the task of preserving the emperor's well-being.

We are not, however, surprised that some historians have hesitated in closely connecting information introduced by Clement to the *taurobolium*. If Clement really was alluding to the *taurobolium* when he spoke of Deo's mysteries, this would imply that the ritual (at least between the second and third centuries) had nothing to do with the description Prudentius would give in approximately the year 400. Prudentius's "description" is usually cited as being the only specific document accounting for the *taurobolium* ritual. The scene is situated during the reign of the emperor Galerius. The hero is Romanus, a young Christian, who is publicly confronted by the prefect Asclepiades. After a long theological argument—more than four hundred verses—in which Romanus mocks the official gods, there follows a no less detailed description of the tortures to which he is subjected. He remains stoic and speaks of the refined working over of his flesh in terms of spiritual liberation. To prove the truth of monotheism, he even manages to persuade Asclepiades to interrogate a child selected from the crowd of spectators. The child proclaims the existence and singularity of the father god. We witness the young boy being tortured in front of his mother. His mother is a Christian who, instead of protesting, reprimands her little son for his weakness and, singing a psalm, receives his little head and the gushing blood in her cloak.[127] After this interlude, the poet returns to Romanus. A flood of water having miraculously extinguished the pyre for which he was destined, his tongue is cut off.

From the blood spurting from this wound, a new miracle occurs: a word is uttered that literally drowns out the story.[128] Deprived of his tongue, Romanus continues to speak in order to explain the distinction between his martyr's blood and the blood shed during animal sacrifices that Asclepiades vainly seeks to associate with his own.[129] From this bloody, tongueless mouth comes the famous description of the *taurobolium*. It is a perfectly emblematic description of the sacrifice. To begin, one dug a hole into which the "great priest" (*summus sacerdos*) descended dressed in his silk toga, worn in Greek ritual fashion and decorated with sacrificial insignia — a crown and strips of cloth. Above his head, there was a split wood platform perforated with many holes, onto which a bull, decorated for the immolation, would be led. Its breast was pierced with a sacred hunting spear (*sacrato uenabulo*),[130] and the blood gushed out and poured through the platform onto the priest, who bathed his body and clothing in it before coming out to be received by the other priests — the *flamines* — and greeted by the crowd. Romanus continues his discussion of pagan sacrifices by mentioning the hecatombs that spread such a quantity of blood that the augurs could barely make their way by swimming through it. He then goes on to mention the mutilations and self-castrations of the *galli* intended to quench the thirst and assuage the wrath of the goddess. Finally, he notes a strange fire-branding ritual.[131]

In essence, the description of the bull sacrifice appears herein as a stylistic exercise. It aims at presenting the group of pagan sacrifices — animal sacrifices and the self-castration of the *galli* — as different kinds of monstrous blood baptisms. These contrast with the martyrs' blood baptism, no less complacently described, but considered as sacred and sanctifying. Prudentius, who mentions it twice, as we have seen, in the same poem, makes no allusion, not even an indirect one, to the Mother of the gods when he describes the sacrifice of the bull.[132] The priests involved in his account are neither *galli* nor *archigalli*, but rather *flamines* and a great pontiff. It is therefore necessary for us to remove this doubtful testimony from the documentation on the *taurobolium*.[133]

Moreover, the *fossa sanguinis*, despite the dreams of some archaeologists,[134] is purely a matter of Christian literature. Firmicus Maternus, who is sometimes invoked to link Prudentius's "evidence" to the taurobolic inscriptions, does not mention a pit for a blood bath:

> It is for the salvation of men that this lamb's holy blood is shed, for the Son of God must redeem his saints by the flowing of his precious blood and the men liberated by the blood of Christ must be consecrated in advance by the majesty of immortal

blood. The blood shed at the feet of idols saves no one, and so that the blood of animals does not fool or lose unfortunate humans, let it be known that blood pollutes, it does not redeem, by a series of catastrophes it destroys a person in death. Unhappy are they who are drenched by the outpouring of sacrilegious blood, that sacrifice of a bull or a ram pours out upon you the stain of wicked blood.[135]

In the following paragraph, Firmicus Maternus exhorts all such "stained" individuals, including those who have been initiated by the *taurobolium*, to purify themselves with holy baptismal water. Rather than a description of the actual rites involved in a *taurobolium*, despite how bloody castration and ritual sacrifice must in fact have been, we have here an illustration of the fourth-century Christian interpretation of baptism. The pit into which the priest descends is a Christian invention, created by extending this interpretation. The pit is only mentioned twice in all of our sources: in the above-mentioned text by Prudentius and in the anonymous poem, *Contra paganos*, that no doubt inspired him. *Contra paganos* is the only source that actually designates this pit as part of the taurobolic ritual.[136] The unknown author evokes the shameful era of Praetextatus and inaugurates, ten or twenty years after the end of the *taurobolia*, the long history of an illusion. The blood pit is a metaphor that ends up being identified with the *taurobolium* and taken literally. As one of the major emblems of the old ritual Roman practice, the *taurobolium* was inextricably linked to the aristocrats' resistance against Christianity. Thus, the *taurobolium* generally takes on the shape given to it by Christian history. Other rituals, and in particular the *lavatio*, outlived it by many years. This is understandable in that, unlike the *taurobolium*, which was a private ceremony reserved for an elite and dedicated to an emperor who was henceforth Christian, the *lavatio* was the continuation of a popular spring festival. These customs were considered indispensable for the well-being of the community at large. At least since the "reforms" of Antoninus Pius, respect for this traditional festival was meant to guarantee the fertility of the fields and the abundance of the harvests.

CHAPTER SEVEN

From Mother of the Gods to Mother of God

The Last Western Processions

Saint Augustine remembered the procession that had carried the Mother of the gods through the streets of Carthage during the *lavatio* in his youth.[1] The goddess bore the poetic name of Berecynthia:

> I myself, when I was a young man, used sometimes to go to sacrilegious entertainments and spectacles; I saw the priests raving in religious excitement and heard the choristers; I took pleasure in the shameful games which were celebrated in honour of gods and goddesses of the virgin Coelestis, and Berecynthia, the mother of all the gods. And on the holy day consecrated to her purification, there were sung before her couch productions so obscene and filthy for the ear — I do not say of the mother of the gods, but of the mother of any senator or honest man — nay, so impure, that not even the mother of the foul-mouthed players themselves could have formed one of the audience.[2]

Augustine recalled the immense crowd of spectators of both sexes. Further on, he observes that

> [Scipio Nasica was chosen] by the Senate as the citizen most worthy to receive in his hands the image of that demon Cybele, and convey it into the city. He would tell us

whether he would be proud to see his own mother so highly esteemed by the state as to have divine honours adjudged to her. . . . Surely he would desire that his mother should enjoy such felicity were it possible. But if we proceeded to ask him whether, among the honours paid to her, he would wish such shameful rites as these to be celebrated, would he not at once exclaim that he would rather his mother lay stone-dead, than survive as a goddess to lend her ear to these obscenities?

Augustine's attitude to "these repugnant ceremonies" is clear in this close-up of the *galli* in another passage in the *City of God:* "Concerning the effeminates consecrated to the same Great Mother, in defiance of all the modesty which belongs to men and women. . . . These effeminates, no later than yesterday, were going through the streets and places of Carthage with anointed hair, whitened faces, relaxed bodies, and feminine gait, exacting from the people the means of maintaining their ignominious lives."

Even after the *galli* had become no more than a distant memory, some aspects inherited from their political ritual, especially the procession of the cult image of the goddess, remained linked for a long time with a goddess referred to in late Christian antiquity as Berecynthia.[3] In Autun [in Burgundy], home of the Aedui, people are reported especially to have venerated this Mother of the gods, who had been transformed into the *mater demonorum,* "mother of demons," and was worshiped alongside Apollo and Diane.[4] During the procession, the idol Bere-cynthia was carried on a chariot throughout the streets of the town amid the crowds. St. Symphorian refused to participate in these celebrations, however, and was brought before Heraclius, the municipal magistrate. Symphorian proclaimed that as a Christian, he refused to adore this demonic image, and he even sardonically asked the magistrate's permission to pulverize the idol.[5] When he was taken out to be executed, his venerable mother encouraged him from the top of the city wall, calling to him by name ("venerabilis mater sua de muro sedula illum voce commonuit dicens: 'Nate, nate, Symphoriane'"): "Raise up your heart, my Son, life is not being taken from you, it is transformed for us [Christians] into a better existence." The appearance of the human mother at the precise moment of the apparent victory of the Mother of the gods is not a coincidence, nor is the precise location of the scene. Substituting herself as a human spiritual guide for the old divine protectress of the city, Symphorian's mother manifests herself, at the moment of his martyrdom, "from the wall." This allusion to an essential attribute of the goddess — her crenellated crown — gives the Christian mother's intervention the character of an epiphany. She appears here as a human substitute for the Mother of the gods, quite as holy as the goddess whom Christians henceforth called a prostitute had been, but bearing an entirely different message.[6]

St. Symphorian was martyred around 179 C.E. However, in his hagiography, written around 590, Gregory of Tours also speaks of Bishop Simplicius (d. 418), another figure linked to the conflicts opposing the Christians of Autun to Berecynthia.[7] Gregory had been to Autun and knew the region well. According to his local sources, the episode relating to Symphorian was already part of a long-standing local tradition. Bishop Simplicius was known for having built a church on the site of St. Symphorian's tomb and was therefore the hero who ended the cult of Berecynthia.

In the middle of the Burgundy countryside, near Autun, we find the very last Western evidence of a ritual precisely described as dedicated to the Mother of the gods, an anecdote marking the apparent end of this religion. One day, the good Bishop Simplicius was walking in the country when he found a great procession in progress, with much singing and dancing. The goddess named Berecynthia was being carried on a chariot called a *carpentum* or a *plaustrum* in order to ensure the bounty of the fields and the vines. Shocked by the idiocy of the idolatrous crowd before him, Simplicius prayed to God: "Enlighten the eyes of this people so that they may know that the image of Berecynthia is nothing." Crossing himself, he then threw the idol to the ground. There she remained, stubbornly attached to the ground, despite all efforts to raise her up again. Even the oxen pulling the chariot could do nothing to move her. The large crowd was confounded. The goddess, they averred, must be outraged. So, they whipped the animals and performed sacrifices, but to no avail. Then, quite spontaneously, four hundred of the men from among this stupid crowd began to say to each other: "If indeed this deity is powerful, she should get up by herself! She has only to order the oxen to stand up and pull. If she cannot move, it is clear then that she is not a divinity at all!" Accepting this proposition, which in effect challenged the goddess to an ordeal, they immolated one of the animals, but in vain. Since Berecynthia showed herself decidedly incapable of moving, they then called for a [Christian] priest and all of them converted on the spot to the Catholic Church. Recognizing the greatness of the true God, they were blessed by holy baptism.[8]

The above story, presented as a report of the last procession of the Mother of the gods to take place in Autun at the beginning of the fifth century, borrows its essential narrative structure from the oldest Roman tradition of Claudia Quinta, a tradition still well known to the Fathers of the Church.[9] Here, too, the obstinate immobility of the cult image of the goddess leads to an ordeal. But here the challenge is no longer addressed to the human and political community. In a rather abrupt reversal of the case in which the Roman matron ceded her role to the divine Mother, the goddess herself is challenged, and the ordeal, unlike the one imposed on Claudia Quinta, leads to failure pure and simple. Following this insulting parody, seven hundred years after her long, hesitant entrance into Rome, the Mater Magna can only depart the scene ashamedly. She is shown to be an impure matron.[10]

The Mother, Attis, Christ, and Mary

Four long centuries had elapsed between the martyrdom of Saint Symphorian and Gregory of Tours's writing of the *Livre sur la gloire des confesseurs* (*Book on the Glory of the Confessors*). Despite Simplicius's episodic intervention and certainly the efforts of many others, the Mother of the gods was not, however, forgotten. In fact, the conflict opposing our goddess to Christianity is inscribed in a history destined to remain unfinished.

Apparently, the goddess emerges from this conflict neither in victory nor in defeat. In order better to grasp the roots and consequences of this contest, we have to follow two converging paths. The first is marked by the stages of the evolution of the cult of the Mater Magna in the Roman empire. There we saw the gradual introduction of public holidays for the ritual into the official calendar. Without always having recognized the implications of the formula, modern scholars have called this the "holy week of Attis." The second path, the Christian polemic against this same ritual, proposes an external perspective closely linked to the first. We have seen that this polemic developed along with the evolution of the metroac liturgy of the month of March, aimed at constituting a new figure of Attis. The paradigm of the priest, divine mourning following the death of a human lover, constituting the founding act of a priesthood (that of Attis and the *galli*), gave way to a new paradigm of resurrection. This movement, without it ever being explicitly formulated, foreshadowed a possible identification of the Phrygian shepherd, a man turned god, with another shepherd, Christ, a god turned man.[11] At the end of this process, victorious Christianity placed Mary, the Mother of God, on a throne strikingly similar to the one used by the Mother of the gods. Moreover, beyond the hieratic image of the heavenly sovereign, Mary's emotions are depicted as those of a loving and suffering mother, paradoxically connected to Eve's sorcery, guilty of the Fall of Man and at the root of all Evil. Eve and Mary are finally united together into a single figure, the Church as Christ's bride.

As we know, the canonical Gospels are not as loquacious as the apocryphal tradition is about the circumstances of the conception, birth, and childhood of Christ, and consequently about his mother. In the latter tradition, from the second century on, a group of stories emerged on the theme of virginal maternity. These constituted a Christian parallel of the traditions relating to the miraculous birth of Attis, also attested in the second century. The theme of Mary's virginity during childbirth appears for the first time in a passage in an apocryphal text called *The Ascension of Isaiah*, which can be dated to the end of the first century.[12] In this, Mary—Joseph's virgin wife—suddenly discovers a small infant next to her. She is troubled by this; "then her womb appeared as before the pregnancy." Did she or did she not give birth? The text, tainted by Docetist thought, leaves the question open.[13] The most important version of the story, from slightly later, is that of "Mary's Nativity" [*Genesis Marias*], traditionally known as the *Protevangelium of James* [*Protevangelium Jacobi*], an extraordinarily widespread text from the second half of the second century that deeply influenced Christian liturgy, prayers, and iconography.[14] Although it comes from a literature parallel to the canon, it nevertheless, as Averil Cameron expresses it so well, manifests "the power of an imaginative world at which the New Testament itself does no more than hint, but which in practice formed the real world of Christian belief."[15]

Before reappearing in connection with Mary, the theme of the Immaculate Conception had already been present in an episode concerning her parents. Joachim and Anne were a sterile couple whose story might have been the first seed—so to speak—of what became the dogma and festival of the Immaculate Conception in the nineteenth century. Humiliated because of his inability to produce descendants of the people of Israel, Joachim retreats to the desert, where he fasts for forty days and forty nights. With a kind of widowhood added to her sterility, Anne, on the Lord's day, washes her face and puts on her wedding Sabbath clothes. She goes into a garden, sits under a laurel tree and prays to the Lord. An angel appears to her announcing that her torture will end, and Anne promises to dedicate the child who will be born to God. Informed by an angel, Joachim returns home two months later. He stays away from Anne in his own home before going to the temple, where an oracle reveals that his wishes will be granted. In her seventh month, Anne gives birth to Mary. The child is raised in the Temple where, living like a dove, she is miraculously nourished by an angel. At the age of twelve, and ostensibly because her passage into puberty has made her impure,[16] her grandfather, Zachariah, has to take her away. Instructed by an angel, he gives her in marriage to Joseph, a widower who has been designated among all others by a miraculous sign. Aware of his age, and because he is already the father of other children, Joseph hesitates before going along with these divine orders. In his prolonged hesitation, but also in accordance with Zachariah's wishes, he does not touch his young bride. He leaves home to work far away as a carpenter for a long period of time. The rest of the text suggests that this absence lasts about four years. In the meantime, Mary is chosen among the seven virgins without a role in David's tribe to weave the "true purple" of the Temple's veil.[17] Leaving her house to go and get water from the well, she hears the voice of an angel say: "Hail Mary, full of grace, the Lord is with you, O blessed among women!" Startled by the Annunciation, whose meaning she does not understand, she returns home to her weaving. An angel then appears to her, reassures her, and predicts that she will conceive the Word of the Lord. Mary remains perplexed: "If I must conceive the work of the Lord, am I going to give birth as all women give birth?" The angel of the Lord answers: "No, Mary, not that way: the power of God will cover you with his shadow,[18] and thus, the being born from this will be called holy, son of the Almighty. You will call him Jesus."

Mary then visits Elisabeth, a relative of hers, the wife of the priest Zacchariah, who is then pregnant with the future John the Baptist. She immediately greets Mary as the mother of her Lord, the mystery of incarnation having been revealed to her through the infant's movements in her womb. Elisabeth makes a gesture of benediction to her visitor. Mary stays with Elisabeth for three months, and her womb grows larger each day. Seized with fear, she returns home and keeps away from the sons of Israel. She is sixteen years old. During the sixth month of her pregnancy, Joseph returns from his construction work. Finding her pregnant, he throws himself to the ground in grief. He cannot believe Mary's claim that she is a pure virgin. He is preparing to take her away in secret when an angel appears to him in his dreams. The angel reveals that the child to be born comes from the Holy Spirit, and that he must accept him as his own and give him the name Jesus. Suspected of not having respected the chastity of the virgin who had been given to him by the Temple — and who was one of the weavers — Joseph must submit to the ordeal of the bitter waters. Mary, too, must undergo the same trial.[19] Found innocent by this test, they leave for Bethlehem, where they must go to obey the imperial order that a census be held. Sitting on a donkey, Mary is sad and then begins to laugh: "I see two peoples in my eyes, one is crying and is in mourning, the other is joyous and is rejoicing." Halfway there, the baby who is in Mary's womb presses to come out. Joseph finds a cave and takes his wife inside. He then goes to look for a Hebrew midwife in Bethlehem, when suddenly, for an instant, everything is immobilized, the sky, the birds, human beings.[20] Then everything returns to normal. Joseph finds the midwife and returns with her to the cave. A luminous cloud covers the cave and then fades away, leaving an intense, blindingly bright light in its place. This light gradually fades, and the infant appears, turning to his mother's breast. The text moves along quickly here and presents the midwife involved in a discussion with Salome, who has not yet been introduced. Salome cannot believe, without testing it herself, that a virgin has given birth without losing her virginity. Salome verifies this with her finger. Her hand is desiccated, until, following a prayer, she takes the baby in her arms. A voice is then heard requesting that she not divulge the marvelous things she has seen before the infant's arrival in Jerusalem.

Only the episodes directly related to the Immaculate Conception and virgin birth have been recounted here. The anonymous author seems to have been a foreigner in the Jewish and Palestinian world, and the story relates to a literary genre very close to that circulating in Greek novels of the period. It appears to be a Christian testimony. Its religious sensibility is analogous to that which, on the Hellenic side, colored stories of Attis's conception and childhood, from Diodoros to Pausanias, and their reformulation in Christian writing by Arnobius.

To better evaluate the scope of a connection that might appear ludicrous to some, a few remarks are in order. First, a reminder: the discourse on chastity — which conditions both the postulate of virginal conception and attitudes to the *galli*'s bloody form of abstinence — comes from preoccupations that were widespread in the second century of our era in both Christian and non-Christian Mediterranean communities. In any case, whereas in the non-Christian world this type of discourse was part of elite philosophies that shied away from extreme practices such as the *galli*'s castration, in the Christian world, the same type of discourse was the subject of general attention and threatened to lead to collective practices of unsettling proportions. The success of the Montanist and Encratist sects show this to be the case.

We know that Mary's virginal maternity has been the subject of numerous interpretations. Early on, it provoked a great deal of speculation, which was soon judged heretical. The Council of Ephesus defined the status of the Theotokos by presenting her maternity exclusively as an incarnation. Christ was born from a real birth, and not from a simulation, as Docetism would have it. Yet it was a childbirth that could not be dissociated from the paradox of virginity. The insistence is on the mysterious nature of this event, without calling it mystic. Mary's tender and maternal qualities do not constitute the center of attention of pious reflection. Instead, the focus is the paradoxical logic implied by the role of the Virgin as an instrument of Christ's birth.[21] The Virgin's maternity only functions to explain the incarnation of an exclusively masculine god. Asceticism and priesthood in the Christian world are directed toward the double figure of a Father and his Son. We have to turn to the Gnostics to see the theme of androgyny referred to, and even here our documentation shows that it relies on a version that radically excludes the female role with regard to conception.[22] As opposed to the Christian position, decidedly simpler for nuns than for monks, the *galli*'s priesthood is entirely oriented toward the Mother. Elsewhere, other religious currents of the same period were directed to Isis or the Dea Syria. Nevertheless, these currents, as opposed to Christianity, were not exclusive and existed alongside other movements coming from the same religious environment that were oriented toward male divinities, such as the Orphic cults of Dionysos, Mithra, and Sol Invictus.

Given this perspective, besides this general tendency toward sexual asceticism, the common ground between Christianity and the other religious movements from the early centuries of the common era lies in this investigation of modes of passage toward the lower, material world from a celestial and immaterial origin. This questioning brought more than abstract responses. In the first centuries of the empire, we find the theme of the virgin also present in evangelical tradition and "Phrygian" mythology, as well as in certain extensions of a Platonic reflection on the Fall and the Incarnation. This virgin's role is to mediate between the heavenly world and the earthly world.

For example, in the *Chaldean Oracles*, this mediating virgin appears in the form of Hecate. The soul-Hecate represents the matrix, the *kolpos*, whose folds, under the influence of the Ideas — the fiery, luminous seed of the paternal Intellect — produce the material worlds.[23] It is remarkable that the Christian and non-Christian discourses introducing such a figure are contemporaneous. It is particularly striking because among these various speculations each envisions the mediating virgin in its own way. Certainly, there are connections, especially with regard to Gnosticism. Yet, notwithstanding this common ground attesting to the desire to respond to the very general question posed by a shared wariness about the body in traditional and mythological terms, the distinctions are more significant than the similarities.

The Dangers of Confusion

The virginal body of Mary was the object of innumerable speculations aimed at preserving the paradoxical mystery of the conception and birth of God. The absolute purity of Mary seems to have been a preliminary condition for affirming so special a form of maternity. Although her body is necessary for the birth of God in this world, the Mother is considered according to a hieratic perspective on celestial sovereignty. Her potential tenderness and entirely human sweetness toward the Child are overshadowed, so to speak, in terms of the official discourse.[24] A mosaic in the apse of the first Roman church to be consecrated to her, Santa Maria Maggiore, shows her as the Empress of Heaven, sitting on a throne.[25]

This sovereign virginity refers to theological and abstract qualities.[26] Yet perhaps, from another viewpoint, it can be seen as the new paradigm for an entirely human chastity that had been made concrete in Christian renunciation. In a passage from the *Pseudo-Titus Epistle*, a fifth-century text referring to the *Acts of John* (the Apostle) from the second century, we can read that those men (and not just those women) who renounced marriage are bound by a superior marriage. They await the arrival of the eternal Bethrothed from Heaven, Christ the Lord.[27] In fact, what goes back to the *Acts of John* is the Encratic type of unequivocal condemnation of marriage. Invited to a wedding, John launches into a vehement diatribe against marriage: "She is the temptation of the serpent, ignorance of doctrine, damage caused to production, gift of death, the act of obliteration, learned division, office of corruption, boorishness . . . flowing of blood, furor of the soul, demise of reason, etc. etc."[28] Following this list, which has no fewer than thirty-six definitions, there is a proposition that comes from an altogether different ideology and must be attributed, not to the *Acts of John*, but rather to the author of the *Pseudo-Titus Epistle:* "Since you have understood that, little children, unite in inseparable, veritable, and holy marriage, while waiting for the unique, incomparable true Spouse, who comes from heaven, Christ, the eternal Spouse." Virginity as the attribute of the spouses of Christ is a theme developed throughout the third century.[29]

In the *Acts of Thomas,* a great apostolic novel of Syriac origin that belongs to this era, we find the story of Mygdonia's baptism. It is one of the first explicit formulations of the marriage of the Christian individual with Christ.[30] Mygdonia explains to Carysios, her earthly husband, that there is a great gulf between their earthly union and true union. She uses a series of contrasts opposing fleeting life and pleasures to immortal life and pleasures, culminating with the mention of the wedding chamber where the bed is not made with perishable covers, but with love and faith, and the mortal husband finally cedes his place to Jesus, the true and everlasting husband. The theme of marriage with Christ is, of course, very much a part of the development of a more ancient tradition going back, via the Epistle to the Ephesians (5:22–33) and the passages of the Gospels qualifying Jesus as a spouse (Matt. 9:15; Mark 2:19; John 2:29–30), to the Song of Songs and the old image of Israel, wife of Yahweh. What is new here is the use of this traditional metaphor to designate, not a collective, but rather an individual relationship between the believer and his God. This transformation into an erotic mystery in turn presupposes the image of Mary as the expression of the Church, as the wife in her relationship to the husband. The genealogical confusion once again verges on the incest theme.

In taking the Mother of God as a model, Christian abstainers effectively readied themselves to receive her Son as the wife waits for her husband.[31] Compared to the fact encountered in the myths and rites relative to the Mother of the gods, this new tendency in Christian sensibility constitutes a noteworthy reversal. No longer is the desire of the Christian mystic oriented toward the Mother; rather, it is now directed toward the Son, conceived of as the lover of a feminized soul. When this process is developed on the Christian side, we observe that, without waiting for any Byzantine scholiast, Attis has already been transformed into the son of the Mother.[32] Once again, the transformations of the metroac religion accompany the emergence of Christian assumptions in a counterpoint that excludes the idea of influence or borrowing. Everything implies that these developments occur in a common context, with mutual interferences.

It is as if the cult of Mary that developed in particular after the Council of Ephesus (431), where Mary was defined as the Theotokos ("genetrix of God"), had to be protected against a dangerous temptation. This dangerous temptation was to accord the Virgin divine status, which would clearly assimilate her, even if in a monotheistic way, to the ancient Mother of the gods.[33] Her cult therefore had to be limited to the religious expression appropriate to a saint and no more.

As proof of the true danger inherent in this possibility, I refer to the fulminations of Epiphanios, bishop of Salamis, half a century before the Council of Ephesus, against the obscure Arab sect of so-called Kollyridians, who adored the Mother of God.[34] The latter took their name from bread rolls (*kollyrides*) that they used to share during a eucharistic type of ritual meal. Epiphanius found these practices to be doubly reprehensible: first, because women performed them, grouped around a priestess, and second, because they addressed their devotions, not to the Father or the Son, but to the Mother. Epiphanius informs us that this sect came out of Thrace and spread throughout Arabia. Insofar as we can rely on this information, one would like to think that the Kollyridians had a certain influence on future events. We know that for Muhammad, and according to Muslim writers, the Christian Trinity consisted of God, Jesus, and the Mother — Allah, Isa, and Maryam.[35]

A Byzantine Epilogue

The danger of seeing the Theotokos take on the attributes of the Mother of the gods was not limited to marginal, and possibly imaginary, populations on the outskirts of the empire. This fusion showed itself to be possible nowhere better than in Constantinople itself. Vasiliki Limberis has been able to show how, in particular the admirable hymn to the Akathistos, one of the most ancient hymns to Mary in the Byzantine liturgy, which apparently dates from the fifth century, derives some of its essential metaphors — notably, those of the divine protectress of the City and the dispenser of agricultural abundance — not from biblical traditions, but rather from those of the ancient Mother of the gods.[36] Even in the eighth century, John of Damascus still wrote, in his *Homilies on the Dormition of the Virgin*, about guarding against possible confusions, specifying that the Christian festival of the Mother of God had to take place without the flutes and corybantes of the "Mother of pseudonymous gods" — that is, the Mother of those who are wrongfully called gods, without *thiasos* (Bacchic dancing) and mystic ritual.[37]

In Constantinople, the new capital city, Constantine himself set up an apparatus favorable to such confusions.[38] We know as well that the "new capital was not as Christian as it was often claimed."[39] For one thing, old sanctuaries — in particular, three temples on the acropolis — were still used, even if less often and only for private, unofficial ceremonies.[40] In addition, there was the introduction of new political and religious symbols that were not entirely bereft of the ancient Greek heritage. Thus, Constantine erected two new religious buildings on the Tetrastoon, the forum with four porticos: a temple of the Roman Fortuna and a temple of Rhea, the Mother of the gods, which can be interpreted and certainly was interpreted by the city's inhabitants as being that of the Fortuna of Constantinople.[41] Indeed, according to a tradition that remained vivid in the Christian era, the city's founding hero, Byzas, had built a sanctuary of Rhea there, a *mētrōon* that Hesychius said was considered a Tychaion, a sanctuary of Tychē-

Fortuna. Constantine thus welcomed the Mother of the gods as the protectress of the city — or perhaps we should say rediscovered her, because her reception simply repeated a legendary action by the city's founding hero.

The historian Zosimus specifies that Constantine ordered that an image of the Mother be brought into his new capital, and that this image recalled the most ancient Hellenic past of the region. He had the statue brought from Kyzikos on the Propontis, the very same place where the Argonauts had long ago founded the most ancient cult of the Mother of the gods. This double reference to the ancestral city and the most distant Greek origins gave Constantine's initiative a hint of nostalgia. He proposed that Byzantium be refounded, as Rome had been before it, with the arrival of an Idaean ancestor. So, instead of the Trojan goddess, he brought in an even more ancient one, the thoroughly Greek Mother goddess of the Argonauts and the Kyzikan initiators of Anarcharsis.

Nonetheless, the new capital aimed at being, above all, a Christian city. Zosimus, with thinly veiled bitterness against the Christians, attributes this to the emperor's lack of regard for the divinity. He reported that Constantine had caused the statue from Kyzikos to be "mutilated." He had had "the lions taken off that flanked her sides and modified the position of the hands: whereas before, she had seemed to hold back the lions, she had now been transformed into a kind of pious figure, her eyes looking toward the city and protecting it with her solicitude."[42]

In the process of metamorphosing into the Fortuna of the new capital, the Mētēr theōn, the Mother of the gods, had lost her ancient attributes and assumed the loving, protective stance of the Mētēr Theou, the Mother of God, her close neighbor. But she did not forget her origins.

Notes

Abbreviations

ANRW   *Aufstieg und Niedergang der römischen Welt*
CCAA   *Corpus Cultus Cybelae Attidisque*, ed. M. J. Vermaseren, Études préliminaires aux religions orientales dans l'Empire romain 50, 7 vols. (Leiden, 1977–89)
CRAI   *Comptes rendus de l'Académie des Inscriptions et Belles Lettres*
IG   *Inscriptiones Graecae*
Jacoby   *Die Fragmente der griechischen Historiker*, ed. F. Jacoby (Berlin, 1923–58)
OGIS   *Orientis Graeci Inscriptiones Selectae*, ed. W. Dittenberger (Leipzig, 1903–5)
PG   Migne, *Patrilogiae Cursus, series Graeca*
PL   Migne, *Patrilogiae Cursus, series Latina*
PMG   *Poetae Melici Graeci*, ed. D. L. Page (Oxford, 1962)
RE   Pauly-Wissowa, *Realencyclopädie der classischen Altertumswissenschaft* (Stuttgart, 1893–)
TAPA   *Transactions and Proceedings of the American Philological Association*

Preface

1. Johann Jakob Bachofen, *Das Mutterrecht* (Stuttgart, 1861), trans. Ralph Manheim in *Myth, Religion, and Mother Right: Selected Writings of J. J. Bachofen*, Bollingen ser. 84 (Princeton, N.J., 1967).

2. See Maarten J. Vermaseren, *Cybele and Attis: The Myth and the Cult*, trans. A. M. H. Lemmers (London, 1977), 13–16, and pl. 5.

3. Michael P. Carroll, *The Cult of the Virgin Mary: Psychological Origins* (Princeton, N.J., 1986), esp. 100–112.

4. See Paul Bernard, *CRAI* 1970: 339–47. A splendid photograph of this disk can be found in Madanjeet Singh, ed., *Le Soleil: Mythologies et représentations* (Paris, 1993), 94, fig. 170. See also Henri-Paul Francfort, *Fouilles d'Aï Khanoum*, vol. 3: *Le Sanctuaire du temple à niches indentées*, pt. 2, *Les Trouvailles*, Mémoires de la délégation archéologique française en Afghanistan, vol. 27 (Paris, 1984), 93–104, with pl. 41.

5. Francfort, *Fouilles d'Aï Khanoum*. See Claude Rapin, "Les Sanctuaires de l'Asie centrale à l'époque hellénistique: État de la question," *Études de Lettres: Revue de la faculté des Lettres, Université de Lausanne* 4 (Oct.–Dec. 1992): 101–24, esp. 116.

6. See the voluminous classic study by Erich Neumann, *The Great Mother: An Analysis of the Archetype*, trans. Ralph Manheim, Bollingen ser. 47 (New York, 1955).

7. Henri Graillot, *Le Culte de Cybèle, mère des dieux, à Rome et dans l'Empire romain* (Paris, 1912); Friederike Naumann, *Die Ikonographie der Kybele in der phrygischen und der griechischen Kunst*, Istanbuler Mitteilungen, 28 (Tübingen, 1984); and *CCAA*.

O N E : An Itinerant Mother

1. There is evidence of a historical Midas; a royal tomb dating from approximately 700 B.C.E. that is very likely Midas's has been excavated at Gordion. See M. Mellink, "The Native Kingdoms of Anatolia," vol. 3, pt. 2, of *The Cambridge Ancient History* (Cambridge, 1991), esp. 633–34, and sources cited there. See also Lynn E. Roller, "The Legend of Midas," *Classical Antiquity* 2 (1983): 229–313, for Greek discourse on this subject, and id., "Phrygian Myth and Cult," *Source* 7 (1988): 43–50.

2. This is at least Ovid's version of events in *Metamorphoses* 11.142 et seq. Midas starved to death, a victim of his power of transmutation, according to Lykophron, *Alexandra* 1401, with Tzetzes ad loc., and schol. Aristophanes, *Plutus* 287.

3. Tyrtaeus fr. 12.6. On the relationship between Sparta and Lydia in terms of figurative art, see Beatrice Palma, "ARTEMIS ORTHIA?" *Annuario della Scuola archeologica di Atene* 52–53, 1974–75 (1978): 307, with n. 2. An ancient tradition holds that Alcman, a poet from Sparta, was originally of Lydian origin, specifically, from Sardis; see Claude Calame, *Alcman: Introduction, texte critique, témoignages, traduction et commentaire* (Rome, 1983), xv.

4. Plato, *Laws* 660e; see also *Republic* 408b. Midas was sometimes considered to be the son of the Phrygian goddess: Hesiod, fr. 251 Rzach = fr. 352 Merkelbach-West; Hyginus, *Fabulae* 191 and 274; Plutarch, *Caesar* 9.3.

5. Hesychius's *Mida theos* specifies that Midas's subjects venerated the "goddess of Midas," and that some contended that this goddess was his mother. The *Suda* (s.v. *elegos*) reports on a tradition, tainted with euhemerism, according to which the flute accompanying the procession around the altar (the *aulos peribomios*) was invented by Midas, son of Gordion, because he wanted to ensure the apotheosis of his deceased mother. This speculation can be connected to an account by Polyaenus (*Poliorketika* 7.5) that clearly links the sovereignty of Midas to a ritual in honor of the Great Gods. Midas gained power by cunning in warfare closely linked to rituals performed during the mysteries: "Pretending to be completing the mysteries in honor of the Great Gods [Megaloi Theoi], at night, Midas led the Phrygians with flutes, tympanums, and symbols. Under their ritual costumes, Midas's Phrygians hid their swords. The inhabitants of the town came out to watch the show. All the while still playing the tympanon and the cymbals, Midas's companions massacred the spectators, before laying siege to the homes left open, and they proclaimed Midas tyrant [Midan turannon anegoreusan]." The Great Gods are without a doubt the Cabiri of Samothrace, whose mythic connections to Phrygia (and Macedonia, another land where Midas's presence was known) are numerous. We know that they were associated with the Corybantes and with a Mother in the traditions of Samothrace. The musical instruments mentioned by Polyaenus are characteristic of those used in "corybantic" and "metroac" (see n. 7 below) rituals.

6. In the version reported by Arrian, *Anabasis* 2.3. See Philippe Borgeaud, "Du mythe à l'idéologie: La Tête du Capitole," *Museum Helveticum* 44 (1987): 86–100.

7. I use the adjective "metroac," derived from Greek, to qualify the Mother of the gods; "maternal" would obviously be inappropriate.

8. Telestes fr. 810 (*PMG*).

9. Dionysos returns from Lydia and Phrygia via Iran, India, and Arabia: see Euripides, *Bacchantes* 13–17.

10. In this way as well, Midas prefigures Croesus.

11. Pausanias 5.13.7.

12. Pausanias 3.22.4 reports a dispute over which was the older, the Laconian or the Asian sculpture of the Mother goddess. See also *CCAA*, vol. 1, no. 440; and cf. E. Akurgal, *Ancient Civilizations and Ruins of Turkey*, 4th ed. (Istanbul, 1978), 132 and pl. 41b.

13. Based on the Marmor Parium, this first epiphany on the "Cybele" hilltops occurred in 1505–1504 B.C.E.: *IG* XII, 5, 444; 239 A 10 Jacoby.

14. The epitaph of Midas is a traditional writing exercise referred to and commented on by Socrates in Plato, *Phaedrus* 264d. Also, there is a well-preserved example of this writing by Kleobulos of Lindos, a contemporary of Simonides (Diogenes Laertius 1.89; cf. *PMG* 298–99). For Midas as the slave of comedy, see Aristophanes, *Wasps* 433; cf. *IG* II/III² 1673, 46; Strabo 7.3.12.

15. Strabo 1.3.21; Plutarch, *Life of Flaminius* 20.5; Plutarch, *De superstitione* 8 = *Moralia* 168; cf. also on this theme Diodoros Siculos 11.58.3; Plutarch, *Themistocles* 31.5.

16. See n. 33 below and related text.

17. For the dating, see Keith De Vries, "Gordion and Phrygia in the Sixth Century B.C.," *Source* 7, nos. 3–4 (1988): 51–59. I have opted for an average chronology in an attempt to include the positions of both the archaeologists, who study the iconography and base their arguments on stylistic considerations (see, e.g., Naumann, *Ikonographie der Kybele*, and I. Fakri, "Die Entstehung der frühen Kybelebilder Phrygiens . . . ," *Jahresh. Österr. Arch. Inst. Wien* 57 [1986–87], suppl., pp. 41–107), and the linguists, who attempt to compare the Phrygian and Greek alphabets (see the next note).

18. At least that is the traditional theory. An upward revision of the dating of the first Phrygian inscriptions would lead to serious questioning of this view of things: see Rodney S. Young, "Old Phrygian Inscriptions from Gordion: Toward a History of the Phrygian Alphabet," *Hesperia* 38 (1969): 252–96. Observing that the Greek alphabet, as such, does not fit in with the Indo-European languages of Anatolia, Roberto Gusmani speaks of a complex network of primary and secondary relationships to describe how the alphabets of Asia Minor (Lydian, Phrygian, and Carian) spread (Gusmani, *Neue epichorische Schriftzeugnisse aus Sardis, 1958–1971* [Cambridge, Mass., 1975], 59–60). Rather than direct borrowing, either from the Greeks or the Phoenicians, he prefers the thesis of reciprocal influences: "the routes through which the Semitic alphabet reached the West were crossed more than once." See L. H. Jeffery, "Greek Alphabetic Writing," *Cambridge Ancient History*, 2d ed., vol. 3, pt. 1 (1982), 819 et seq.; Olivier Masson, "Anatolian Languages," ibid., pt. 2 (1991), 666–76, cites Michel Lejeune, "Discussion sur l'alphabet phrygien," *Studi micenei ed egeo-anatolici* 10 (1969): 19–47, and "Les Inscriptions de Gordion et l'alphabet phrygien," *Kadmos* 9 (1970): 51–74. He notes that the oldest Phrygian inscriptions, a graffito from Gordion dating from at least 750 B.C.E. and later graffiti from approximately 720 B.C.E., are contemporary with the most ancient Greek alphabets known to us. Rather than deducing that both had their origin in the Phoenician alphabet, without any mutual interaction, he regards it as more plausible to postulate that Phrygian writing was based on a Greek model. See also Barry Powell, *Homer and the Origin of the Greek Alphabet* (Cambridge, 1991).

19. C. Brixhe and M. Lejeune, *Corpus des inscriptions paléophrygiennes* (Paris, 1984), B-01, W-04, M-01c, M-01d, M-01e.

20. See K. De Vries, "Gordion and Phrygia in the Sixth Century B.C.," 57–58.

21. The reference on rupestrian monuments remains the two-volume study by C. H. Emilie Haspels, *The Highlands of Phrygia* (Princeton, N.J., 1971).

22. Naumann, *Ikonographie der Kybele*.

23. These attributes include a headdress, the *polos;* an animal, the lion; and, in light of a famous statuary group found at Bogazköy, certain acolytes: ibid., pl. 7.1 and cat. no. 23, with bibliography (see p. 295) referring to the significant studies by Kurt Bittel.

24. In general, see G. M. A. Hanfmann, *From Croesus to Constantine* (Ann Arbor, Mich., 1975); and more specifically, G. M. A. Hanfmann and N. H. Ramage, *Sculpture from Sardis: The Finds Through 1975* (Cambridge, Mass., 1978), 14, 19.

25. Hipponax, fr. 127 West; Herodotus 5.102. On the Lydian evidence of Kufav(a) or Kuvav(a), see Gusmani, *Neue epichorische Schriftzeugnisse aus Sardis,* 28–29. The most impressive monument in terms of its iconography is the one known as "Cybele's shrine," a votive *naiskos* representing the goddess (Kuvav — Cybebe) standing at the entrance to the sanctuary. It can be dated from between 540 and 530. The monument is stylistically influenced by Ionian art. Also, the presence of dancers, long-haired acolytes of the Dionysian sort, and young girls on the sides can be noted. See Hanfmann and Ramage, *Sculpture from Sardis,* no. 7, fig. 20–50 and pp. 15 et seq., 43–51. Naumann, *Ikonographie der Kybele,* cat. no. 34. The archaic temple of Cybele burned down by the Greeks in 499 (see Herodotus 5.102) has not been found by archaeologists. The goddess (characterized by her hairstyle, a *polos,* and by the fact that she carries a lion) is shown next to Artemis (who is holding a doe). They appear inside a *naiskos* and in the presence of two worshipers (a man and a woman) on a stele from Sardis dating from approximately 400 B.C.E. G. M. A. Hanfmann and J. C. Waldbaum, "Kybele and Artemis: Two Anatolian Goddesses at Sardis," *Archaeology* 22 (1983), fig. 1, p. 223 (relief from Sardis), fig. 2, p. 225 ("model of the Temple of Cybele"). As for Carchemish, see E. Laroche, "Koubaba, déesse anatolienne, et le problème des origines de Cybèle," in *Élements orientaux dans la religion grecque ancienne* (Paris, 1960), 113–28, confirmed by J. D. Hawkins, "Kubaba. A. Philologisch," in *Reallexikon der Assyriologie und vorderasiatischen Archäologie,* vol. 6 (Berlin, 1980–83), 257–61. I thank Professor Gerd Steiner who was kind enough to point out that the famous basalt relief from Carchemish in the museum in Ankara, often reproduced as a representation of Kubaba, does not in fact represent this goddess, as the inscription read by Piero Meriggi proves. See Meriggi, *Manuale di eteo geroglifico* (Rome, 1975), pt. 2, *Testi e tavoli,* 188, pl. 32, A 33 g.; cf. *Reallexikon der Assyriologie,* "Kubaba. B. Ikonographie," 262 with fig. 2.

26. Marmor Parium 239 A 10 Jacoby; Diodoros Siculos 3.58; Strabo 12.567; schol. Aristophanes, *Birds* 877; Stephanus of Byzantium s.v. "Kubeleia"; Hesychius s.v. "Kubela"; *Suda* III K 2588; *Etymologicum Magnum* 542.54; Aelius Herodianus (Herodian) and Pseudo-Herodianus (Pseudo-Herodian), *De prosa catholica,* p. 278, 39; p. 322, 6; p. 381, 18–19 Lentz.

27. Claude Brixhe, "Le Nom de Cybèle: L'Antiquité avait-elle raison?" *Die Sprache* 25 (1979): 40–45. Cf. Ladislav Zgusta, "Weiteres zum Namen der Kybele," ibid. 28 (1982): 171–72.

28. See Pindar fr. 80; Aristophanes, *Birds* 877; Euripides, *Bacchantes* 79; Theokritos, *Idylls* 20.43.

29. On the iconography of the Mother of the gods in general, see Naumann, *Ikonographie der Kybele,* and *CCAA.* See also Erika Simon, "Kubele," in the *Lexicon Iconographicum Mythologiae Classicae,* suppl. (1997).

30. On the presence of the Mother in Peloponnesian (and especially Laconian) sculpture of the sixth century, see the impressive documentation collected and analyzed by Juliette de la Genière, "Le Culte de la Mère des dieux dans le Péloponnèse," *CRAI* 1986:

29–48. Supporting Fritz Graf's hypothesis in "The Arrival of Cybele in the Greek East," in *Actes du VIIe Congrès de la FIEC* (Budapest, 1983), 1: 117–20, the author believes in the possible influence of Phrygian models on Peloponnesian sculpture dating back to a period preceding the Cimmerian invasion (see p. 30). This would put us in the eighth century B.C.E., that is, in fact, during a period in Greece for which we have no evidence of this type of representation. There is no need to go back any further. The observable *terminus post quem* as far as the Phrygian-Peloponnesian mutual "interferences" are concerned is exemplified by the stylistic relationship present both in the famous group from Bogazköy (the Phrygian Mother flanked by two little musicians) and in a sculpture from Sparta (the goddess on her knees, accompanied by a little *aulos* player). See Maria Pipili, *Laconian Iconography of the Sixth Century* B.C. (Oxford, 1987), 58–60; cf. José Dörig, "Eleuthía," in *Sculpture from Arcadia and Laconia*, Oxbow Monograph 30, ed. O. Palagia and W. Coulson (1993), 145–51. For the Ionian cults of the Mother (mainly in Smyrna, Phocia, Klazomenae, Erythria, Chios, and Kolophon), see the ample research done by Fritz Graf, *Nordionische Kulte* (Rome, 1985). The Locri shard is the oldest evidence of the presence of the Anatolian goddess in Magna Graecia. According to Graf, "Arrival of Cybele," developing a hypothesis formulated by Marguerita Guarducci, "Cibele in un'epigrafe arcaica di Locri Epizefirî," *Klio* 52 (1970): 133–38, the goddess arrived in Italy by way of the Ionian coast of Asia Minor (more specifically, through Kolophon). On the other hand, Juliette de la Genière, "De la Phrygie à Locres épizéphyrienne: Les Chemins de Cybèle," *Antiquité* 97 (1985): 693–718, believes that her importation to Locri was from Sparta. Absent any evidence of rituals in the Ionian milieu, the goddess's name, Cybele, might favor the second hypothesis. For more on the statue sculpted by Agorakritos in the sanctuary of the Mother in the Athenian Agora and the iconography that relates to it, see Naumann, *Ikonographie der Kybele*, 159–69.

31. Certain acolytes or companions appear on the front of the *naiskos* in mainland Greece: Pan, or rather a young cupbearer (Hermes), and a young girl (identified by her torch as Hecate). Instead, there are two different acolytes present on the reliefs in Asia Minor and in the islands (Samos, Chios): a young man (sometimes also a cupbearer), and an older, bearded character. This transformation, when we get closer to Athens, might reveal the intent of incorporating the Mother into the context of Demeter, marked by the Eleusian myth. Oriental acolytes are sometimes mentioned in the texts: Titias and Cyllenos (= Hermes?), schol. Ap. Rhod. 1.1126 (= Maiandros, 491 F 3 Jacoby, fourth century C.E.); with these two characters (the old, bearded man and the young beardless one), it seems that we reconnect with the documentation on the Cabiri of Samothrace: cf. F. Chapouthier, *Les Dioscures au service d'une déesse* (Paris, 1935), 172–75; B. Hemberg, *Die Kabiren* (Uppsala, 1950), 97–98, 249, 256. Strabo 11.8.4 notes that the Iranian goddess Anaïtis, elsewhere identified with the Mother of the gods in Asia Minor, is accompanied by two male "demons": Omanes (= Vohumano?) and Anadates.

32. Graillot, *Culte de Cybèle*, 33–34 and n. 4.

33. Salomon Reinach, "Statues archaïques de Cybèle découvertes à Cymè (Eolide)" *Bulletin de correspondance hellénique* 13 (1889): 543–60. See also the iconographical research on this issue in Ernst Langlotz, *Studien zur nordostgriechischen Kunst* (Mainz, 1975), pl. 60.

34. Pindar, *Nem.* 6.1 et seq.: "Hen andrōn hen theōn genos ek mias de pneomen matros amphoteroi."

35. Aeschylus, *Choephoroi* 828 et seq.; Sophocles, *Inachos*, fr. 268 Nauck; [Homer] *Hymn* 30.17; Solon, fr. 24, 4 Diehl.

36. [Homer], *Hymn* 9.7.

37. The fact that Pindar calls this divinity Cybele and has her originate in Arcadia leads me to believe that for him, in the context of the Theban cult attached to her name, she was the same mother goddess that Genière, "Culte de la Mère des dieux," locates in the Peloponnesos. The route would have been from Phrygia to Sparta, via Lydia, and then from the Peloponnesos to Thebes. A completely different itinerary leads to Athens from the Ionian coast, even if there are theoretically some "interferences" that should not be excluded. The most ancient representation of the Mother discovered in Athens is a sixth-century B.C.E. "sculpture in the round" (*en ronde-bosse*) excavated on the northeastern side of the Acropolis, which corresponds to a well-known typology from the same period in Asia Minor and in the Peloponnesos (see Naumann, *Ikonographie der Kybele*, 145, no. 111; 308 and pl. 19.3) as do numerous figurines in terra-cotta (references in ibid., 145, no. 140).

38. Plutarch, *Themistocles* 30.1; Strabo 14.1.40 tells a similar story. Note that Themistocles belonged to the *genos* of Lykomides, who were the co-owners of the sanctuary of Phyle in Attica where the mysteries were performed and where the Earth was worshiped as the "Great Goddess" (Pausanias 1.31.4; cf. 1.22.7).

39. English translation by A. D. Godley from *Herodotus, Histories*, bk. 4, Loeb Classical Library (Cambridge, Mass., 1921; reprint, 1982), 2: 274–77.

40. Apollonius Rhodius, *Argonautika* 1.1079–1152. As for the cult of the Mother in Kyzikos, see F. W. Hasluck, *Cyzicus* (Cambridge, 1910), 214–22.

41. An inscription on a vase fragment from Olbia dating from the middle of the sixth century B.C.E. (that is, a century before Herodotus) confirms the importance of Hylaia in the local cult (of Milesian origin, perhaps transmitted via Kyzikos) of the Mother of the gods. See *CCAA*, 6: 151, no. 515 (with bibliography). I thank Yuri Vinogradov for familiarizing me with the meaning of this text. On the well-documented cult of Mētēr in archaic Olbia, see A. S. Rusyaeva, "Investigations of the Western Temenos of Olbia," *Ancient Civilizations from Scythia to Siberia* 1 (1994): 80–102, esp. 87–89.

T W O : In the Athenian Agora

1. See Homer A. Thompson and R. E. Wycherley, *The Agora of Athens* (Princeton, N.J., 1972). The documentation on the Mother of the gods in Athens has been presented in a useful fashion by Ronda Rae Simms in "Foreign Religious Cults in Athens in the Fifth and Fourth Centuries B.C." (Ph.D. diss., University of Virginia, 1985), 59–123. See also Robert Parker, *Athenian Religion: A History* (Oxford, 1996), whom I thank for allowing me to read the manuscript version of his chapter "The Fifth Century: The New Gods." Most of the epigraphical documents concerning the *mētrōon* are collected in R. E. Wycherley, *Literary and Epigraphical Testimonia*, American School of Classical Studies at Athens, The Athenian Agora, vol. 3 (Princeton, N.J., 1957), 150–60.

2. The law of Chairemonides is itself mentioned in a law from 353–352 (= *IG* II², 140, 11.31–35) concerning the offering of firstfruits in Eleusis.

3. In other words, the honors were to those who liberated Athens from the tyranny of the Thirty. See Aeschines 3 = Ctesiphon 187.

4. See S. C. Todd, *The Shape of Athenian Law* (Oxford, 1993), 56 (which does not exclude that this might have occurred earlier).

5. H. A. Thompson, "Buildings on the West Side of the Agora," *Hesperia* 6 (1937): 1–

226, at 215–17. See A. L. Boegehold, "The Establishment of a Central Archive at Athens," *American Journal of Archaeology* 76 (1972): 23–30, at 28. Andocides 2.23 would have us go back a bit earlier than 411 B.C.E.

6. Literally, "of all the rights and duties that figure in the writings": "he panton tōn en tois grammasi dikaion phulax tei polei kathesteke" (Dinarchos, *Against Demosthenes* 86).

7. Leokrates 67.

8. Timarchos 60–61.

9. See H. A. Thompson's studies.

10. A small annex assumed to be a kitchen was discovered at the north end of the building.

11. See Gerhard Kuhn, "Das neue Bouleuterion von Athen," *Archaeologischer Anzeiger,* 1984: 17–26; John M. Camp, *The Athenian Agora* (London, 1986), 38, 90–94.

12. A decree from approximately 450 (*IG* I², 27) specifies that the names of foreigners honored by the city will be conserved in the *bouleuterion* and on a stele, of which an example was deposited on the Acropolis.

13. Even if we do suppose, along with H. A. Thompson, that it was already Mētēr, or possibly Demeter.

14. [Ps.-]Arrian, *Periplous Ponti Euxini* [Periplus of the Black Sea] 9; Pausanias 1.3.5; Pliny, *Nat. hist.* 36.17. We can get an idea of this statue through its influence on later art. I am thinking in particular of the imposing cult statue discovered at Moschaton near Piraeus in 1971 and the iconography of the votive reliefs dedicated to the Mother that developed in Attica as early as the fourth century.

15. This concurs with Karl Schefold's hypothesis, in "Statuen auf Vasenbildern," *Jahrbuch des Deutschen archäologischen Instituts* 52 (1937): 30–75, at 38, concerning a black figure amphora in the British Museum dating from approximately 530 B.C.E., which shows a female figure in profile (an idol?) in a building that could be a temple; there is a lion on the roof (*Corpus Vasorum Antiquorum* III, He, pl. 35, 2a).

16. Giovanni Cerri, "La Madre degli Dei nell'*Elena* di Euripide: Tragedia e rituale," *Quaderni di storia* 9 (1983): 155–95.

17. P. Roussel, *Délos, colonie athénienne* (Paris, 1916), 45. The fake money taken out of circulation was dedicated in the *mētrōon* of Athens according to a decree from 375–374. See R. S. Stroud, "An Athenian Law on Silver Coinage," *Hesperia* 43 (1974): 157–88, at 174–78. The logic underlying such a procedure might be clarified by the deposit in different sanctuaries in the Greek world. These deposits contained tablets dedicated to a goddess of stolen money or money borrowed and not repaid. One of these texts, from Knidos (but whose dating is unfortunately quite imprecise: between 100 B.C.E. and 200 C.E.) was deposited in one of the sanctuaries of the Mother of the gods. At least one example comes from southern Italy, from the third century B.C.E. See H. S. Versnel, "Beyond Cursing: The Appeal to Justice in Judicial Prayers," in *Magika hiera: Ancient Greek Magic and Religion*, ed. Christopher A. Faraone and Dirk Obbink (New York, 1991), 73–74. By dedicating the counterfeit money in the sanctuary of the Mother, the Athenian magistrates religiously condemned counterfeiters to repay to the goddess what they had stolen from the city.

18. This piece of information can be confirmed, if need be, by epigraphy: a decree from 184–183 B.C.E. honoring the *prytaneis*, discovered in 1970; see John S. Trail, "Greek Inscriptions Honoring Prytaneis," *Hesperia* 40 (1971): 308–11 (line 10).

19. Theophrastus, *Characters* 21; Immanuel Bekker, *Anecdota Graeca*, 3 vols. (Berlin, 1814–21), 1: 229, 25; Hesychius, s.v. *galaxia*.

20. Varro, *De lingua latina* 5.105 explicitly cites the Athenian Apollodoros in this connection. On the *pultes* and the *polenta* of the Romans, see J. André, *L'Alimentation et la cuisine à Rome* (Paris, 1981), 60–61.

21. See Allaire Chandor Brumfield, *The Attic Festivals of Demeter and Their Relations to the Agricultural Year* (Salem, N.H., 1981).

22. *IG* XI², 203 A 31; cf. Ph. Bruneau, *Recherches sur les cultes de Délos* (Paris, 1970), 508. The rites for the same goddess in Rome took place exactly between the end of March and the beginning of April. The date of the rite in Athens is perhaps a small concession that was accorded to the idea of an eastern origin, an idea manifested explicitly by the cult images (framed by lions) and the poetic discourse.

23. The *homogalaktes*: see Aristotle, *Politics* 1252b18; *Suda*, s.v. *orgeones;* Harpokration, s.v. *gennetai.*

24. See Jean-Louis Durand, "Formules attiques du fonder," in *Tracés de fondation*, ed. Marcel Detienne (Louvain, 1990), 271–87.

25. *IG* XI², 79, ll. 9–12.

26. Athenaeus 5.214d–e. It is possible that these were not only administrative texts. We know from Pseudo-Plutarch in the *Lives of the Orators* 841 that by law copies of tragedies by Aeschylus, Sophocles, and Euripides were kept in an official building. Unfortunately, he does not mention in which building.

27. Athenaeus 9.407b–c, citing Chamaeleon of Heraclea Pontica (third–fourth centuries B.C.E.).

28. See Aristotle, *Constitution of Athens.*

29. Aeschylus, *Prometheus Bound* 209: "Themis kai Gaia, pollōn onomatōn morphē mia."

30. *Corpus Inscriptionum Antiquarum* III, 318, 350. The sanctuary of Themis, at the foot of the Acropolis, adjoined the sanctuary of Gē Courotrophē and Demeter Chloē (Pausanias 1.22.1).

31. See R. E. Wycherley, *The Stones of Athens* (Princeton, N.J., 1978), 178–79.

32. W. Dörpfell, *Athenische Mitteilungen* 19 (1894), 148.

33. For verses 1301–69, I refer to Richard Kannicht's edition and commentary, *Euripides, Helena* (Heidelberg, 1969).

34. Henri Grégoire and Louis Méridier in their edition of Euripides, Collection des universités de France, vol. 5 (1950), 11–17. In his edition (*Euripides, Helena*), Kannicht refuses to play this game.

35. Euripides, *Helen* 1301–2.

36. Ibid., 1324.

37. Ibid., 1327–37: the drought making farming useless, the suffering of human populations and livestock, famine in the cities, the end of animal sacrifices (*thusiai*) and cereal offerings (*pelanoi*, ritual cakes), and the drying up of springs.

38. Ibid., 1343.

39. Ibid., 1320 and 1340; finally, *megalē Matēr,* "Great Mother," in 1355–56.

40. Ibid., 1301–12, trans. Arthur S. Way, in the Loeb *Euripides* (New York, 1912; reprint, 1930), 1: 579–81. Among the virgin companions mentioned in the corrupted text are the huntress Artemis (with her arrows) and the warrior Athena (named *Gorgōpis,* "with the face or look of Gorgon"). On the possible allusion to an attempt on the part of these

two goddesses to get rid of Hades, see the commentary by Kannicht, *Euripides, Helena,* 1414–18 (2: 342–43).

41. See Kannicht, *Euripides, Helena,* 1317–18. For an English verse translation, but one that does not emphasize the linguistic aspects that are of interest here, see Euripides, *Helen,* trans. Arthur S. Way, in the Loeb *Euripides* (New York, 1912; reprint, 1930), 1: 1319–52 (pp. 581–83).

42. *Alalē:* a cry of joy or of pain, sometimes of victory, attested to in connection with rituals dedicated to Cybele and Dionysus. See Kannicht's commentary in id., *Euripides, Helena,* 2: 350–51.

43. Euripides, *Helen* 1342–43: "Tan peri parthenoi Deo thumosamenan."

44. Probably the cymbals: see Kannicht, *Euripides, Helena.*

45. Way's Loeb translation, 583, has "skin-strained tambourine."

46. Ibid. has "flute of the deep wild notes"; perhaps a *bombyx.*

47. Euripides, *Helen* 1364–65.

48. On this reference, see also the fifth-century poet Melanippides (*PMG,* fr. 764), cited by Philodemus, *De pietate,* which also refers to Telestes and perhaps to Stesimbrotos (see text and remarks by R. Philippson, *Hermes* 55 [1920]: 277–78): "Dēmetra kai Mētera theōn phēsin mian huparchein" ("Demeter and the Mother of the gods are one and same"). Telestes, or Stesimbrotos, adds Rhea, and in a similar list, the Derveni papyrus includes Deo (col. 18 in *Zeitschrift für Papyrologie und Epigraphik* 47, 1982 = col. 22 of the new arrangement resulting from the Princeton conference, 1993).

49. It is the same in Arcadia with Erinye or Melaina of Telephusa (or Telphussa) and Lykosura.

50. It is Zeus who, in the Homeric version to which Euripides' chorus refers, and from which it differentiates itself, decides to give Persephone to Hades without consulting Demeter.

51. Verses 1353 and 1357 deal with this fault or tragic error, presented as a transgression (*ou themis outh' hosia* [1353]) committed on the occasion of a sacrifice (*thusias* [1356]) accomplished as part of a domestic ritual (*en thalamois* [1354]). The nature of this error, which is unconnected with anything else in the play itself or in the traditions relative to Helen, remains a mystery. Let us note that because verses 1353–54 are terribly fragmented, we cannot tell whether the error committed by Helen was presented as an established fact (which seems unlikely) or as a simple supposition on the part of the chorus, without any foundation, perhaps in the form of a question. (A parallel to this in Euripides' *Hippolytos* 141–47 would also involve a Mother.)

52. The relationship between Aphrodite and Helen has not, to my knowledge, been emphasized in this context.

53. A contemporary description of this procession in tragedy is known in the fragment of the *Semele* by Diogenes of Athens (*Tragicorum Graecorum Fragmenta,* Snell no. 45, 1). Here we see women with eastern hairdos, companions of the oriental Cybele, daughters of rich Lydians whose song resounds to the rhythm of bronze cymbals, accompanied by rhombs and tympanums. The ritual (and especially musical) proximity of the Mother of the gods and Dionysos has been widely evidenced. See the ecstatic dances represented on the famous Ferrara crater: Naumann, *Ikonographie der Kybele,* cat. no. 134; Claude Bérard and Jean-Louis Durand, in *La Cité des images: Religion et société en Grèce antique* (Paris, 1984), 18–21; I. Loucas, "Meaning and Place of the Cult Scene on the Ferrara Krater T 128," in *The Iconography of Greek Cult in the Archaic and Classical Periods,* ed. R. Hägg

(Athens, 1992), 73–83. Cf. Euripides, *Palamedes*, fr. 586 (Dionysus on Mount Ida, with the Mother and the sound of the tympanum); *Bacchae* 72–82. On *Helen*, see Giovanni Cerri, "Il message dionisiaco nell'*Elena* di Euripide," *Aion* 9–10 (1987–88): 43–67.

54. Cf. Maurice Olender, "Aspects de Baubō: Textes et contextes antiques," *Revue de l'histoire des religions* 202 (1985): 3–55.

55. See Philippe Borgeaud, *Recherches sur le dieu Pan* (Rome, 1979), 206–21, trans. Kathleen Atlass and James Redfield as *The Cult of Pan in Ancient Greece* (Chicago, 1988).

56. For this text and commentary on it, see Robert Wagman, *Inni di Epidauro* (Pisa, 1994), 108–42. See also M. Pizzocaro, "L'inno di Epidauro alla Madre degli Dei," in *L'inno fra rituale e letturatura nel mondo antico* (Naples, 1991).

57. And so close to Hesiod's Hecate in this way!

58. Wagman, *Inni di Epidauro*, 125.

59. Thucydides 8.6.4.

60. Thucydides 8.7.1.

61. Thucydides 8.9.

62. See *RE*, col. 2249, s.v. "Isthmia" (K. Schneider, 1916).

63. Thucydides 8.14.2 (Chios and Erythrea); 8.19.1 (Miletus).

64. The prototypes of the Athenian image are specifically evidenced in this area. See E. Will, "Aspects du culte et de la légende de la Grande Mère dans le monde grec," in *Élements orientaux dans la religionne grecque ancienne* (Paris, 1960); Naumann, *Ikonographie der Kybele*, 101–58. See also Graf, *Nordionische Kulte*, index, s.v. "Mētēr."

65. Froma Zeitlin tells me that the allusion in Euripides to a ritual innovation was not unique; see P. Carrara, *Euripides, "Eretteo"* (Florence, 1977), on the cult of Praxithea in the Erechtheion.

66. See Giulia Sfameni Gasparro, "Connotazioni metroache di Demetra nel Coro dell'*Elena* (v. 1301–65)," in *Hommages à Maarten J. Vermaseren*, ed. Margreet B. de Boer and T. A. Edridge (Leiden, 1978), 3: 1148–87.

67. Sophocles, *Philoctetes* 391 et seq.

68. Aristophanes, *Birds* 876 et seq.

69. See Naumann, *Ikonographie der Kybele*, no. 123 (and pl. 22.1 and bibliography) and numerous votive reliefs dedicated to the Mother from the Piraeus area. See also I. Petrocheilos, "Votive Reliefs of Cybele in Piraeus" (in Greek), *Archaeologikē ephēmeris* 131, 1992 (1993): 21–65, for an inventory.

70. William Scott Ferguson, "The Attic Orgeones," *Harvard Theological Review* 37 (1944): 61–140.

71. *IG* II², 1273.

72. With the one intermediary exception, chronologically speaking, of *Inscriptiones Graecae* II², 1316, dating from 246–245, where we find *orgeones* and *thiasotai* side by side.

73. *IG* II², 1315, from 211–210 (*tas theas*); *IG* II², 1328 I (later).

74. Naumann, *Ikonographie der Kybele*, cat. no. 348.

75. See St. Lattimore, "Double Cybele," *American Journal of Archaeology* 84 (1980): 120; M. Carla Giammarco Razzano, "Il culto di Cibele e il problema dei doppi *naiskoi*," *Miscellanea greca e romana* 9 (1984): 63–88.

76. I. N. Svoronos, catalogue of the Greek National Museum in Athens, first published in Greek (1903) and then in German under the title *Das Athener Nationalmuseum* (Athens, 1908–37), 624 et seq.

77. On this *Mētēr theōn autochthon*, see *Bulletin épigraphique* 364 (1969), and 401 (1971);

cf. Louis Robert, in *Bulletin de correspondance hellénique* 106 (1982): 361; F. Papazoglou, "Affranchissements par consécration et hiérodulie," *Ziva Antika* 31 (1981): 171–79; Ph. Petsas, "The Dated Inscriptions from the Sanctuary of the Autochthonous Mother of the Gods at Leukopetra" (in Greek), in *VIIIᵉ Congrès international d'épigraphie, 1982* (Athens, 1984), 1: 281–307.

78. W. R. Paton, *Classical Review* 16 (1902): 290–91; and see the careful edition by E. Schwyzer, *Dialectorum graecorum exempla epigraphica potiora* (Leipzig, 1923), no. 633; cf. F. Sokolowski, *Lois sacrées des cités grecques* (Paris, 1969), 219–20 (no. 124). The *galli*, and the women who would like to *gallazein*, appear in lines 11–12, as part of a long list of prohibitions. The deity of the sanctuary is not named. Some have thought of Apollo and also of Themis, because there is mention (lines 18–20) of a priestess and a prophetess.

79. Ovid, *Metamorphoses* 6.313–81. Peter Frei, "Konflikt und Synkretismus: Leto und die Frösche," in *Le Temple lieu de conflit: Actes du colloque de Cartigny, 1991* (Louvain, 1994). Cf. Emmanuel Laroche, "Les Dieux de la Lycie classique d'après les textes lyciens," in *Actes du colloque sur la Lycie antique, Istanbul, 1977* (Paris, 1980), 3–4.

80. Plato, *Republic* 1.327a. Cf. R. Garland, *Introducing New Gods: The Politics of Athenian Religion* (Ithaca, N.Y., 1992), 111–14.

81. Aristotle, *Rhetoric* 1405a. This opposition between *daidouchos* and *mētragurtēs* reproduces the one already presented in Aeschylus, apropos of Cassandra, between *mantis* and *agurtria* (Aeschylus, *Agamemnon* 1273). For more on the torch-bearing Callias, see Xenophon, *Hellenica* 63.3.

82. See I. M. Linforth, "Corybantic Rites in Plato," *University of California Publications in Classical Philology* 13 (1946): 121–62.

83. Demosthenes, *On the Crown* 259. Cf. Strabo 10.3.18 (C 471) ("tauta gar esti ta sabazia kai metroia").

84. See *Bulletin épigraphique* 624 (1976): 289–91, and Chapter 5, n. 34.

85. See Chapter 5, n. 35.

86. *Prostagma*, in the inscription of the relief dedicated to Agdistis.

87. Schol. Pindar, *Pythian Odes* 3.137 et seq.: "Kathartria tes manias he theos."

88. She would be "enthusiastic," *entheos*: Euripides, *Hippolytos* 141; cf. Borgeaud, *Recherches sur le dieu Pan*, 156–66.

89. Cf. Borgeaud, *Recherches sur le dieu Pan*.

90. *Mētera theōn* on a curse tablet *(tabella defixionum)* from Attica (fourth–third centuries B.C.E.): Richard Wünsch, "Neue Fluchtafeln," *Rheinisches Museum* 55 (1900), no. 18; A. Audollent, *Defixionum Tabellae . . .* (Paris, 1904), 100, no. 72; John G. Gager, *Curse Tablets and Binding Spells from the Ancient World* (Oxford, 1992), 165, no. 74.

91. On the dedication of counterfeit money in the sanctuary of the Mother, see n. 17 above.

92. Christiane Dunant, "Sus aux voleurs!" *Museum Helveticum* 35 (1978): 241–44. See esp. the corrected text commented on by Versnel, "Beyond Cursing," in *Magika hiera*, 74.

93. The goddess appears as Anaitis, Hipta, Leto, or simply the Mother of the gods in fifteen or so documents collected, edited, and commented on in the very useful study by Georg Petzl, *Die Beichtinschriften Westkleinasiens* (Bonn, 1994); see index, 150, s.v. "Mētēr."

94. Diogenes of Athens, fr. 1, *Tragicorum Graecorum Fragmenta*, 2d. ed., 776.

95. See esp. the Hippocratic treatise *On the Sacred Disease (De morbo sacro)*.

96. Besides the dedication to Agdistis and the myth reported by Diodoros, see Chapter 4, n. 63, on the ex-voto from the Palatine.

97. See Pausanias 5.3.2 on the Mētēr Athena in Elis (with the meaning of midwife). The famous Sicilian Mothers (Plutarch, *Life of Marcellus* 20; cf. Diodoros Siculos 4.79 et seq.; Aratus 31 et seq.; Pseudo-Eratosthenes, *Catast.* 2) are wet nurses.

98. *Matere teija*, in the dative, is the equivalent of the classical Greek *Matrei theiai*, in an inventory of Pylos oil offerings: Pylos tablet PY fr. 1202.

99. See H. S. Versnel, *Inconsistencies in Greek and Roman Religion*, vol. 1, *Ter Unus: Isis, Dionysos, Hermes* (Leiden, 1990), 105–11.

THREE: The Invention of a Mythology

1. The Mermnades's empire was crumbling at this time, and Croesus's pyre was being prepared.

2. Herodotus 1.34–45. In passing, Ed. Meyer postulated a hypothesis relayed by Hugo Hepding in *Attis: Seine Mythen und sein Kult* (Giessen, 1903), 5: "Herodotus. . . narrat fabulam de Atye et Adrasto ex mytho de Attide ab apro interempto derivatam." The relationship between the episode in Herodotus and the mythology of Attis is accepted, with excellent arguments, but not developed, by A. S. F. Gow in "The Gallus and the Lion (*Anth. pal.* VI, 217–220, 237)," *Journal of Roman Studies* 80 (1960): 88–93, whose last sentence is: "The stories are not identical, but I think that Ed. Meyer and Hepding were right in calling attention to their resemblance." On Adrasteia, see Hepding, *Attis*, 101 n. 6. For a more recent commentary by David Asheri, see *Erodoto: Le storie* (Milan, 1988), 1: 287–88. Known as early as the *Phoronides* (fr. 2 Kinkel) as a Phrygian Mountain Mother, surrounded by dactyli, who were her servants, Adrasteia is placed by Aeschylus (fr. 158) among the Berecynthians in Phrygia. According to Antimachus (fr. 43), cited by Strabo (12.1.13), the hero Adrastus founded the cult of the Great Goddess (*megalē theos*) Nemesis in the city of Adrasteia in Mycia. In the fourth century, the comics Nikostratos (fr. 37 Kock) and Menander (fr. 321) associate Nemesis (the redeemer) with Adrasteia (the inevitable, the infallible one). From the third century on, there is abundant evidence of their identification with each other. Let us note that at Rhamnous in Attica, where Nemesis is connected to Themis (they are both *sunnaoi: Corpus Inscriptionum Antiquarum* II, 1570), there is evidence of a cult of the Phrygian Mother venerated under the Pessinontian name of Agdistis in the first century B.C.E. See P. Roussel, "Un Sanctuaire d'Agdistis à Rhamnonte," *Revue des études anciennes* 32 (1930): 5–8.

3. Although it is introduced as a story coming from elsewhere, developed at the junction between Lydia and Phrygia, the story of Atys is nevertheless perfectly situated within the logic proper to the whole body of Herodotus's writing. In the interest of following a good scientific method, the comparison between this episode and the Phrygian rites known through later sources should therefore be preceded by an analysis of this same episode in the *Histories*. In fact, there are curious connections to be discovered there between the "lack of communication" on the part of Croesus's sons and the castration theme. The examination of these connections leads us from Lydia to Corinth, and possibly also to Cyrene in North Africa. For more on this point of view, see Thomas A. Sebeok and Erika Brady, "The Two Sons of Croesus: A Myth about Communication in Herodotus," *Quaderni urbinati di cultura classica* 30 (1979): 7–22; Pauline Schmitt-Pantel, "Histoire de tyran, ou comment la cité grecque construit ses marges," in *Les Marginaux et les exclus dans l'histoire* (Paris, 1979); J.-P. Vernant, "Le Tyran boiteux: d'Oedipe à Périandre" (1981), in *Mythe et tragédie en Grèce ancienne*, ed. id. and Pierre Vidal-Naquet (Paris, 1986). Christiane Sourvinou-Inwood

kindly allowed me to read her manuscript of a key study on this issue, "Myth and History: On Herodotus III, 48 and 50 53," *Opuscula Atheniensia* 17 (1988): 167–82. See also Dario M. Cosi, "Jammed Communication: Battos, the Founder of Cyrene, Stammering and Castrated," in *The Regions of Silence: Studies on the Difficulty of Communicating*, ed. M. G. Ciani (Amsterdam, 1987), 115–44, and Claude Calame, "Mythe, récit épique et histoire: le récit hérodotéen de la fondation de Cyrène," in *Métamorphoses du mythe en Grèce antique*, ed. id. (Geneva, 1988), 105–25.

4. Hermesianax, fr. 8 Powell = Pausanias 7.17.9.

5. Walter Burkert, *Structure and History in Greek Mythology and Ritual* (Berkeley, Calif., 1979), 198 n. 20, suggests that the name of Kalaos evokes *gallos*, i.e., one of the *galli*. Unfortunately, this does not seem very likely, given that the *galles* (named as such) did not appear in literature until after the establishment of the Galatians in Asia Minor, and probably not before the expansion of Rome into this region.

6. Schol. Nikander, *Alexipharmaka* 8e.

7. These *thalamoi* might constitute an additional indication of the link between Herodotus's account and the Anatolian traditions concerning Attis. The word evokes a sanctuary of the Mother whose priest is Attis. See nn. 16 and 68 below.

8. See Lynn E. Roller, "Attis on Greek Votive Monuments: Greek God or Phrygian?" *Hesperia* 63 (1994): 245–52, p. 247 n. 12, for a nonexhaustive list of these observers. See also Pieter Lambrechts, *Attis: Van herdersknaap tot God* (Brussels, 1962).

9. For the first evidence of the name, see Brixhe and Lejeune, *Corpus des inscriptions paléophrygiennes*, M-O1a. *Ates* first appears as the dedicant on the famous façade sculpted in the so-called City of Midas (Yazilikaya), a votive monument dedicated to the Phrygian Mother.

10. See Roller, "Attis on Greek Monuments." Cf. Chapter 5, n. 35, below.

11. Theopompos fr. 27 Edmonds (1: 858), cited by the *Suda*, s.v. "Attis." Cf. Bekker, *Anecdota Graeca*, 461.

12. Hesiod, *Theogony* 988–991.

13. See Strabo 10.3.7–23 (C466–C474).

14. Literally, *boukolos* (herdsman, cattleman), a well-known priestly title.

15. Theokritos, *Idylls* 20.40.

16. Nikander, *Alexipharmaka* 6–8, cf. 217–21 and schol. ad loc. The Lobrinon near Kyzikos, situated not far from Dindymon, is also a mountain dedicated to the Mother. The scholiast interprets these "chambers," *thalamai*, as subterranean places dedicated to Rhea, where the priests of the Mother and Attis deposit testicles they have cut off themselves or others. Next, he reports the death of Attis, killed by a boar, the Mother's lamentations over the corpse, the funeral and Phrygian spring ritual of lamenting Attis. See Pseudo-Theokritos 20.40 (Rhea's crying over the *boukolos*) and Lucian, *Dialogues of the Gods* 12 (Attis's burial).

17. There are a few rare exceptions, such as the *megabyzoi* from Ephesus (Xenophon, *Anabasis* 5.3.6.), who also represent a priesthood of eunuchs. See Ch. Picard, *Éphèse et Claros* (Paris, 1922).

18. See Chapter 5, "*Galli* and Gauls."

19. Kratinos, fr. 82 Kock-Hesychius, s.v. *kubebis*.

20. Semonides, fr. 36 West, and Cratinos fr. 87, cited by Photios, *Lexicon*, s.v. *kubebos*.

21. A. Quattordio Moreschini, "Per un etimologia di *korúbantes/kúrbantes*, sacerdoti di Cibele," *Aion* (ling.) 8 (1986): 207–17, proposes that *kubaba* was also the origin of *corybantes*

(the name of the classical companions of the Mother of the gods). The derivation would be as follows: *kubabantes kubantes kurbantes korurbantes.*

22. Hipponax fr. 120–21; cf. Tzetzes, *ad Lyk.* 1170. In Lysippos, fr. 6 Kock L 702 (= Hesychius, s.v. *agersikubelis;* cf. Athenaeus 8.344e), *agersikubelis* appears again, as an archaic and pretentious equivalent of *mētragurtēs,* mocking the famous fortune-teller Lampoon.

23. The word *menagurtēs* appears in the titles of lost comedies by Menander and Antiphon. The confusion with *mētragurtēs* would later be compounded by the confusion identifying the Mother's *galli* with the Syrian goddess's *galli* (cf. Apuleius and Lucian). This says a great deal about the contempt weighing on these different marginal and foreign currents, which ended up being lumped together for condemnation. On the *menagurtēs* being confused with the *mētragurtēs,* cf. E. Lane, *Corpus Monumentorum Religionis Dei Menis,* vol. 3 (Leiden, 1976), 110, 117–18.

24. See the epigram by Alexander the Aetolian (beginning of the third century, B.C.E.) concerning the Spartan lyric poet Alcman from Sardis, in the *Anthologia Palatina* VII, 709. If he had remained in his home country, Alcman would not have become a poet, but would have remained an obscure *kernas* or *bakelas,* a player of the *tumpana.* The *bakeloi* appear again in *IG* XII, 3, 812 (Thera, fifth–fourth centuries); in comedy by Antiphon (*The Carians,* cited by Athenaeus 4.134b), and, finally, in Lucian (*Saturnales* 12 = ed. Jacobitz III, 308). This Greek satirist has a passage where Cronos (who has already castrated Ouranus) finds it funny to have the same fate allotted to rich people who mock the laws, thereby transforming them into *bakeloi,* begging for alms for the Mother, with their flutes and tympanums.

25. See the bilingual inscription in Sardis dedicating a votive stele to Artimul (in the dative; the name would be *Artimush = Artemis), ca. 350 B.C.E. The stele was dedicated by Nannas, son of Bakivalis (in the genitive), corresponding to Dionysokleos (*Sardis VII* [1932], no. 85; cf. Hanfmann and Ramage, *Sculpture from Sardis,* 177, no. 274 (= figs. 465–66).

26. The two major texts are Plato, *Republic* 2.364b, and Hippocrates, *De morbo sacro* 1.10 Grensemann = Littré, 6: 354 (cf. p. 359). Cf. *RE,* 1, pt. 1 (1893), cols. 915–17, s.v. "Agyrtes" (P. Stengel).

27. *Agurtēs* is a noun of agency constructed on the verb *ageirō.*

28. See the paintings and mosaics commented on in the *Lexicon Iconographicum Mythologiae Classicae,* vol. 1, s.v. "Agyrtes": the *agurtēs* trumpeter appears with this name next to the daughters of Lykomedes.

29. Hesychius, s.v. *agurmos (tōn musterion hēmera protē),* can be connected to the same lexicon, s.v. *agurtēs (ochlagogos).*

30. Aeschylus, fr. 168.

31. A common Ionian practice, designated by the verb *ageirō:* Herodotus 4.35.

32. Homer, *Odyssey* 19.284.

33. Plato, *Republic* 2.364b.

34. Plato, *Laws* 10.908d–909b.

35. Aristotle, *Rhetoric* 1405a, 20.

36. Plutarch, *Kleomenes* 36.

37. Klearchos, fr. 47 Wehrli, *Die Schule des Aristoteles* III, 23–24 = Athenaeus 12.541c–d; Aelian, *Various Stories* 9.8.

38. Antiphanes fr. 159.8 (Kock II, p. 12).

39. Dionysius of Halicarnassus, *Roman Antiquities* 2.19.

40. Apuleius, *Metamorphoses* 8.24–30; Lucian, *Lucius* 35 et seq.

41. Babrius 137 (14.1.1), cited by Natale Conti, *Mythologiae sive explicationis fabularum libri decem* 9.5 (Hannover, 1605), 968.

42. The Scythian eunuchs in Herodotus 4.67–69; see Alain Ballabriga, "Les Eunuques scythes et leurs femmes," *Métis* 1 (1986): 121–38. The *megabyzoi* in Xenophon, *Anabasis* 5.3.6. The interpretation of the pseudo-polymasty of Artemis of Ephesus in sacrificial terms (the goddess would in reality wear a pendant made from the scrotum of sacrificed bulls) can be added to the paltry documentation on this subject. See G. Seiterle, "Die grosse Göttin von Ephesos," *Antike Welt* 19, 3 (1979): 3–16, and Burkert, *Structure and History*, 130. We should specify that if the examples of castration recognized by the Greeks as being ritual in nature are quite rare, castration as a practice linked to perhaps orientalizing forms of tyranny cannot be ignored: see, e.g., Herodotus 3.49: to revenge himself on the inhabitants of Corcyra (Corfu), Periander of Corinth deported three hundred young aristocrats from that island to Sardis with the intention of making eunuchs of them; and see also 6.32 and 8.105.

43. I do not agree completely with the conclusions of M. Carla Giammarco Razzano, "I galli di Cibele nel culto di età ellenistica," *Miscellanea greca e romana* 9 (1982): 63–88.

44. Atys is spelled this way in Herodotus and often in later poetry.

45. *Anthologia Palatina* VI, 220; A. S. F. Gow and D. L. Page, *Hellenistic Epigrams* (Cambridge, 1965), 1: 85–86, 2: 246–48. See also Gow, "*Gallus* and the Lion."

46. The remarks of the scholiast on Nikander's *Alexipharmaka* about the subterranean chambers of Rhea where the *mēdea* were deposited after a ritual castration shed light on the title *thalamēpolos* of Cybele.

47. Gow, "*Gallus* and the Lion," 92 n. 33.

48. We cannot deduce much from Plutarch's mention in *Nikias* 3.2 of a madman who castrated himself on the altar of the twelve gods in 415.

49. There is also, however, other, older evidence, both iconographic (the relief at Piraeus with Agdistis and Attis) and implicit (see the story of Scipio Nasica in Chapter 4).

50. Neanthes is considered to be a significant source of *logos mustikos* (myths connected with the ritual mysteries) relating to Attis, the servant (*prospolos*) of the Mother of the gods, according to Harpokration, s.v. "Attēs" (= *Fragmenta Historicum Graecorum* III, 8, fr. 26 Müller = FgrHist. 84 F 37 Jacoby).

51. Marinus, *Life of Proclus* 19. Merino di Neapoli, *Vita di Proclo: Testo critico introduzione traduzione e commentario*, ed. Rita Masullo (Naples, 1985), 75. Greek text with English and French translations in Marinos of Neapolis, *Extant Works*, ed. Al. N. Oikonomides (Chicago, 1977).

52. Marinus, *Life of Proclus* 33 (pp. 89–90, ed. Masullo).

53. See also Alexander Polyhistor, in a work *On Phrygia* (273 F 73–78), mentioned by Stephanus of Byzantium and Pseudo-Plutarch, *De fluviis* 10.1.

54. Diodoros derives his information from Dionysos Skytobrachion (32 F 7 Jacoby).

55. Diodoros 3.55.8–9: "En aporretoi kata ten teleten."

56. Diodoros 5.48.4–50. Iasion, a famous figure, will be struck by lightning or immortalized; the version emphasized by Diodoros and his source is a variation of the facts from Hesiod and Homer, where Iasion is loved by Demeter (Hesiod, *Theogony* 969–71); Homer, *Odyssey* 5.125–28. In the classical version (also known to Diodoros), the fruit of this union is not Korybas, but Ploutos.

57. This is a title found in a hymn preserved on a papyrus drafted during Diodoros's

times. See Vittorio Bartoletti, "Inni a Cibele," in *Dai papyri della Società italiana* . . . (Florence, 1965), 13, line 10 (whose commentary refers to Schwenn in *RE*, 9, pt. 2 [1922], cols. 2294–95).

58. Cybele and Apollo's association perhaps goes back to an oriental context in which the Mother's *galli*, from Hierapolis (near Aphrodisias), presided in a place dedicated to Apollo. See Chapter 6, n. 18.

59. Diodoros 3.58–59.

60. See Eustathios's commentary on the *Iliad* 5.408.

61. See esp. Antoninus Liberalis, *Metamorphōseōn sunagōgē* 26.5.

62. See Herodotus 7.74–77 and also 1.7 (a passage implying the reign of a Meion before that of Lydos, son of Atys).

63. This binomial was spotted by E. Laroche and cited in his article "Asianiques (religions)," in *Dictionnaire des mythologies* (Paris, 1981), 1: 96, col. 2.

64. See Chapter 7, n. 32.

65. Ovid, *Fasti* 4.223–44.

66. Ibid., 224: *casto amore*; cf. Hesiod, *Theogony* 988–91.

67. Ovid, *Fasti* 4.229.

68. Ibid., 233; cf. "the chambers [*thalamoi*] of Rhea Lobrina and the sanctuary of the mysteries [*orgasterion*) of Attis" alluded to in Nikander, *Alexipharmaka* 6–7.

69. The torches and whips evoke the Furies. The Palestinian goddesses seem to lead us toward the Syrian goddess, linked early on to the Phrygian Mother.

70. Long hair (characteristic of Curetes, Corybantes, and *galli*) refers to the idea of virginity. It was believed that eunuchs could not be bald, because baldness was only a condition of people who had already had a sexual experience. See Pliny, *Nat. his.* 11.47 (131).

71. ". . . Onus inguinis aufert / Nullaque sunt subito signa relicta uiri."

72. See Pliny, *Nat. his.* 11.262 (109).

73. See Albert Henrichs, "Der rasende Gott: Zur Psychologie des Dionysus und des Dionysischen in Mythos und Litteratur," *Antike und Abendland* 40 (1994): 31–58, on the account of a physician of the first century c.e.: Aretaios 3.6.11, *Corpus Medicorum Graecorum*, ed. C. Hude (Berlin, 1958), 2: 43 et seq.

74. Pliny, *Nat. his.* 35.165. Cf. Martial 3.81. On the use of shards (*ostraka*) as cutting tools, see Gabriel Herman, "How Violent Was Athenian Society?" in *Ritual, Finance, Politics: Athenian Democratic Accounts Presented to David Lewis* (Oxford, 1994), 99–117. The Mother's *galli* belonged to the category of *castrati*, that is, eunuchs deprived of both penis and testicles. This extreme type of castration distinguished them from *spadones*, who were only deprived of their testicles (through ablation), and *thlasiae*, whose testicles had been crushed. *Spadones* and *thlasiae* were both capable of having an erection, and this is the category of eunuchism to which the *galli* of the Syrian goddess evidently belonged (Lucian emphasizes their heterosexual abilities). See G. Vorberg, *Glossarium eroticum* (Stuttgart, 1932), esp. 169.

75. The nymph is the daughter of the river Sangarios.

76. Pausanias 7.17.9. He himself opposes this second version to the one he took from Hermesianax, the so-called Lydian version.

77. Arnobius, *Adversus nationes* 5.5–7.

78. For the state of the question, see Fabio Mora, *Arnobio e i culti di mistero* (Rome, 1994), 125, n. 64, who suggests two possible identifications: a pontifex of the first century b.c.e., author of a work on the auspices, and a pontifex around the beginning of the second

century (for whom no works are mentioned). The exact identity of Valerius is thus very hypothetical.

79. Alexander Polyhistor, 273 F 74 Jacoby, cited by Stephanus of Byzantium, s.v. "Gallos."

80. See Andreas Alföldi, "Redeunt Saturnia regna, VII: Frugifer/Triptolemos im ptolemäisch-römischen Herrscherkult," *Chiron* 9 (1979): 553–606.

81. As minor discrepancies with regard to the main source, we can note the transposition from Midas to Gallos throughout the story as well as the name of the *virgo*, Ia, explicitly borrowed from the enigmatic pontifex Valerius. With regard to the sources, Mora, *Arnobio e i culti di mistero*, 116, 128, proposes to distinguish the body of the story (referring to Timotheos the Eumolpid via Alexander Polyhistor), the initial section (with the mention of Deucalion and Pyrrha, and the oracle of Themis referring to Ovid), and the final section (vegetable metamorphoses and ritual developments, referring to a Roman source, Valerius).

82. In Pausanias's version, the tree is an almond tree (which also plays a key role in the Gnostic account). Theophrastus (*History of Plants* 1.13.1) observes that the almond has something in common with the pomegranate, in that both have red flowers, which is unusual in cultivated trees. The saffron flowers of the pine, which, like the almond tree, plays a role in the conclusion of Arnobius's story, are analogous, and the pine is a symbolic element that is part of the ritual.

83. Arnobius, *Adversus nationes* 5.5.6: *in sinu reponit* (*sinus* corresponds to the Greek *kolpos*, on which see Chapter 6, n. 43 and related text).

84. See Chapter 6, n. 76 and related text.

85. Arnobius, *Adversus nationes* 5.7: "Tibi Acdesti haec habe, propter quae motus tantos furialium discriminum concitasti."

86. According to Ovid, *Metamorphoses* 1.383, these stones are in fact the bones of the Great Mother (*ossa magnae parentis*), which conforms with the oracle of Themis.

87. By title of his Eleusinian origins: Timotheos had been born into the priestly family of the Eumolpidae.

88. Scott Littleton, "The *Kingship in Heaven* Theme," in *Myth and Law Among the Indo-Europeans*, ed. J. Puhvel (Berkeley, Calif., 1970), 83–121; Walter Burkert, "Von Ullikumi zum Kaukasus: Die Felsgeburt des Unholds," *Würzburger Jahrbücher für die Altertumswissenschaft*, n.s., 5 (1979): 253–61; and id., *Structure and History*.

89. See H. G. Güterbock, "The Hittite Version of the Hurrian Kumarbi Myths," *American Journal of Archaeology* 52 (1948): 123–34.

90. J. G. Frazer, *Adonis, Attis, Osiris* (London, 1907), 237.

91. Burkert, *Structure and History*, 110–11.

92. See the translation of the Sumerian story in Jean Bottéro, *Lorsque les dieux faisaient l'homme: Mythologie mésopotamienne* (Paris, 1989), 86–289.

93. Burkert, *Structure and History*, 198 n. 20

94. Jean Bottéro and H. Petschow, "Homosexualität" (in French), in *Reallexikon der Assyriologie und vorderasiatischen Archäologie*, vol. 4 (Berlin, 1975), 459–68; cf. Jean Bottéro, "L'Amour libre à Babylone et ses servitudes," in *Le Couple interdit: Entretiens sur le racisme*, ed. L. Poliakov (Paris, 1980), 27–42. Stefan M. Maul, "*Kurgarrû* und *assinu* und ihr Stand in der babylonischen Gesellschaft," in *Aussenseiter und Randgruppen*, ed. V. Haas (Constance, 1992), 159–71, reviews the documentation and introduces a comparison with shamanistic practices. On the category of eunuchism, see n. 74 above.

95. Translation based on Bottéro's rendering in *Lorsque les dieux faisaient l'homme*, 323.

96. On this type of character, see Georges Dumézil, "Les Énarées scythiques et la grossesse de Narte Hamyc," *Latomus* 5 (1946): 249–55; Ballabriga, "Les Eunuques scythes et leurs femmes"; Will Roscoe, "Priests of the Goddess: Gender Transgression in Ancient Religion," *History of Religions* 35 (1996): 195–230; Pierrette Désy, "L'Homme-femme (les berdaches en Amérique du Nord)," *Libre* 3 (1978): 57–102; Ch. Callender and L. M. Kochems, "The North American Berdache," *Current Anthropology* 24 (1983): 443–70; W. L. Williams, *The Spirit and the Flesh: Sexual Diversity in American Indian Culture* (Boston, 1986). Cf. Ph. Borgeaud, "Le Problème du comparatisme en histoire des religions," *Revue européenne des sciences sociales* 24, 72 (1986): 59–75, esp. 60–63.

97. Firmicus Maternus, *De errore profanorum religionum* 3.1; cf. Hippolytus, *Refutation of All Heresies* 5.8.23–24 (and 5.9.8).

98. Porphyry, *Peri agalmatōn (On Images)* 6–7 Bidez, cited by Eusebius, *Praeparatio evangelica* 3.11 (110c) and Augustine, *De civitate Dei* 7.25.

99. Julian, *Discourse on the Mother of the Gods* 161c–176a; Sallustius, *De deis et mundo* 7.

100. Sallustius, *De deis et mundo*.

101. In what very well might be the last version of the myth, an eastern (Phoenician) version proposed by Damascius at the beginning of the sixth century in his *Life of Isidorus* (Photios, *Bibliothēkē*, codex 242, sect. 302), death is once again dodged. The beautiful adolescent Esmounos (a Cabire, son of Sadukos) is loved by the Mother of the gods, here named Astronoë: "He had the habit of hunting in the valleys of the country. Then he says that the goddess pursued him as he escaped and that when she was about to seize him, he cut off his genitals with an axe. The goddess, afflicted by this drama, called the young man Pean. She brought him back to life thanks to her creative warmth and made him into a god, whom the Phoenicians called Esmounos for his vital warmth." Based on Photios, *Bibliothēkē*, French trans. by René Henry (Paris, 1971), 6: 55.

102. Hepding, *Attis*, 110, n. 3.

103. Erwin Rohde, "Sardinische Sage von den Neunschläfer," in id., *Kleine Schriften* (Tübingen, 1901), vol. 2, 198 et seq.; and see id., *Psyche: Seelencult und Unsterblichkeitsglaube der Griechen* (Freiburg i.B., 1894), trans. W. B. Hillis as *Psyche: The Cult of Souls and Belief in Immortality Among the Greeks* (New York, 1966).

104. W. H. Roscher, *Ausführliches Lexikon der griechischen und römischen Mythologie* (Leipzig, 1884–1937), s.v. "Agdistis."

105. Ibid., s.v. "Attis" (W. Rapp).

106. *RE*, s.v. "Agdistis" (Knaack).

107. *RE*, s.v. "Attic" (Cumont). There is no mention at all of this in Cumont's *Les Religions orientales dans le paganisme romain* (4th ed., Paris, 1929).

108. Mora, *Arnobio e i culti di mistero*, 124, just notes this "simulacrum of life."

109. Otto Gruppe, *Griechische Mythologie und Religionsgeschichte* (Munich, 1906), 2: 933 n. 7.

110. M. Fritze, "Der Attiskult in Kyzikos," *Nomisma* 4 (1909): 33–42.

111. M. J. Vermaseren, *The Legend of Attis in Greek and Roman Art* (Leiden, 1966), 34.

112. Pausanias 8.34.1. Cf. also the tomb of Heracles' finger in Sparta, where the digit was deposited after having been bitten off by the Nemean lion (Ptol. Heph. 2.14–15 Roulez).

113. Felix Liebrecht, "Deutscher Aberglaube," *Heidelberger Jahrbuch*, 1869: 805; a text reprinted in *Zur Volkskunde: Alte und neue Aufsätze* (Heilbronn, 1879), 343–44. See also a

lecture by Chr. Belger in the *Berliner Philologische Wochenschrift* 12, no. 20 (1892): 638–40 (a summary of the "Februarsitzung" of the Archäologische Gesellschaft zu Berlin).

114. Amélie Bosquet, *La Normandie romanesque et merveilleuse* (Paris, 1845), 263.

115. [Pseudo-]Apollodoros, *Bibliothēkē* 3.5.1.

116. See n. 70 above and related text.

117. Michel Meslin, "Agdistis ou l'androgynie malséante," in *Hommages à Maarten J. Vermaseren*, ed. Margreet B. de Boer and T. A. Edridge (Leiden, 1978), 765–76; id., "Agdistis ou l'éducation sentimentale," *Bulletin de l'Association Guillaume-Budé* 4 (1979): 378–88.

118. Ezio Pellizer, *Favole d'identità, favole di paura* (Rome, 1982), 134–35, 138–39.

119. C. E. Colpe, "Zur mythologischen Struktur der Adonis- Attis- und Osiris-Überlieferungen," in *Lišān mithurti: Festschrift Wolfram Freiherr von Soden zum 19.4.1968 gewidmet von Schülern und Mitarbeitern*, ed. W. Röllig (Kevelaer and Neukirchen-Vluyn, 1969).

120. Pellizer, *Favole d'identità*, 136 n. 13.

121. Servius in Virgil, *Aeneid* 9.115.

122. See Schmitt-Pantel, "Histoire de tyran, esp. 227.

123. Here I stand by the conclusion expressed in my essay "L'Écriture d'Attis: Le Récit dans l'histoire" (in *Métamorphoses du mythe en Grèce antique*, ed. Claude Calame [Geneva, 1988], 87–103), despite the (partial) dissatisfaction of Mora, *Arnobio e i culti di mistero*, 123, who, although he does not offer one himself, would prefer an analysis that accounts better for the complexity of the story. Since I freely recognize that complexity, I shall attempt to respect it by returning to the subject further on, where it belongs, in the context of the religious world of the Roman empire in the second and third centuries.

FOUR: The Mother's Entrance into the Roman Republic

1. See K. Ziegler, "Mater Magna oder Magna Mater," *Latomus* 101 (1969).

2. Livy 29.10.5. This is the *carmen* according to which "from the moment that a foreign enemy introduced war onto the land of Italy, he would be beaten and chased from Italy if the Idaean Mother is brought from Pessinos to Rome" ("Quandoque hostis alienigena terrae Italiae bellum intulisset, eum pelli Italia vincique posse, si Mater Idaea a Pessinunte Romam advecta foret"). On the "manufacture" of the Sibylline oracles, see J. Scheid and J. Svenbro, *Le Métier de Zeus* (Paris, 1994), 155–57.

3. Also in 205, M. Pomponius Matho and Q. Catius went to Delphi to Apollo's sanctuary to deposit rich offerings commemorating the victory over Hasdrubal's army. A 200-pound gold crown and silver figurines weighing 1,000 pounds in all constituted the booty (Livy 28.45.12). They then proceeded to perform a sacrifice in which the examination of the entrails was favorable and heard an oracular response emitted from the depths of the *adyton*. This oracle proclaimed that Rome would have an even greater victory than the one for which these offerings were being given. That same year, Scipio Africanus declared that he knew how to make Africa a province of Rome (Livy 28.40).

4. Led by a specialist in Greek affairs, the two-time consul M. Valerius Laevinus, this embassy included the following magistrates: the praetor, M. Caecilius Metellus, the aedile, Ser. Sulpicius Galba, and the two quaestors, Cn. Tremellius Flaccus and M. Valerius Falto. In order to make manifest the *"majestas* of the Roman name," the Senate decreed that each of these five delegates would have a ship with five rows of rowers. See G. Clemente,

"Esperti, ambasciatori del Senato e la formazione della politica esterna romana tra il III et il II secolo a.C.," *Athenaeum* 54 (1976): 319–52, esp. 326–27, 333.

5. "Consultatio de Matre Idaea accipienda."

6. John Scheid, "D'indispensables *étrangères:* Les Rôles religieux des femmes à Rome," in *Histoire des femmes en occident*, ed. Georges Duby and Michelle Perrot, vol. 1, *L'Antiquité*, ed. Pauline Schmitt Pantel (Paris, 1991), 405–37.

7. The entire itinerary from the sea to the Palatine Hill (*in Palatium a mare*) is nevertheless emphasized as having taken place under the auspices of Scipio Nasica by Livy, recalling the episode in 36.36.3.

8. The documentation was assembled by Ernst Schmidt in *Kultübertragungen* (Giessen, 1909), 1–30. A statue of Claudia Quinta, miraculously saved from the flames that twice destroyed the temple of the Mother (in 111 B.C.E. and 3 C.E.), stood in the vestibule of this building (Valerius Maximus 1.8.11; cf. Tacitus, *Annals* 4.64). A famous relief in the Capitoline Museum dedicated to the ship that carried the goddess to safety, and depicting the miracle performed by Claudia Quinta, has been the subject of many commentaries: see *CCAA*, vol. 3, no. 218.

9. See the episode of Coriolanus in Livy 2.40.

10. See Livy 1.4.2: "Vi compressa Vestalis cum geminum partum edidisset, seu ita rata seu quia deux auctor culpae honestior erat, Martem incertae stirpis patrem edidisset."

11. Tradition holds that the image of the Mother "fell" into Pessinos (see 90–92, 113, 213 n. 27). For the most detailed description of this stone, see Arnobius, *Adversus nationes* 7.49): "allatum ex Phrygio nihil quid aliud scribitur missum rege ab Attalo, nisi lapis quidam non magnus, ferri manu hominis sine ulla impressione qui posset, coloris furvi atque atri, angellis signo oris loco positum, indolatum et asperum et simulacro faciem minus expressam simulatione praebentem."

12. See *Inscriptiones Italiae* 13.2.438, with J. Brisco, *A Commentary on Livy* (Oxford, 1981), 2: 274–75, and A. Manuelian's notes on bk. 36 of Livy in the Collection des universités de France, 115–16.

13. *Ex senatus consulto* (Livy 36.36.4).

14. See Livy 29.37. Contradicting himself, in 36.36.3, Livy curiously dates the goddess's arrival and reception by Scipio Nasica to the consulate of Publius Cornelius Scipio (later Scipio Africanus) and Publius Licinius Crassus, that is, in 205.

15. Diodoros 34.33.2.

16. Ovid, *Fasti* 4.347.

17. Ibid., 293–96.

18. Ibid., 326.

19. Ibid., 291–330.

20. Clausus Attius.

21. Ovid, *Fasti* 4.297–329. *Ovid's* Fasti: *Roman Holidays*, trans. B. R. Nagle (Bloomington, Ind., 1995), 113. See also the more poetic Loeb translation by Sir James Frazer, in Ovid, *Fasti* (New York, 1931), 210–13.

22. Dionysius of Halicarnassus, *Roman Antiquities*, 2.19.4, Loeb ed., trans. Earnest Cary, based on Edward Spelman (Cambridge, Mass., 1937), 1: 365–67.

23. Lucretius, *De rerum natura* 2.598–643; cf. the Loeb translation, ibid., lines 618–38, 142–45, starting: "The taut tomtoms thunder under the open palm. . . ." The lions pulling the Mother's chariot correspond to the two docile animals flanking the Mother's throne in classical Greek iconography. The chariot pulled by lions is often represented in

Roman times. It is not necessarily an idealization. Twelve of the chariots in the famous procession of Ptolemy II Philadelphus (Ath. 5.32) were pulled by lions, and Aelian, *De natura animalium* 17.26, reports the presence of tame lions in the sanctuary of Anaïtis, a goddess close to the Mother of the gods, in Elymais (Iran). Aelian also notes that the Indians used lions to hunt (ibid. 17.26). For more on lions and the *galli*, see Dioscorides 65.

24. Cicero, *De legibus* 2.9.22: "Praeter Idaeae Matris famules eosque iustis diebus ne quis stipem cogito"; cf. 2.16.40, where it is repeated that this exception accorded the Idaean Mother is only for "a few days" (*paucos dies*). We can estimate that this short period lasted from the *lavatio* (March 27) to the opening of the Megalesia (April 4).

25. Ovid, *Fasti* 4.181–86. *Ovid's Fasti*, trans. Nagle, 110. See also the Loeb *Ovid* 4.181–86, 201–3.

26. See Ovid, *Fasti* 4.215–18.

27. The poet assimilates the Idaean Mother to Rhea's tree.

28. Ovid, *Fasti* 4.339–42. *Ovid's Fasti*, trans. Nagle, 114.

29. Martial, *Epigrams* 3.47.1 et seq., evokes the Porta Capena, where water seeps through, and the Almo River, which washes and purifies the knife used to castrate the *galli*: "Capena grandi porta qua pluit gutta / Phrygiumque Matris Almo qua lavat ferrum."

30. Ovid's mention of two different processions perfectly corroborates what Cicero tells us of the *galli*'s solicitations (taken together over a few days, they are indeed plural).

31. While accepting neither the existence in Rome of a Phrygian ritual nor one of Attis before Claudius, Danielle Porte, "Claudia Quinta et le problème de la *lavatio* de Cybèle en 204 av. J.-C.," *Klio* 66 (1984): 93–103, nonetheless arrives at a conclusion similar to my own.

32. John Scheid, "Les Sanctuaires de confins dans la Rome antique," in *L'Urbs*, Collection de l'École française de Rome 48 (Rome, 1987), 583–95, has called my attention to the fact that the Almo joins the Tiber at Santo Paolo "outside the walls," that is, near the "ideal" borders of the city, marked by the presence of military sanctuaries on the left bank of the Tiber.

33. Arrian, *Technē taktikē* 33.

34. See E. Habel in *RE*, suppl. 5, 626–28.

35. Dedication made by the *praetor urbanus* M. Iunius Brutus: Cicero, *De haruspicum responsis* 24.

36. The first games were presided over by the aediles and were organized as of the goddess's arrival in Rome in 204 (Livy 29.14.13–14, with the correction *pridie Nonas* instead of *Idus Apriles:* note in Ovid, *Fasti* 4.247 in R. Schilling's edition in the Collection des universités de France; cf. Livy 34.54.3). From 22 B.C.E. on, the praetors took over the role of the aediles (Dio Cassius 54.2.3). According to Livy 34.34.3, the theatrical representations appeared as of 194; according to Valerius Antias, as of 191, the date the Palatine sanctuary was dedicated, and on which Plautus's *Pseudolus* was first performed before the temple. A generation later, plays by Terence were put on there.

37. Cicero, *De sen.* 13.45. Cf. Pliny, *Nat. hist.* 2.24.2; Aulus Gellius 18.2.11. See also the *Fasti Praenestini, Corpus Inscriptionum Latinarum* I², pp. 231–39, Mommsen.

38. See Schilling's edition of Ovid's *Fasti* in the Collection des universités de France, 2: 118, n. 128, and Angelo Brelich, "Offerte e interdizione alimentari nel culto della Magna Mater a Roma," *Studi e materiali di storia della religione* 36 (1965): 27–41.

39. On Julius Obsequens, see *T. Livi Periochae omnium librorum, Fragmenta Oxyrhynchi reperta, Iulii Obsequentis prodigiorum liber*, ed. O. Rossbach (Leipzig, 1910), 166. Valerius

Maximus 7.7.6. For a legal examination of the two cases, see Danilo Dalla, *L'incapacità sessuale in diritto romano* (Milan, 1978), 46, 204 et seq.

40. On ex-votos that give evidence of this piety, see P. Romanelli, "Magna Mater e Attis sul Palatino," in *Hommages à J. Bayet* (Brussels, 1964), 619–26; cf. id., *Mon. Ant. Lincei* 46 (1963): 202–330, figs. 32–37; F. Coarelli, "I monumenti di culti orientali in Roma," in *La soteriologia dei culti orientali* (Leiden, 1982), 33–67, at 40 et seq.; and P. Pensabene, "Cibele la Grande Madre," *Archeo: attualità del passato* 48 (1989): 74–82.

41. Ovid, *Fasti* 4.251–54: "cum Troiam Aeneas Italos portaret in agros, / est dea sacriferas paene secuta rates, / sed nondum fatis Latio sua numina posci / senserat, adsuentis substiteratque locis."

42. Sources and bibliography can be found in Naumann, *Ikonographie der Kybele*, 283–90; see Graf, *Nordionische Kulte*, 305. Cicero, Strabo, Livy, Diodoros, Valerius Maximus, Arrian, Dio Cassius, Herodian, Arnobius, and Ammianus Marcellinus explicitly mention that she originates from Pessinos. The *Fasti Praenestini*, Silius, Festus, Solinus, and Julian (although Julian does make a detour via Pessinos) generally cite the goddess as coming from Phrygia. Only Ovid gives Trojan Ida as her origin. Only Varro, *De lingua latina* 6.15, which presents some textual difficulties (see Chapter 5, n. 21), affirms Pergamon to be her place of origin. (Noted by Graf, *Nordionische Kulte*, and Erich S. Gruen, *Studies in Greek Culture and Roman Policy* [Leiden, 1990], 5–33.)

43. Dionysius of Halicarnassus, *Roman Antiquities* 2.20, Loeb ed., 366–69.

44. See François Hartog's preface to Dionysius of Halicarnassus, *Les Antiquités romaines: Livres I et II (Les Origines de Rome)*, trans. and ed. Valérie Fromentin and Jacques Schnäbele (Paris, 1900), "Le Choix de Denys et l'identité des Romains."

45. The equation of Cybele with the fertile earth is not only philosophical in nature. See *Corpus Inscriptionum Latinarum* XIV, and T. Gesztelyi, "Tellus–Terra Mater in der Zeit des Principats," *ANRW* II, 17, 1 (1981), 429–56. On Lucretius 2.598–643, see Leon Lacroix, "Texte et réalités à propos du témoignage de Lucrèce sur la Magna Mater," *Journal des savants*, 1982: 11–43. Varro, *Ant. Div.*, fr. 267 Cardauns, cited by Augustine, *Civ. Dei* 7.24: "She [Tellus] is the one, said he, whom we call the Great Mother. She carries a tambourine to signify that she is the terrestrial disk. The towers she wears on her head are the cities. She is represented sitting down for, although everything moves all around her, she does not move. The *galli* serve her. This means that those who have no seed must be attached to the earth; it is within her that all things are found. If they move around before her, it is, said he, because farmers must not sit down, since they always have something to do. The cymbals clashing symbolizes the beating of iron weapons and the noise made by working hands and bronze while tilling the soil in a field. The cymbals are made of metal because the ancients laboured with a bronze plowshare before the discovery of iron. A free, unchained lion is placed beside Tellus to show that there is no kind of land, no matter how vacant or wild that cannot be worked on and cultivated." Varro would not have ignored the presence of Attis *in the temple*, at least if we are to believe the correction made by Lachmann to fr. 132 of the *Menippean Satires*: "Cum illoc uento, uideo Gallorum frequentiam in templo, qui, dum messem hornam [essena hora nam *codd.*] adlatam imponunt Attidis [Lachmann; aedilis *cett.*, cum *codd.*] signo deae, deum et deam [signosiae et deam *codd.*] gallantes uario recinebant studio" (= *Eumenides* 16, pp. 530, 562–64, 614 et seq. of J.-P. Cèbe's edition in the Collection de l'École française de Rome 9, vol. 4 [1977]).

46. Ovid, *Fasti* 4.353–60.

47. The Mater Magna was as Roman as she was Trojan: see her numerous appearances

in the *Aeneid*, esp. 9.80 et seq. Augustus, a member of the gens Iulia, descended from Aeneas the Trojan, rebuilt the Palatine temple (which had once again been destroyed since its reconstruction in 111), dedicated it in 3 c.e., and made the Idaean Mother one of the divinities protecting the imperial house. Livia, who belonged to the gens Claudia (i.e., the tribe of Claudia Quinta), had herself represented as Cybele. See T. P. Wiseman, "Cybele, Virgil and Augustus," in *Poetry and Politics in the Age of Augustus*, ed. Tony Woodman and David West (Cambridge, 1984).

48. Erika Simon, *Die Götter der Römer* (Munich, 1990), 150–51 and fig. 191, believes she has recognized Attis and Cybele on a cistern from Praeneste dating from the end of the fourth century. However, an "Attis" armed with a sword in the presence of a "Cybele" without lions is doubtful in my view.

49. Graf, *Nordionische Kulte*, mentions this episode.

50. H. Le Bonniec has very clearly shown this in *Le Culte de Cérès à Rome des origines à la fin de la République* (Paris, 1958), 365–67, two luminous pages summarizing the antagonism and rivalry between the plebian goddess (Ceres) and the "protector of nobility" (Cybele).

51. Servius on Virgil, *Georgics* 2.394.

52. Virgil, *Aeneid* 9.619–29, English translation from Bellessort's French version in the Collection des universités de France (cf. the English of the Loeb edition, which begins: "But ye are clothed in embroidered saffron and gleaming purple; sloth is your joy").

53. See *Iliad* 2.235; 7.96: *Achaiides ouket'Achaioi*, "Acheans and no longer Acheans."

54. This is found in a fragment of a Hellenistic poem often attributed to Callimachus, as well as in Catullus.

55. This territory is signified by the Mother's sacred wood on Trojan Ida, a wood that ensures that Aeneas reaches Italy, before returning, after a metamorphosis, to the divine realm.

56. In an indirect fashion, the figure of the Mother of the gods (conceived of as Rhea, mother of the Olympians) here encounters Rhea Silvia, mother of Romulus and Remus, once again. We have already observed this type of similarity with regard to the episode of Claudia Quinta.

57. Dionysius of Halicarnassus, *Roman Antiquities* 2.19.5, opposes the *autigeneis (ingenui)*, high-born citizens' practice of the official rites of the Megalesia, to the *mētragurtai, galli* who partake in the bloody, exotic procession. On the ambivalence of the Roman attitude toward the Mother, see Mary Beard, "The Roman and the Foreign: The Cult of the Great Mother in Imperial Rome," in *Shamanism, History, and the State*, ed. Nicholas Thomas and Caroline Humphrey (Ann Arbor, Mich., 1994), 164–90.

58. J. N. Bremmer, "Slow Cybele's Arrival," in *Roman Myth and Mythography*, ed. id. and N. M. Horsfall (London, 1987), 105–11.

59. Even according to Livy (29.14.8–9), the participation of young Scipio Nasica poses a problem: "The Fathers declared that the best of all the citizens of Rome was Publius Scipio Nasica, son of Gnaeus Scipio who died in Spain. He was not yet old enough to be a quaestor [thus less than twenty-seven years old]. As for the reasons guiding this choice, if they had been passed down to us by witnesses of the period, I would not hesitate to repeat them for all posterity. However, I do not want to penetrate a secret covered up by years by allowing myself to make conjectures." Th. Köves, "Zum Empfang der Magna Mater in Rom," *Historia* 12 (1963): 321–47, at 330, had already spotted "a kind of Roman Attis" in Scipio Nasica. Garth Thomas, "Magna Mater and Attis," *ANRW* II, 17, 3 (1984),

1506, reacts against such an unlikely assimilation. In reality, he must be interpreted in terms of a transformation (with camouflage). Not literally a Roman Attis, but rather someone who in Rome acts as an echo of the eastern myth, he functions to obliterate Attis. For a position similar to my own, see Eva Stehle, "Venus, Cybele, and the Sabine Women: the Roman Construction of Female Sexuality," *Helios* 16 (1989): 143–64, at 163 n. 82.

60. Valerius Maximus 1.8.11. E. S. Gruen, *Culture and National Identity* (Ithaca, N.Y., 1992), 118–19, suggests that the statue was placed there during the dedication of the temple in 191. See also the following note.

61. J. Gérard, "Légende et politique autour de la Mère des dieux," *Revue des études latines* 58 (1980): 153–75, believes that the Roman legend, as we know it, did not take shape until the middle of the first century B.C.E..

62. See Arnobius 5.5–7.

63. See Varro, n. 45 above, for a possible explanation. Numerous terra-cotta ex-votos dating from the Republican era have been found at this site, proving that ritual there involved Attis. See also Romanelli, "Magna Mater e Attis," and Pensabene, "Cibele la Grande Madre." This popular piety in the Palatine sanctuary developed at the end of the second century B.C.E. with the reconstruction of the temple, destroyed by fire in 111.

64. Ovid, *Fasti* 4.223–44.

F I V E : The Origin of the Mater Magna

1. The phrase *hostis alienigena* includes both Carthaginians and Gauls.

2. Polybius 21.20.3: *philias kai summachias.*

3. The connections between Delphi and Attalos I are well known: see G. Roux, "La Terrasse d'Attale Iᵉʳ à Delphes," *Bulletin de Correspondance hellénique* 76 (1952), 141 et seq., and École française d'Athènes, *Fouilles de Delphes, II*, fasc. 17, *La Terrasse d'Attale Iᵉʳ* (Paris, 1987).

4. On the historical context and the nature of these alliances, see Erich S. Gruen, *The Hellenistic World and the Coming of Rome* (Berkeley, Calif., 1984), 2: 530 et seq.

5. Livy 29.12.14. Modern historians hesitate about including the presence of Ilium, and also Athens and Sparta, on the list of the *adscripti*. They believe it possible that these were added later on by Roman commentators. See André Piganiol, *La Conquête romaine* (1927; reprint, Paris, 1944), 196; Gruen, *Hellenistic World*, with documentation). No such skepticism is shown by Domenico Musti, *Storia greca*² (Rome, 1990), 821 *in fine*.

6. Gruen, *Hellenistic World*, 2: 531 n. 8. Gruen modifies the position he adopted in this work, dating from 1984, in his subsequent books *Studies of Greek Culture and Roman Policy* (1990), 5–33 ("The Advent of the Magna Mater"; see esp. 30–32) and *Culture and National Identity* (1992), where he concedes that the contested list of *adscripti* were authentic co-signers of the peace of Phoenice:

> The episode had diplomatic, military, and religious implications. But all were joined by the golden thread of the Trojan legend that announced Rome's cultural credentials to the nations of the Hellenistic world. . . . The conclusion is reinforced by the Peace of Phoenice in 205, which brought a formal terminus to the First Macedonian War. The signatures framed that treaty in the same year as Cybele's cult was transferred to Rome. And there can be no coincidence in the fact that the two states who headed the list of Rome's *adscripti* in the document were Ilium and

Pergamum. . . . Ilium, a small and impotent town in the politics of the Hellenistic titans, had had no imperial ambitions by associating her fortunes with that community. The value of Ilium lay on a symbolic plane. It accorded to Rome the cultural stature that could not be won on the battlefield. (*Culture and National Identity*, 47– 48)

Gruen adds (ibid., 48 n. 196) that denying the authenticity of the presence of Ilium as a signatory to the peace of Phoenice, as does C. Habicht, *Studien zur Geschichte Athens in hellenistischer Zeit* (Göttingen, 1982), 138–41, amounts to neglecting the cultural dimension of this whole affair. In my opinion, although I refuse to distinguish between the cultural and the political or the strategic (see the next note), I cannot decide between the two opposing views. It is altogether possible that ideological expectations or cultural constraints only became involved later on, thereby prompting a *post eventum* reworking of the history connected to the Peace of Phoenice (and introducing Ilium).

7. In *Culture and National Identity*, Gruen once again underscores the importance of this Trojan ideology in the Roman reception of the Mother. The myth of Trojan origins connects the Roman Urbs, culturally (on a symbolic level) to the prestigious ancient legends of Greek epics. In this perspective, Rome is situated on equal ground with its Near Eastern partners. See also the admirable synthesis on this issue by Arnaldo Momigliano, *Saggi di storia della religione romana* (Brescia, 1988), 171–83: "La leggenda di Enea nella storia di Roma fino ad Augusto." In contrast, Gruen does not recognize any implications for a strategy of conquest. Cf. Köves, "Zum Empfang der Magna Mater in Rom"; Gérard, "Légende et politique"; and F. Bömer, "Kybele in Rom," *Römische Mitteilungen* 71 (1964): 130–51.

8. H. Kuiper, "De Magna Matre Pergamenorum" (1902), notwithstanding the solid arguments advanced by A. Körte in *Athenische Mitteilungen* 22 (1897): 15 et seq. Kuiper's thesis, reiterated by Schmidt, *Kultübertragungen*, 23–24, and Graillot, *Culte de Cybèle*, 25– 26, 46–51, is only rarely contested; see the documentation of Biagio Virgilio in *Il "Tempio Stato" di Pessinunte* . . . (Pisa, 1981), 45, who, although he rallies to the *communis opinio*, admits that "è difficle decidere quale sia la posizione giusta" ("it is difficult to decide which position is right").

9. Strabo 12.5.3 (C 567): the Attalids provided the sanctuary (*temenos*) of Pessinous with a temple (*naos*) and a white marble portico (*stoai leukolithoi*).

10. There is a great deal to say about the image of the Gauls in Hellenistic tradition. Besides their being identified as exemplary adversaries, like the Giants in the mythical cosmos and the Persians in the historical world, we see an entirely new discourse arise. They become very fragile warriors, predestined victims of their panicky fears. (Note the episode in Delphi and their defeat at Lysimacheia, under the sign of Pan.) A myth of origin is attributed to them, playing on the etymology, and presenting them as the descendants of Galatea and the pitiful Polyphemus.

11. On all of this, see Karl Strobel, "Die Galater im hellenistischen Kleinasien: Historische Aspekte einer keltischen Staatenbildung," in *Hellenistische Studien*, ed. J. Seibert (Munich, 1991), 101–34, and Stephen Mitchell, *Anatolia: Land, Men, and Gods in Asia Minor*, vol. 1, *The Celts and the Impact of Roman Rule* (Oxford, 1993), 21.

12. See the Pessinontian inscriptions GAL TOL PESSINOUTION (nos. 34, 35) and SEBA TOLISTOBO PESINOUNTION (nos. 53, 69, 82), dating from the reigns of Marcus Aurelius and Augustus, in the catalogue established by J. Devreker, in J. Devreker and M. Waelkens, *Les*

Fouilles de la Rijksuniversiteit te Gent à Pessinonte, 1967–1973 (Bruges, 1984), 173–215 ("Le Monnayage de Pessinonte").

13. See Livy 38.16.12.

14. Lynn E. Roller, "The Great Mother at Gordion: The Hellenization of an Anatolian Cult," *Journal of Hellenic Studies* 111 (1991): 131 n. 14, and 138–39.

15. See also Strobel, "Galater im hellenistischen Kleinasien."

16. Livy 38.17.9.

17. The Tolistobogiae were still Pergamene allies in 189 (Livy 38.18.1); one of them was apparently Eposognatos, "the only Gaulish chief to have retained Eumenes' friendship," as Richard Adam notes in the commentary to his translation in the Collection des universités de France (1982), 133, 134.

18. See Kurt Bittel, "Die Galater in Kleinasien, archäologisch gesehen," in *Assimilation et résistance à la culture gréco-romain dans le monde ancien*, ed. D. M. Pippidi (Paris, 1976), 241–49, at 243.

19. *IG* XI, 4, 1299; see P. Roussel, *Les Cultes égyptiens à Délos. . . .* (Nancy, 1916); H. Engelmann, *The Delian Aretalogy of Sarapis* (Leiden, 1975).

20. See Pseudo-Plutarch, *De fluviis* 9, 10, 11, and 13. Graillot, *Culte de Cybèle*, 18 n. 4, 328–30, provides ample documentation on these autoglyph "stones to which the caprice of nature or the effect of the elements attributed the strange shape of idols" (329).

21. Varro, *De lingua latina* 6.15. "That Varro was able to write that that way, even an ignorant person would doubt, unless one were to claim that Varro knew nothing of syntax" ("Haec ita scripsisse Varroneum vix quispiam vel leviter doctus sibi persuaserit, nisi qui Varronem soloikizein velit"), Scaliger declared (in Varro, *De lingua latina cum Jos. Scaligeri conjectaneis* [Paris, 1565]). As for the name given to the April ritual of the goddess (the Megalesia), three lines by Varro, a short notice written in a style one is tempted to call "telegraphic," are inserted in a list of the etymologies of the Roman festivals, as follows: "Megalesia dicta a Graecis quod ex libris Sibyllinis arcessita ab Attalo rege Pergama ibi prope murum Megalesion id est templum eius deae unde aduecta Romam" (Collection des universités de France [Paris, 1985]; punctuation deleted). Scaliger corrects *Pergama* to *Pergami* and consequently feels obliged to suppose a lacuna, which he fills with the ablative deriving from *Pessinunte* (justified in his eyes by the historical tradition relating the provenance of the cult image). The meaning then becomes: "The Greeks called the festival of the Great Mother the Megalesia because, after consultation of the Sibylline books, she [the goddess] was sought out by King Attalos of Pergamon in Pessinos, where there is, next to a wall, a *megalesion*, that is, a sanctuary of this goddess; from there, she was taken to Rome" ("quod ex libris Sibyllinis arcessita ab Attalo rege Pergami, Pessinunte, ubi . . . Megalesion"). But however clever it may be, the conjecture is not very economical and fails to clear everything up. L. Bloch, in *Philologus* 52 (1893): 580, followed by Varro's translators Elisabetta Riganti (Bologna, 1978) and Pierre Flobert (Paris, 1985) simply emended *Pergama* to *Pergamou*, whence the translation proposed by Flobert: "The Megalesia (festivals of the Great Mother) owe their name to the Greeks, because, according to the Sibylline books, the goddess was brought from Pergamon, by requesting her of King Attalos; there, near a fortified wall, there is the *megalesion*, that is, the temple of this goddess, from where she was transported to Rome." The question remains: should *Pergama* necessarily be corrected. As is, it is a neuter accusative in the plural form indicating the direction of Ilium. (In Latin, *Pergamum*, in the singular, designates the city of Attalos, whereas *Pergama*, in the

plural, always indicates Troy.) In order to understand Pergamon, Attalos's city, *Pergama* (from the manuscript evidence) was transformed into *Pergami* or *Pergamo*. Is this judicious when we know that the oracle reported by Livy explicitly concerns the Trojan goddess (the Idaean Mother)?

22. *Pergama* thus depends on *advecta*, as does *Romam*.

23. As Naumann, *Ikonographie der Kybele*, 249, judiciously remarks.

24. Representations of Mētēr from Ilium from the archaic era exist: see D. B. Thompson, "The Terracotta Figurines of the Hellenistic Period," in *Troy*, suppl. 3 (Princeton, N.J., 1963), 58–60, and *Der kleine Pauly* (Stuttgart, 1975, s.v. "Troia," cols. 982–83 (Konrat Ziegler); cf. *American Journal of Archaeology* 1937: 588 et seq.; 1939: 218 et seq. The doubts of Graf, *Nordionische Kulte*, 114 and n. 59, do not appear conclusive to me.

25. Theopompus, 115 F 260 Jacoby, cited by Ammianus Marcellinus 27.9.6–7 (which also refers to more recent historians). In Diodoros Siculos 3.59.8, Midas encourages the construction of the temple in Pessinos; cf. Arnobius, *Adversus nationes* 2.73.

26. Herodian 1.11.2.

27. Herodian also mentions the etymology according to which Pessinos (from *pessein*, "to fall") owes its name to the fact that an idol of the Mother fell from the sky there. This cult image, a stone not worked by human hands, evoking the image of the goddess, is also the object of yet another eschatological myth, mentioned by Pseudo-Plutarch, *De fluviis* 12. It is an autoglyph (i.e. self-sculpted) stone found in the Sangarius River.

28. See notes to *Herodian*, trans. C. R. Whittaker, 2 vols., Loeb Classical Library 454 (Cambridge, Mass., 1969–70).

29. Pseudo-Plutarch, *De fluviis* 13.2. The name Agdesthios (codd. *Aigesthios*) is restored as per corrections proposed by Roberto Gusmani, "AGDISTIS," *Parola del passato* 14 (1959): 202–11, at 205 with n. 18. The text does not mention upon whom or what Agdesthios's seed falls. Apparently, one is supposed to understand the Mother of the gods, or a rock. The peak of Gargaron, sometimes also known as Gargara, is a summit in the south of the Troad, in the Idaean chain of mountains. The *Iliad* frequently alludes to the summit of Mount Ida (14.292), a favorite resort of Zeus (15.152; 14.352, etc.).

30. Arnobius, *Adversus nationes* 2.73.

31. See Devreker and Waelkens, *Fouilles de la Rijksuniversiteit te Gent*, esp. 13–28, "Pessinonte dans l'Antiquité" (Devreker); 51–54, "Description générale du site" (Waelkens); and 173–215, "Le Monnayage de Pessinonte" (Devreker).

32. See Strabo 12.5.3 (C 567). The cult of Agdistis in Asia Minor is evidenced, aside from at Pessinos, in Ephesus (*Jahresheft* 1926, *Beibl.* 259); in the Phrygian establishments of Eumenia (*Corpus Inscriptionum Graecarum* III, 3886); the "City of Midas" (*Monumenta Asiae Minoris Antiqua*, nos. 390–94, 396–99, 395; cf. Haspels, *Highlands of Phrygia*, 1: 154–55, 199–200); and Dokimeion (Louis Robert, *CRAI* 1980: 527; cf. id., "À travers l'Asie Mineure," *Bulletin de l'École française d'Athènes et de Rome* 299 [1980]: 266–99), as well as at Iconium in Lycaonia (*Corpus Inscriptionum Graecarum* III, 3993); see F. Hiller von Gaertringer, "Eine verkannte Gottheit," *Archiv für Religionswissenschaft* 24 (1926–27): 169–70; P. Roussel, "Un Sanctuaire d'Agdistis à Rhamnonte," *Revue des études anciennes* 32 (1930): 5–8; Gusmani, "AGDISTIS"; Robert, "À travers l'Asie Mineure."

33. The best example is the "city of Midas" (Yazilikaya, Midas Kale, Midas Sehri) on the very spot where the most ancient devotion of the Matar Kubileia took place. It was not until the middle of the second century B.C.E. (as the analysis of the shards shows) that a

Hellenistic sanctuary was created. Numerous inscriptions (from the Roman imperial period) attest to the fact that it was dedicated to Agdistis: see Haspels, *Highlands of Phrygia*, 1: 154–55, 199–200.

34. L. Robert, "Une Nouvelle Inscription de Sardes," *CRAI* 1975: 306–30, a decree from the thirty-ninth year of the reign of Artaxerxes II Mnemon (second century C.E.): Zeus Baradates (Ahura Mazda) is obliged by his priests to shun the rites of Ma, Agdistis, and Sabazios. Cf. *Bulletin épigraphique* 624 (1976): 289–91.

35. Staatliche Museum, Berlin, inv. no. 1612 (= *IG* II², 4671), dedication on a votive relief from Piraeus, ca. 300–350 B.C.E.

36. The temple dedicated to Agdistis Epēkoos was built between 274 and 270; see Jouguet, *Bulletin de Correspondance hellénique* 20 (1896): 398; *Sammelbuch griechischer Urkunden aus Ägypten* (Strasbourg, 1915), 1: 306; *OGIS*, 1, no. 28. On the epithet, see O. Weinreich, "ΘΕΟΙ ΕΠΕΚΟΟΙ," *Athenische Mitteilungen* 37 (1912): 1 et seq. The name Agdistis appears in the Greek literature of Egypt (on a papyrus from the first century B.C.E., which transmitted more ancient texts) with two fragmentary hymns dedicated to the Mother of the gods, also designated as Phrygian Queen, Cretan Mountain Mother, and Agdistis: Bartoletti, "Inni a Cibele"; see Carlo Pavese, "Un frammento di mimo in un nuovo papiro fiorentino," *Studi italiani di filologia classica* 38 (1965): 63–69.

37. Pausanias 1.7; schol. Callimachus, *Hymn in Del.* 173: see Marcel Launey, *Recherches sur les armées hellénistiques*, vol. 1 (Paris, 1949), 511–16. Strobel, "Galater im hellenistischen Kleinasien," dates the episode to 275 B.C.E.; *Supplementum Hellenisticum*, ed. Hugh Lloyd-Jones and Peter Parsons (Berlin, 1983), 459–60, no. 958 (fragment of a poem celebrating this victory by Ptolemy II), to ca. 274–272 B.C.E.; and Luigi Beschi and Domenico Musti to between 274 and 269 B.C.E. at the latest, in *Pausania: Guida della Grecia* (Milan, 1982), 1: 284.

38. The Gauls of Egypt evidently spoke and wrote Greek correctly: "Les stèles d'Alexandrie établissent qu'ils avaient adopté les moeurs et les goûts des Grecs" (Launey, *Recherches sur les armées hellénistiques*, 528).

39. In addition to the literature (especially Callimachus), there were monuments commemorating the victory of Ptolemy that were disseminated in the form of reproductions as far as the Egyptian countryside. See P. Laubscher, *Antike Kunst* 30 (1987): 148 et seq. (the head of the Gaul in the Cairo Museum).

40. Attesting to the fame of the sanctuary of Pessinos in the third century B.C.E. (in addition to the interest of Timotheos the Eumolpid), a poem by Dioscorides (*Anthologia Palatina* VI, 220) describes the voyage of a chaste Atys, Cybele's attendant, from Pessinos to Sardis and his encounter with a lion.

41. Roller, "Great Mother at Gordion," 1329, suggests that it was perhaps the Gauls who substituted the Greek alphabet for the ancient Phrygian alphabet in the third century B.C.E. Spoken Phrygian did not, however, disappear and continued to be used, coexisting with the Greek at least until the fifth century C.E., and possibly up until the Arab invasion in the seventh century. See Claude Brixhe, *Essai sur le grec anatolien au début de notre ère* (Nancy, 1984); id., "La Langue comme critère d'acculturation: L'Exemple du grec d'un district phrygien," *Hethitica* 8 (1987): 45–80. Moreover, the epigraphy shows that a celtophone population conserved its language up until at least the second century C.E. See Strobel, "Galater im hellenistischen Kleinasien," 128.

42. The bibliography for all these episodes is quite extensive. What interests me here is simply their fame, spread by poetry, the minor arts, and decorative sculpture. Examples

include the arrival of the Celts in Asia Minor, prophesied in verse by Phaenno of Epirus (Zosimus 2.37.1; cf. the commentary by François Paschoud, Collection des universités de France [1971], 109–10, 237–41); the role of the gods and Pan in the victories of Delphi (Pausanias 10.23.608; Diodoros Siculos 22.9) and Lysimacheia (*Hymn to Pan* dedicated by Aratos on this occasion to Antigonos Gonatas; cf. Borgeaud, *Recherches sur le dieu Pan*, 169 n. 135 = id., *Cult of Pan in Ancient Greece*, 237 n. 138); a fragment of the poem commemorating the victory of Ptolemy I over the mercenary Galatians of Alexandria (see n. 37 above); Callimachus's *Hymn to Delos* 171 et seq.; Simonides of Magnesia ad Sipylum's epic poem commemorating the victory of Antiochos and his elephants (*Suda* s.v. "Simonides"; cf. B. Bar-Kochva, *Proceedings of the Cambridge Philological Society* 199 [1973]: 1–8), which may be the source of Lucian's *Zeuxis;* terra-cotta figures from Asia Minor celebrating that victory (S. Reinach, *Bulletin de correspondance hellénique* 9 [1885]: 484–93; P. Bienkowski, *Les Celtes dans les arts mineurs gréco-romains* [Kraków, 1928], 141–50); the gift of Attalos to Athens (Beatrice Palma, "Il piccolo donario pergameno," *Xenia* 1 [1981]: 45–84; cf. C. Habicht, "Athens and the Attalids in the Second Century B.C.," *Hesperia* 59 [1990]: 561–77); and the monuments of Pergamon (W. Radt, *Pergamon* [Cologne, 1988], 182–87; cf. Marina Mattei, *Il Galata Capitolino* [Rome, 1987]).

43. See Mommsen, *Römische Geschichte* I⁸ (Berlin, 1888), 869, and also Jerome, *Hos.* 1, 4 (*PL* 36, 41). F. Cumont, *RE,* s.v. "Gallos," challenges this explanation, however illuminating, and asserts that the word *gallos* is Greek, dating from at least the third century B.C.E. He backs this thesis with evidence of a fragment carelessly attributed to Callimachus (see n. 45 below) and a quotation (by Diogenes Laertius 4.43) of an expression that would go back to Arcesilas of Pitane. Let us note that Diogenes Laertius knew of no writings by this philosopher, a contemporary of Eumenes I of Pergamon. Even if the joke was authentic, nothing proves that the word *galle* rather than "eunuch" was used. Diogenes Laertius expresses this as follows: "People still speak of this agreeable feature of his. When he was asked why many of his disciples left his teaching to join the sect of Epicurus, and why no Epicurian ever came to him, he said: "It's because eunuchs [*galles*] come from men, but men do not come from eunuchs."

44. The name "Keltoi," found in Herodotus 2.3, is more ancient than "Galatai," most likely introduced to specify Gauls from the East, and Aristotle distinguishes between the two (fr. 35 Rose = 661 Gigon; in *Historia animalium* 606b4, moreover, Aristotle calls Gaul "Keltikē").

45. "Gallai metros oreies philothursoi dromades / hais entea patageitai kai chalkea krotala": Rudolf Pfeiffer, *Callimachus,* vol. 1, *Fragmenta* (Oxford, 1949), fr. 761, p. 478 (in the part dealing with the *Fragmenta Incerti Auctoris*). Cf. Catullus 63.12; Virgil, *Aeneid* 9.619–29.

46. Hephestion, *Enchiridion* 12.39; p. 39 Consbruch.

47. Wilamowitz, *Hermes* 14 (1879): 194 et seq.

48. Otto Weinreich, "Catulls Attisgedicht" (1961): 467; Pfeiffer, *Callimachus,* vol. 1, *Fragmenta,* ad loc.

49. Polybius 21.39.5; E. Schwyzer, *Dialectorum graecorum exempla epigraphica potiora* (Leipzig, 1923), no. 633.11.

50. See Chapter 3 above.

51. In Latin, the word *gallus* had three meanings: rooster, eunuch (*galle*), or Gaul. The satirical poets would often use and abuse the multiple meanings of this term.

52. Livy 38.17.4.

53. This is François Hartog's term in *Le Miroir d'Hérodote* (Paris, 1980), 225–69.

54. See Strobel, "Galater im hellenistischen Kleinasien," on the Greek view of the Celts. And see also Arnaldo Momigliano, *Alien Wisdom: The Limits of Hellenization* (Cambridge, 1975).

55. I take this term in the way Michel Tardieu means it in his *Leçon inaugurale* at the Collège de France (Paris, 1991), 17. See also V. Pirenne-Delforge, "Du 'bon usage' de la notion de syncrétisme," *Kernos* 7 (1994): 11–27.

56. Tacitus, *Germania* 45.3.

57. Pliny, *Nat. hist.* 2.149.

58. This Celtic Andraste is probably identical with the *dea Andarta* of the Voconces, whose name indicates that she was linked to the bear, like the *dea Artio* of the Muri bronze in the Berne Museum. See Jan de Vries, *Keltische Religion* (Stuttgart, 1961), trans. L. Jospin as *La Religion des Celtes* (Paris, 1963), 122; and on the Muri bronze, see also Carlo Ginzburg, *Storia notturna: Una decifrazione del sabba* (Turin, 1989), trans. Raymond Rosenthal as *Ecstasies: Deciphering the Witches' Sabbath* (New York, 1991). At Die, under the Antonines, Andarta ended up being confused with the Mater deum or the Dea Augusta Vocontiorum (Graillot, *Culte de Cybèle*, 459).

59. Dio Cassius, *Roman History* 6.1 et seq.

60. See J. Vendryes, *La Religion des Celtes* (Paris, 1948), 275–78; de Vries, *Religion des Celtes*, 128–32; Paul Marie Duval, *Les Dieux de la Gaule* (rev. ed., Paris, 1976), vol. 3 (1920), 243–53. The *interpretatio* is sometimes explicit; cf. a dedication "to the Mater Magna," in the sanctuary of the Matrons at Pesch: E. Schwertheim, *Die Denkmälern orientalischer Gottheiten im römischen Deutschland* (Leiden, 1974), no. 40 with pl. 74.

61. *Ana.i. mater deorum hibernensium*, according to the translation cited by J. Vendryes, *Religion des Celtes*, 277; cf. Kuno Meyer, "*Sanas Cormaic:* An Old Irish Glossary," in *Anecdota from Irish Manuscripts*, ed. O. J. Bergin et al. (Halle, 1912), 4: 83, sec. 97 et seq.; bibliography in C.-J. Guyonvarc'h, *Textes mythologiques irlandais*, vol. 1 (Rennes, 1980), 79. Although the image is perhaps commonplace, it is noteworthy that the Greeks also saw breasts (*mastoi*) in the two peaks of Dindymus consecrated to the Mother of the gods; the name of the mountain is etymologically explained as deriving from these *didumoi mastoi*, or "twin breasts" (schol. Ap. Rhod. 1.985).

62. W. H. Roscher, *Omphalos: Eine philologisch-archäologisch-volkskundliche Abhandlung über die Vorstellungen der Griechen und anderer Völker vom "Nabel der Erde"* (Leipzig, 1913).

63. J. Loth, "L'Omphalos chez les Celtes," *Revue des études anciennes* 17 (1915): 193–206.

64. W. H. Roscher, *Der Omphalosgedanke bei verschiedenen Völkern, besonders den semitischen: Ein Beitrag zur vergleichenden Religionswissenschaft, Volkskunde und Archäologie* (Leipzig, 1918).

65. Jan de Vries, "Der irische Königsstein," *Antaios* 1 (1960): 73–80.

66. In any case, see Jean-Louis Brunaux, "Les Bois sacrés des Celtes et des Germains," in *Les Bois sacrés* (Naples, 1993), 57–65, at 60.

67. Caesar, *De bello gallico* 6.13: "Hi (druides) certo anni tempore in finibus Carnutum quae regio totius Galliae media habetur considunt in loco consecrato."

68. Strabo 12.5.1.

69. A British parallel might be the Stone of Scone, a talisman of Scottish royal power that was incorporated into the royal throne of England (see de Vries, "Irische Königsstein").

70. The (Celtic) theme of the royal chariot can be found in Gordion: see Peter Frei, "Der Wagen von Gordion," *Museum Helveticum* 29 (1972): 110–23.

71. Translated from de Vries, "Irische Königsstein," 248.

72. See Bernard Sergent, "Les Premiers Celtes d'Anatolie," *Revue des études anciennes* 90 (1988): 329–58.

73. Bormos in Nymphis of Heraclea, 432 F 5 Jacoby; Arganthoneion in Euphorion of Chalcis, fr. 75 Powell, and in Apollonius Rhodius, *Argonautika* 1.1178. For the legend of the heroine Arganthone, who became the companion of the Homeric Rhesos, see Philippe Borgeaud, "Rhésos et Arganthoné," in *Orphisme et Orphée*, ed. id. (Geneva, 1991), 51–59.

74. C. B. Welles, *Royal Correspondence in the Hellenistic Period* (New Haven, Conn., 1934), 241–53; Virgilio, *"Tempio Stato" di Pessinunte*.

75. Strabo 12.5.3.

76. Pausanias 1.4.5.

77. Strabo 12.5.5.

78. Cicero, *De haruspicum responsis* 28.

79. Ammianus Marcellinus, 22.9.5–8; Libanios, *Ad Iulian. cons.*, ed. Reiske, 1: 398; cf. H. Graillot, *Culte de Cybèle*, 548. Julian made this pilgrimage a few months after writing the famous *Discourse on the Mother of the Gods* on the night after the *lavatio* of March 27. See also Dario M. Cosi, *Casta Mater Idaea: Giuliano l'Apostata e l'etica della sessualità* (Venice, 1986), 77–87.

80. Livy 37.9.8–11; English trans. by Evan T. Sage in the Loeb *Livy* (Cambridge, Mass., 1919), 10: 316–17. Cf. Polybius 21.6.7.

81. On the two *galli* presented to C. Livius Salinator before Sestos, see Polybius 21.6.7. The same paraphernalia can be found adorning the *galles* in the Roman procession described by Dionysius 2.19. The costume and the attributes (attached images) are already mentioned in Herodotus's description of Anacharsis's involvement with the cult of the Mother in Hylaia (4.76). On these ritual attributes (plaques engraved with the image of a *naiskos*) also present in the iconography, see Gow, "*Gallus* and the Lion," pl. VIII.1 and fig. 1.

82. Polybius 21.37, which in Greek says "the galles" and not "the Galatians." Cf. Livy 38.18.9–10: "Transgressis ponte perfecto flumen, praeter ripam euntibus, Galli Matris Magnae a Pessinunte occurrere cum insignibus suis, uaticinantes fanatico carmine deam Romanis uiam belli et uictoriam dare imperiumque eius regionis. Accipere se omen cum dixisset consul, castra eo ipso loco posuit. Postero die ad Gordium peruenit." Obviously, Livy's Latin is ambiguous and could mean either *galles* or Gauls or both at the same time.

83. Diodoros 36.13; Plutarch, *Marius* 17.

84. Versnel, *Inconsistencies in Greek and Roman Religion*, 1: 105 n. 35.

85. The *Suda*; Photios, *Bibliothēkē*; the scholiast on Aristophanes' *Plutus* 431; and the emperor Julian, in his *Discourse on the Mother of the Gods*, are among the many later sources for this legend. See D. M. Cosi, "L'ingresso di Cibele ad Atene e a Roma," *Centro ricerche e documentazione sull'antichità classica. Atti* 11, n.s., 1 (1980–81): 81–91; Nicoletta Frapiccini, "L'arrivo di Cibele in Attica," *Parola del passato* 42 (1987): 12–26; A. Ruiz Pérez, "Un Oracle relatif à l'introduction du culte de Cybèle à Athènes," *Kernos* 7 (1994): 169–77.

86. We know that the *barathron* was actually reserved for those condemned to death after a crime committed against the whole community, but it was not in the Agora. See L. Gernet, *Anthropologie de la Grèce ancienne* (Paris, 1976), 302–29.

87. This type of comparison was already present in the Derveni papyrus and is part of a philosophical reflection on the mysteries.

88. Cerri, "La Madre degli Dei nell'*Elena* di Euripide." A scholion on Aeschines 3 (Ctesiphon 187) apparently attributes this legend to a fourth-century author of philippics, whom Cerri proposes we identify as Anaximenes of Lampsacus, who wrote a history of the Athenian archives. The scholion specifies that this writer of philippics says that a part of the *bouleuterion* became the *mētrōon* after the misadventure of the famous Phrygian. But see also n. 89 below.

89. The scholiast on Aeschines is probably referring to a late commentary on Demosthenes's *Philippics*. See Parker's argument in *Athenian Religion*, 190 n. 137.

s i x : Attis in the Imperial Period

1. See Polemius Silvius's calendar, *Corpus Inscriptionum Latinarum* I², 261. The possible coincidence of Christian Easter with the pagan mysteries, in terms of a diabolical imitation, is the subject of a commentary by Pseudo-Ambrose (Ambrosiaster), *Quaestiones Veteris et Novi Testamenti* (127, ed. Souter, *Corpus Scriptorum Ecclesiasticorum Latinorum*, 50, 145).

2. *Corpus Inscriptionum Latinarum* I², 263.

3. Ibid., 261.

4. Ibid., 260.

5. The enigmatic *initium Caiani*, slated for March 28, does not seem to belong to this group of holidays. See Duncan Fishwick, "The *Cannophori* and the March Festival of Magna Mater," *TAPA* 97 (1966): 193–202.

6. See Julian, *Discourse on the Mother of the Gods* 5.163B and 180A; Sallustius, *De deis et mundo* 4.

7. See Vermaseren, *Cybele and Attis*, 123; Graillot, *Culte de Cybèle*, 136.

8. See Johannes Lydus, *De mensibus* 4.49 regarding the day designated as *canna intrat* which introduces the March cycle: "To the Ides of March, Jupiter's festival because of the half-moon [*mesomenian*], and public prayers for a healthy year. It is also necessary to sacrifice a six-year-old bull for the good of the plantings on the mountain [or fields: *agron*], under the supervision of the *archiereus* and the Mother's cannephori." Fishwick, *Cannophori*, 196 et seq., interprets the *archiereus* as being the *archigallus* and the sacrifice of the bull as a *taurobolium*. He supports his thesis with an inscription from Ostia (*Corpus Inscriptionum Latinarum* XIV, 40) mentioning a *taurobolium* performed along with the *cannophoroi*'s intervention for the well-being of the imperial family (Marcus Aurelius and his family). That the *cannophoroi* might be involved in a *taurobolium* (thereby conferring an air of solemnity on it) does not, however, imply that the sacrifice of a six-year-old bull on March 15 was a *taurobolium*. The *archigallus* (if indeed he was the priest involved, which is doubtful) could perform rituals besides a *taurobolium*.

9. Pieter Lambrechts, "Les Fêtes 'phrygiennes' de Cybèle et d'Attis," *Bulletin de l'Institut historique belge de Rome* 27 (1952): 141–70; id., *Attis*. The conclusions reached by Lambrechts are refined by Fishwick, "*Cannophori*," esp. 200–202; echoed by Vermaseren, *Cybele and Attis*, 122; and reiterated by Thomas, "Magna Mater and Attis," 1517 et seq.

10. Against the view propounded by A. von Domaszewski, "Magna Mater in Latin Inscriptions," *Journal of Roman Studies* 1 (1911): 56, see on this particular point J. Carcopino, *Aspects mystiques de la Rome païenne* (Paris, 1941), 49–171; however, Carcopino erroneously attributes the holy week of Attis as such to Claudius, in contradiction to the documentation. The key document (if not the only one) is a note by the Byzantine author

Johannes Lydus, *De mensibus* 4.59, to the effect that on that day, the *dendrophoroi* carried a pine tree up the Palatine Hill, and that the holiday had been established by the emperor Claudius. Domaszewski thought that this meant Claudius II Gothicus (r. 268–70) and not the Julio-Claudian emperor of the same name.

11. Cf. Martial (ca. 40–104 C.E.), 3.47.1–2: "Capena grandi porta qua pluit gutta/Phrygiumque Matris Almo qua lavat ferrum." And see also Valerius Flaccus (d. 92/93 C.E.), *Argonautica* 8.239–42: "sic ubi mygdonios planctus sacer abuit Almo / laetaque iam Cybele festaeque per oppida taedae / qui modo tam saevos adytis fluxisse cruores / cogitet aut ipsi qui iam meminere ministri?" ("So from the moment that the sacred Almo has cleansed the Mygdonian [i.e., Phrygian] lamentations and Cybele rejoicing is now borne through the town, accompanied by festive torches, who would still remember that that bloody wounds were recently inflicted in the temples?" [trans. Vermaseren, *Cybele and Attis*, 120]).

12. On Antoninus Pius's "reform," see J. Beaujeu, *La Religion romaine à l'apogée de l'Empire*, vol. 1, *La Politique religieuse des Antonins* (Paris, 1955), 312–20. Ramsay MacMullen, *Paganism in the Roman Empire* (New Haven, Conn., 1981), 103, is critical. But see also Karl Schillinger, *Untersuchungen zur Entwicklung des Magna Mater-Kultes im Westen des römischen Kaiserreiches* (diss., Constance, 1979), cited by J. B. Rives, *Religion and Authority in Roman Carthage from Augustus to Constantine* (Oxford, 1995), 73 n. 114. The cult of the Mother and Attis was particularly well developed in Ostia during the second century; see Maria Floriani Squarciapino, *I culti orientali ad Ostia* (Leiden, 1962), 1–18.

13. Although its chronology is based on specious and impossible reconstitution of a scabrous text by Pliny the Elder, the classic study of the *archigallus* is Carcopino, *Aspects mystiques de la Rome païenne*, which gives a fascinating and accurate account, noting "that if the individuality of the *galli* is lost in the shadow of small streets where, because of a vague tolerance, more than because of explicit right, they circulated as beggars, the *archigallus* emerges in the brilliant light of public ceremonies as one of the supports of the empire" (ibid., 80). See also Arnaldo Momigliano, "Archigallus," *Revista di filologia e di istruzione classica* 10 (1932): 226–29.

14. See Vermaseren, *Cybele and Attis*, 119 et seq.; Robert Turcan, "Les Dieux de l'Orient dans l'*Histoire Auguste*," *Journal des savants*, Jan.–June 1993, 21–32, at 26 et seq. The evidence on the *hilaria* is analyzed by Hepding, *Attis*, 168. See also Macrobius, *Saturnalia* 1.21.7; St. Maximus's scholion on Dionysius the Areopagite, *Epist.* 8.6 (*PG* 4, 320), which cites a treatise on the sacrifices and holidays of the ancients by an otherwise unknown author called Demophilos.

15. Firmicus Maternus, *De errore profanorum religionum* 3.1, with Robert Turcan's commentary in the *Collection des universités de France*, ad loc., n. 5 (and see also article cited by Turcan).

16. Sallustius, *De deis et mundo* 4.

17. Damaskios, *Vita Isidori* 131: "Ten ex haidou gegonuian hemon soterian." See *Das Leben des Philosophen Isidoros von Damaskios aus Damaskos*, ed. Rudolph Asmus (Leipzig, 1911), 78, 174–75; Clemens Zintaen, *Damascii Vitae Isidori Reliquiae* (Hildesheim, 1967), 176; and Photios, *Bibliothēkē*, Greek text and French translation (not altogether convincing) by René Henry, 6: 34–35.

18. Strabo had already described Hierapolis's Plutonium in the first century C.E., reporting that he himself had released sparrows over the abyss with the deadly vapors, only "to see them immediately fall down breathless and lifeless." Cybele's *galli* officiated there, he notes:

We see them approach a hole, bend over it and descend to a certain depth (for which they must hold their breath, as evidenced by their suffocated expressions). So is this an effect of castration that can be observed in all eunuchs? Or should we see it as a privilege reserved for the servitors of the temple, who have either the special protection of the goddess (as is natural to suppose by analogy with what happens in the cases of enthusiasm) or the use of certain secret preservatives? (Strabo 13.4.14)

The remarkable coexistence of the Greek Apollo (god of the colonists) and the ancient Phrygian Mother of the gods at Hierapolis in an oracular (oneiromantic) context has been examined by Leo Weber in "Apollon *Pythokthonos* im phrygischen Hierapolis," *Philologus* 69 (1910): 178–251. When all is said and done, it is perhaps this type of guild relationship that is reflected in the version of the myth of Attis and Dindymene given by Diodoros (see Chapter 3 above). Frédéric Amsler, who has reviewed the documentation, adds the *Acts of Philip* (particularly Act 8), an Encratite text from the fourth or fifth century attesting to the influence exerted by the ancient religious practices of Hierapolis on the development of Christianity in Phrygia and the traditions connected with the Apostle Philip. See *Acta Philippi*, vol. 2, in *Corpus Christianorum, series Apocryphorum*, no. 12 (Turnhout, 1999).

19. Arnobius cites earlier sources, confirmed by the prior, independent testimony of Pausanias.

20. This has to be specified, because Attis, alongside Agdistis, is the dedicatee of an ex-voto at Piraeus dating from as early as the end of the fourth century B.C.E. (cf. the relief cited in Chapter 5, n. 35, above).

21. Lambrechts, "Fêtes," leans toward a later date, echoed by Thomas, "Magna Mater and Attis," 1519. However, in his youth (ca. 180 C.E.), Tertullian had already seen theatrical depictions of the god Attis: "Attis deum a Pessinunte" (*Ad nationes* 1.10 [*PL* 1, col. 647]). See also Minucius Felix, *Octavius* 22.4, and perhaps Plutarch, *De Is. et Os.* 69: "The Phrygians believing that the god sleeps in winter and wakes up in summer, practice for him, in a manner similar to the bacchantes, both 'sleepings' [*Kateunasmous*] and 'wakings' [*anegerseis*]." Even if these practices are not specifically linked to Attis, Plutarch's observations relate to a Phrygian context to which Attis was no stranger.

22. See Chapter 7, n. 32.

23. On the impact of Christianity on non-Christian literature of the imperial period, especially for authors who do not explicitly mention it (but "of whom we can suspect that they know more than their silence indicates"), see Arnaldo Momigliano, "Roman Religion: The Imperial Period," in *The Encyclopedia of Religion*, ed. Mircea Eliade (New York, 1986), 195. See also Glen Bowersock, *Fiction as History: Nero to Julian* (Berkeley, Calif., 1994), esp. chaps. 5 and 6.

24. Children were apparently regularly abandoned. See W. H. Harris, "Child-Exposure in the Roman Empire," *Journal of Roman Studies* 84 (1994): 1–22.

25. Justin Martyr, *Apology* 1.27.

26. Martial 5.41.1–3: "Even more effeminate that a wavering eunuch, or the lover of Celene [a Phrygian town that was, according to Catullus, Attis's birthplace] whose ecstatic, castrated *gallus* of the Mother screams out the name." This invective shows that the term *gallus* was frequently used in daily life as a metaphor.

27. Seneca, *De superstitione* (fr. 34 Haase), as quoted in St. Augustine, *De civitate Dei* 6.10.

28. To quote G. Sanders, "Les Galles et le gallat devant l'opinion chrétienne," in

Hommages à Maarten J. Vermaseren, ed. Margreet B. de Boer and T. A. Edridge (Leiden, 1978), 3: 1962–91, a very useful study to which I owe a great deal.

29. Tertullian, *Contre Marcion* 1.13.4; on Lucretius and Varro, see Chapter 4, n. 45.

30. See Minucius Felix, *Octavus* 24.12: he who cuts off his genitals with a hatchet outrages God in the very act meant to appease him, for if God had wanted there to be eunuchs, he would have had them born as such.

31. On castration in antiquity, see Aline Rousselle, *Porneia: De la maîtrise du corps à la privation sensorielle: IIe–IVe siècles de l'ère chrétienne* (Paris, 1983), 157–60.

32. Eusebius, *Ecclesiastical History* 6.8.2–3. See Peter Brown, *The Body and Society: Men, Women, and Sexual Renunciation in Early Christianity* (New York, 1988), 168–69. A Christian sect that practiced castration, the *skoptzy*, flourished in Russia in the nineteenth century and reportedly survived until 1930. See Nikolai Volkov, *La Secte russe des castrats* (Paris, 1995).

33. Brown, *Body and Society;* see Justin Martyr, *Apology* 1.29.2.

34. See É. Beneviste, "La Légende de Kombabos," *Mélanges syriens* (Paris, 1939), 1: 249–58.

35. "Ou gar ta organa esti blaptika tōi anthrōpōi all' hai aphaneis pēgai di' hōn pasa kinēsis aischra kineitai kai eis to phaneron proeisin" (*Acta Iohannis, Corpus Christianorum, series Apocryphorum* 1, 236). The terms used to describe the agitation caused by sexual desire are remarkably close to those placed in the mouth of Attis at the moment of his castration in Ovid's version, Arnobius's story, and the Naassene interpretation in Hippolytus.

36. Jerome, *Epist.* 41 *ad Marcellam* 4 (cited by Sanders, "Galles et le gallat devant l'opinion chrétienne," 1070–71). On the valorization of sexual constancy (and especially the obligation not to remarry, "monogamy") among the Montanists, see E. Schepelern, *Der Montanismus und die phrygischen Kulte: Eine religionsgeschichtliche untersuchung* (Tübingen, 1929), 53–59; Schepelern (89–91) establishes a relationship between Jerome's remark and a remark of Didymus's (*De Trin.* 3.41) indicating that Montanus was the priest of an idol before he became a Christian. He deduces that Montanus had been a *gallus* of the Phrygian goddess. According to Schepelern, the metroac religion strongly influenced the development of many aspects of Montanism (fasting, sexual abstinence, prophecy). Schepelern also studies the metroac religion attested to in the second and third centuries c.e. by numerous inscriptions discovered at the birthplace of Montanism, on the border between Phrygia and Lydia-Mysia (92–105).

37. Sanders, "Galles et le gallat devant l'opinion chrétienne," 1073.

38. See Brown, *Body and Society,* esp. 8–10, 19–22. This mistrust of sex had nothing to do with the cult uses of chastity, sexual bans limited to the time and space of the ritual, in pre-Christian antiquity. See E. Fehrle, *Die kultische Keuschheit* (Giessen, 1910), and R. Parker, *Miasma* (Oxford, 1983), 74–103.

39. See *RE*, 3 (1877), 1772–73, s.v. "Castratio" (Hitzig). This ban related to castrating either oneself or someone else. Roman law, since Republican times, had already from another point of view limited the rights of castrates.

40. It was not until the third century that, exceptionally, an emperor, Elagabalus, had his testicles tied for religious reasons, inspired by the cult of the Mother (Aelius Lampridius, *Vita Heliogabali* 7.2, in the *Historia Augusta*).

41. Michel Foucault, "Le Combat de la chasteté," *Communications* 25 (1982): 15–25; *Le Souci de soi* (Paris, 1984); *L'Usage des plaisirs* (Paris, 1984); and see translation by Robert

Hurley as *The History of Sexuality*, vol. 1: *An Introduction;* vol. 2: *The Use of Pleasure;* vol. 3: *The Care of the Self* (New York, 1978–86). See too Robin Lane Fox, *Pagans and Christians* (New York, 1986), and Pierre Chuvin, *Chronique des derniers païens* (Paris, 1990). And see, inter alia, on the theme of asceticism, James A. Francis, *Subversive Virtues: Asceticism and Authority in the Second-Century Pagan World* (University Park, Pa., 1995).

42. Brown, *Body and Society*, is entirely dedicated to this question. The choices proposed are remarkably varied in second- and third-century Christianity: faithfulness and monogamy, definitive renunciation (absolute chastity) within marriage, celibacy, and communal practices of renunciation of all sexual activity. The discrepancy between Eastern Christianity (where the ground was being readied for the development of Monachism) and Western Christianity is already present in this context (see ibid., 82).

43. For references, see n. 74 below.

44. On this type of spectacle, see Kathleen M. Coleman, "Fatal Charades: Roman Executions Staged as Mythological Enactments," *Journal of Roman Studies* 80 (1990): 44–73.

45. Minucius Felix seems to borrow this feature from Lucian: cf. *De sacrificiis* 7.1 and *Deorum dialog.* 12, two texts that present Rhea as the mother of numerous gods, but smitten with a younger man, like an old woman forgetful of her age.

46. Minucius Felix, *Octavius* 22.4.

47. The theme of *imitatio diabolica* can be found explicitly connected to the cult of the Mother, apropos of the resemblance between fasting in Phrygian ritual and fasting in Montanist practice, as early as Tertullian (*De jejunio* 16.7). It was soon extended to other ritual elements. Thus, the ritual of the *arbor intrat* is connected to the theme of crucifixion in Firmicus Maternus, *De errore profanorum religionum* 27.1–2. See also n. 1 to this chapter and related text, on Easter and the "day of blood."

48. Tertullian, *De exhotatione castitatis* 10.1–2; and see Brown, *Body and Society*, 77.

49. Brown, *Body and Society*, 86.

50. J. Laplanche and J.-B. Pontalis, *Vocabulaire de la psychanalyse* (Paris, 1967), 78.

51. What, one can only wonder, would Father Joseph-François Lafitau, the author of *Moeurs des sauvages amériquains comparées aux moeurs des premiers temps* (Paris, 1724), who wished so much to prove the primordial connections between pagan mysteries and the Christian mystery, have made of Hippolytus's *Refutation of All Heresies*, had he had access to it?

52. Michel Tardieu suggests this in his article "Naassènes" in the *Dictionnaire des mythologies*, ed. Yves Bonnefoy (Paris, 1981), 2: 150–51.

53. On Papas (which, as has been noted, is one of the names of Attis in the version of the myth reported by Diodoros), see the inscriptions collected by Thomas Drew-Bear and Christian Naour, "Divinités de Phrygie," *ANRW* II, 19, 3 (1990), 2018–22. Papas, "father," is an epithet used of Zeus, as well as of Attis (whose name means the same thing).

54. Hippolytus, *Refutation of All Heresies* 5.6.1, 5.7.1, ed. Miroslav Marcovich (New York, 1986), 141–42.

55. Ibid., 5.10.2; cf. Miroslav Marcovich, "The Naassene Psalm in Hippolytus (*Haer.* 5, 10, 2)," in *The Rediscovery of Gnosticism*, ed. B. Layton, vol. 2, *Sethian Gnosticism* (Leiden, 1981), 770–78; Thielko Wolbergs, *Griechische religiöse Gedichte der ersten nachchristlichen jahrhunderte*, Beiträge zur klass. Philol. 40 (Meisenheim am Glan, 1971), 1: 8, 60–75, trans. Miroslav Marcovich in *Studies in Graeco-Roman Religions and Gnosticism* (Leiden, 1988), 81.

56. Hippolytus, *Refutation of All Heresies* 5.7.6–11.

57. In the process, Hippolytus revives a type of argument used against the Gnostics that the Jews had used against the Christians during Justin's time (see Justin Martyr, *Apology* 1).

58. "I will reveal all the mysteries / and show the forms of the gods."

59. Hippolytus, *Refutation of All Heresies* 5.7.9.

60. A gloss by Hesychius — "Adamnein: to philein; kai Phruges tōn philōn Adamna legousin" — indicates the Phrygian meaning of the name "Adamna": the "well-loved," or the "near one," equivalent to the Greek *philos*, and frequently used in the vocabulary of prayer. The list of mysteries evoked by the Naassenes corresponds rather precisely to that found in Clement of Alexandria, Arnobius, and Firmicus Maternus, which leads one to suppose the same archetype. For more extensive analysis, see D. M. Cosi, "*Adamna:* Un problema e qualche proposta," *Atti e memorie dell'Accademia pattavina* 88, pt. 3 (1975–76): 81–91.

61. Hippolytus, *Refutation of All Heresies* 5.7.11–13.

62. Ibid., 5.7. 13–15.

63. Ibid., 5.9. 10.

64. Rom. 1:20–27; the Jerusalem Bible translation, slightly modified.

65. The verb *pauein* generally refers to the idea of abstinence. With regard to the allusion to the wild movements preceding castration, it must be connected to an element in the Attis myth that we find both in Ovid and Arnobius.

66. Hippolytus, *Refutation of All Heresies* 5.8.22–25.

67. Ibid., 5.8.31–38.

68. Ibid., 5.8.39–40. A traditional image without any relationship to Eleusis beyond that of the "*galli's* harvest"; see remarks in Chapter 4, n. 45, and related text, on Varro and Lucretius.

69. Ibid., 5.9.3–6.

70. Ibid., 5.9.8. Quotation from Hippolytus, *Refutation of All Heresies*, ed. Marcovich, slightly modified.

71. Ibid., 5.9.9. Quotation from Hippolytus, *Refutation of All Heresies*, ed. Marcovich, slightly modified.

72. In Pausanias, the tree is also an almond. Arnobius mentions a pomegranate tree at the origin of the conception of Attis, but refers to an almond tree at his death. The erotic connotations of the pomegranate are well known; see Vinciane Pirenne-Delforge. *L'Aphrodite grecque* (Liège, 1994), 411–12.

73. Hippolytus, *Refutation of All Heresies* 5.9.1: "Aoraton, kai akatonomaston kai arreton."

74. See Paola Migliorini, "*Kolpos* e *Sinus* nella lingua medica," *Prometheus* 7 (1981): 254–62; Maurice Olender, "Aspects de Baubô," *Revue de l'histoire des religions* 202 (1985): 3–55, at 19 and n. 71.

75. Arnobius, *Adversus nationes* 5.8–17.

76. Ibid., 5.13. Understandably, I do not introduce as sole commentary here — although I seem to be the first to comment on it — the following report from Reuters, dated February 10, 1995: "NABLUS, West Bank — A Palestinian shepherd is milking his billy-goat for all it's worth. *Kol al-Arab*, an Arabic language weekly, reported Friday that dozens of Israelis and Arabs are on a waiting list to drink its milk, believing it will cure them of impotency. Shepherd Mufid Abdel-Ghafer is charging them a cool $33 a glass. The news-

paper said that the goat was a male in every respect—the animal has sired 50 kids—except for one teat, which gives just two glasses of milk a day." I thank my friend Sarah Johnston for this valuable information.

77. Arnobius, *Adversus nationes* 5.13.

78. Lactantius, *Div. inst.* 1.21.16.

79. Ibid., 1.17.7.

80. Glen Bowersock, *Julian the Apostate* (London, 1978). See also Cosi, *Casta Mater Idaea*.

81. See Cosi, *Casta Mater Idaea*, 88 et seq.

82. For the dating of Firmicus Maternus's *De errore profanorum religionum*, see Robert Turcan's 1982 edition in the Collection des universités de France, 24–27.

83. Burkert, *Structure and History*, 202 n. 17, recognizes the relationship between the two, without delving into it.

84. On the *taurobolium*, see two essential studies that appeared almost at the same time, more than twenty-five years ago: Jeremy B. Rutter, "The Three Phases of the Taurobolium," *Phoenix* 22 (1968): 226–49; Robert Duthoy, *The Taurobolium: Its Evolution and Terminology* (Leiden, 1969). Duthoy provides a very useful table summarizing all the inscriptions and their contents in chronological order (78–80). I also refer to his catalogue (5–53), which is organized according to geography (and therefore can sometimes be misleading). A bit less rich than Duthoy's, Rutter's catalogue (243–49) is just as inconvenient. His analysis, on the other hand, is generally very clear.

85. Cf. *elaphēbolos*, which has meant "doe hunter" at least since Homer. And cf. also *lagobolon*, an instrument for hunting rabbits.

86. Duthoy, *Taurobolium*, no. 2 (Pergamon, ca. 135 B.C.E.); no. 1 (Ilium, first century B.C.E.); no. 4 (Pinara in Asia Minor, first century B.C.E.); no. 3 (Pergamon, ca. 105 C.E.).

87. "Ludum vel certamen epheborum quo aries captus et domitus ad aram adduceretur ibique mactaretur, simillimum illum quidem ei exercitationi quae taurokathapsion nomine significaretur" (*OGIS*, 764, 25, commentary ad loc.).

88. See Louis Robert, *Les Gladiateurs dans l'Orient grec* (Paris, 1940), 315 n. 3.

89. Duthoy, *Taurobolium*, no. 4. An inscription from Pisidia from after the reign of Nerva (*Supplementum epigraphicum Graecum* [1923–], 2: 727; cf. Robert, *Gladiateurs*, 316–18) shows that these practices still existed in the eastern part of the empire between the first and second centuries.

90. Duthoy, *Taurobolium*, no. 50.

91. This concerns 128 out of 133 inscriptions catalogued by Duthoy. The first evidence of the *taurobolium* in connection with the cult of the Mother of the gods dates from Lyon in 160 C.E. (*Corpus Inscriptionum Latinarum*, XIII, 1751 = Duthoy, *Taurobolium*, no. 126). The four literary testimonies traditionally mentioned—Firmicus Maternus, *De errore profanorum religionum* 27.8; Anon., *Carmen contra paganos* (see n. 136 below); Aelius Lampridius, *Vita Heliogabali* 7.1 (with commentary by Turcan, "Dieux de l'orient dans l'*Histoire Auguste*"); and Prudentius, *Peristephanon* 10.1006–50—date from 350 to 400 C.E.

92. We should understand this as meaning that it followed an order, a divine injunction (in a dream or otherwise) transmitted or interpreted by the *archigallus*, whose role it was to be prophetic.

93. Lambrechts, "Fêtes," 157–58. Duthoy, *Taurobolium*, 68, catalogues thirty-two taurobolic inscriptions explicitly including the formula *pro salute imperatoris*.

94. Rutter, "Three Phases of the Taurobolium," 243.

95. Twelve examples of inscriptions are provided in Duthoy, *Taurobolium*, 58 (the two most ancient ones we can date go back to 370).

96. Duthoy, *Taurobolium*, 67: *hostis suis; de suo; ex stipe conlata; sua pecunia; suo sumptu; sumptibus suis; suo impendio.*

97. See Thomas, "Magna Mater and Attis," 1524. (He too prefers to see an evolution from bourgeois to aristocratic.)

98. Duthoy, *Taurobolium*, nos. 71, 73, 127: "Ex vaticinatione archigalli"; nos 96, 98, 126 (cf. 50): "ex imperio matris deum"; nos. 54, 74, 94, 132: "ex iussu matris deum."

99. See their famous and reciprocal posthumous elegy engraved on the funerary monument housed in the Capitoline Museum (*Corpus Inscriptionum Latinarum* VI, 1779 = H. Dessau, *Inscriptiones Latinae Selectae*, no. 1259). On the milieu evolving around Praetextatus, see Herbert Bloch, "The Pagan Revival in the West at the End of the Fourth Century," in *The Conflict Between Paganism and Christianity in the Fourth Century*, ed. Arnaldo Momigliano (Oxford, 1963), 193–218; cf. T. D. Barnes, "Religion and Society in the Age of Theodosius," in *Grace, Politics and Desire*, ed. H. A. Meynell (Calgary, 1990), 157–75.

100. See Rolf Biering and Henner von Hesberg, "Zur Bau- und Kultgeschichte von St. Andreas apud S. Petrum. Vom Phrygianum zum Kenotaph Theodosius d. Gr.?" *Römische Quartalschrift* 82 (1987): 145–82. The circular temple of the Mother (the Phrygianum), built in the reign of Severus, was destroyed following the Edict of Theodosis (promulgated on February 24, 391). It was replaced by the Rotunda of St. Andreas, contemporary with the Rotunda of St. Petronillo. For the vicissitudes previous to this cult, during the fourth century, see Margherita Guarducci's study, "L'interruzione dei culti nel Phrygianum del Vaticano durante il IV Secolo," in *La soteriologia dei culti orientali* (Leiden, 1982), 109–22.

101. Bloch, "Pagan Revival in the West," 203.

102. Dessau, *Inscriptiones Latinae Selectae*, no. 1260: Praetextatus's wife, Pauline, was sanctified for the triple Hecate and Eleusis: "apud Eleusinam deo Iaccho Cereri et Corae, apud Laernam deo Libero et Cereri et Corae, apud Aeginam deabus" (see the parallel formulae in Dessau, no. 1259, ll. 28–29).

103. Archelaos at Lerna: *IG* IV, 666 = Kaibel, *Epigr.* 821. Archelaos at Phyle: Duthoy, *Taurobolium*, no. 5 (cf. also no. 6); cf. *CCAA*, 2: 389 (cf. also 390); see n. 112 below. For Phosphorius, see A. H. M. Jones, J. R. Martindale, and J. Morris, *The Prosopography of the Later Roman Empire* (Cambridge, 1971–), 1: 700, "Phosphorius 2." See also the early article by Theodore Reinach, "Un Nouveau Proconsul d'Achaïe," *Bulletin de correspondance hellénique* 24 (1900): 325. I am grateful to Marcel Piérart who kindly called my attention to (and guided me through) the network connecting the Lerna mysteries to those of Phyle in Attica via Archelaos (cf. M. Piérart, "Le Grand-père de Symmaque, la femme de Prétextat et les prêtres d'Argos"). The same network also includes, as expected, Eleusis: Cleadas, who dedicates a statue of her father Erotios, hierophant in Eleusis (*IG* II², 3674), is also initiated into the mysteries of Lerna (*Anthologia Palatina*, IX, 688). See Giovanni Casadio, *Storia del culto di Dioniso in Argolide* (Rome, 1994), 318–19. On Phyle, see I. Loukas, *He Rhea-Kubele kai hoi gonimikes latreies tēs Phulas* (Athens, 1988); id., "Le daphnéphoreion de Phyla, la daphnéphorie béotienne et l'oracle de Delphes," *Kernos* 3 (1990): 211–18; cf. Giovanni Casadio, "Antropologia gnostica e antropologia orfica nella notizia di Ippolito sui Sethiani," in *Sangue e antropologia nella teologia*, ed. F. Vattioni (Rome, 1989), 1329–44. The last pagans in the Greek world, that is, the Neoplatonists, were the ones who continued this type of regular attendance at different initiation rituals

still in existence. See Chuvin, *Chronique des derniers païens*, and Michel Tardieu, *Les Paysages reliques: Routes et haltes syriennes d'Isidore à Simplicius* (Paris, 1990).

104. With regard to the cremation of these organs, see Duthoy, *Taurobolium*, 74. The place for this ritual is called the Vatican not only in Rome but apparently also, in a symbolic way, in Lyon and in Kastel, in what is now Croatia (ibid., 73).

105. Ibid., 74–76. On the *kernos*, see the classic pages by Jane Harrison, *Prolegomena to the Study of Greek Religion*, 3d ed. (Cambridge, 1922), 158–61; and the recent study by G. Bakalakis, "Les *kernoi* éleusiennes," *Kernos* 4 (1991): 105–17. With regard to the *cernophoroi* in connection with the Mother of the gods, see *Corpus Inscriptionum Latinarum* II, 179 (108 c.e.) and X, 1803 (references given by Rutter, "Three Phases of the Taurobolium," 238 n. 43).

106. Duthoy, *Taurobolium*, 75.

107. Nikander, *Alexipharmaka* 217, with scholium.

108. *Anthologia Palatina* VII, 709: the reference to Alexander the Aetolian brings us very close to Timotheos the Eumolpid, one of Arnobius's sources.

109. Duthoy, *Taurobolium*, 75.

110. "Perfectis sacris cernorum" (ibid., no. 60, third century); "cerno et criobolio acceptis" (no. 68, third century); cf. no. 21 (fourth century).

111. However, this transformation did not last forever, since one was obliged to repeat the ritual every twenty years. Only one inscription seems to affirm that the ritual performed was definitive: "in aeternum renatus" (ibid., no. 23).

112. *Teletē* and *mustipolos*: ibid., no. 22; in Rome in 370. "Sumbolon euageon teleton anetheka": no. 31; in Rome in 377. "Teletēs sunthemata krupta charaxas taurobolou": no. 5; in Phyle near Athens (see n. 103 above) before 387 (*CCAA*, 2: 389). Archelaos had the figurative equivalent (*charaxas*) of these "secret passwords of the taurobolic *teletē*" engraved on the supports of the altar he dedicated. The symbols are well known: torches, tympanum, *pedum*, and *phialē*.

113. Clement (referring to Apollodorius of Athens) mentions another possibility, which he does not, however, develop: *ta musteria* could derive from the name of an Attic hero named Myous who was killed during a hunt.

114. See Mora, *Arnobio e i culti di mistero*, esp. 163–71. Mora supports the thesis of Arnobius's independence with regard to Clement: rather than regarding the one as an amplification of the other, it would be better to recognize the use of sources in common.

115. Literally, "in her *kolpos.*"

116. Clement of Alexandria, *Protrepticus* 2.15.3. *Symbola* ("symboles") is a synonym of *sunthemata* ("passwords"): see the usage of *sunthemata* in the taurobolic inscription in Phyle, n. 112 above.

117. Firmicus Maternus, *De errore profanorum religionum* 18.1. Arnobius, *Adversus nationes* 5.26, reports a very different formula at Eleusis: "I have fasted and I have drunk the *kykeōn;* I have taken from the basket and I have deposited in the *kalathos* [another kind of basket]; I have taken again and carried in the small basket."

118. See Chapter 3 text at n. 41 on the fragment from Babrius on the *agurtai*.

119. This connection is confirmed by Arnobius as well. See also Firmicus Maternus, *De errore profanorum religionum* 6.

120. Pausanias 8.42.1; 8.25.4–5.

121. It may be a matter of a milk dish, similar to the one eaten at the end of the fasting during the holy week of Attis. See Saloustios, *De deis et mundo* 4.

122. Walter Burkert, *Ancient Mystery Cults* (Cambridge, Mass., 1987), suggests a sexual interpretation of this veil or "bed curtain" (*pastos*).

123. The idea that initiation rites were introduced into Rome through the cult of the Mater Magna after the "reform" of Antoninus Pius is supported, with different arguments, by M. van Doren, "L'Évolution des mystères phrygiens à Rome," *L'Antiquité classique* 22 (1953): 79–88. In the Greek East, mysteries centered on the Mother of the gods are attested from a more ancient date by Neanthes of Kyzikos and the papyrological evidence of one of two hymns from Ptolemaic Egypt published by Bartoletti, "Inni a Cibele," 10 and 13, l. 15. The officiant who prepares to celebrate the rite of Agdistis, a "Phrygian and Cretan" Mother of the gods, gets rid of the uninitiated with a formula (*epitethei pulas*) that Plato knew (*Symposium* 218b). Other evidence can be found in van Doren, "Évolution des mystères phrygiens à Rome," and Giulia Sfameni Gasparro, *Soteriology and Mystic Aspects in the Cult of Cybele and Attis* (Palermo, 1979; trans., Leiden, 1985).

124. Schepelern, *Montanismus*, 116.

125. Thomas, "Magna Mater and Attis," 1523.

126. There are numerous epigraphic examples attesting to women's piety with respect to the Mother throughout the Greek and Roman world.

127. Prudentius 841–45. See also Prudentius, *Peristephanon* 10.1006–50, and the Loeb *Prudentius* (Cambridge, Mass., 1961), 2: 294–99.

128. It is actually the blood itself that, in Prudentius's perspective, wrote the martyr's text in imperishable letters; see the comments of Michael Roberts, *Poetry and the Cult of the Martyrs: The Liber Peristephanon of Prudentius* (Ann Arbor, Mich., 1993), 12–13, 40–41, on the *sanguinis notae* of *Peristephanon* 1.3.

129. Prudentius 1007: "Meus iste sanguis uerus est, non bubulus."

130. Ibid., 1027. The name of this instrument (*uenabulum*, which originally designated a hunting weapon) has been connected to the word *taurobolium* (which also originally designated the chase). See Burkert, *Structure and History*, 119. For Prudentius, the choice of this word may have been dictated by a concern to comment on the word *tauroboliatus*, found in his model, the *Contra paganos* (see n. 136 below).

131. See Franz Joseph Dölger, "Die religiöse Brandmarkung in den Kybele-Attis-Mysterien," *Antike und Christentum* 1 (1929): 66–72.

132. In verses 154–60, the *lavatio* is the object of a rather precise description situated between an allusion to the auspices and a mention of the *lupercae*. The Idaean Mother appears here to be closely tied to the most conservative aristocratic cults. Her chariot (*carpentum*), preceded by individuals of high rank (the *togai*), who, however, walk barefoot, is directed toward the waters of the Almo. It bears the black stone inlaid with silver ("lapis nigellus . . . muliebris oris clausus argento") that resembles the goddess's face. This has no more to do with the pit of blood than does the allusion in verses 196–200 to Attis turned *gallus*, whose castration creates a *spado* to whom the lamentations proffered in the rituals of Cybele are addressed. Attis thus appears here as that which dishonors the cult (the sacred wood) of Cybele — just like Hyacinth in respect to Apollo, or Ganymede vis-à-vis Jupiter. The gods are guilty of sexual crimes in each case, and the list goes on to Adonis and Priapus.

133. Back in 1969, before Duthoy's *Taurobolium* (which still did not resolve the problem) had been published and without any knowledge of Rutter's work, Louis Richard had expressed his own serious doubts about the credibility of the "evidence" provided by Prudentius. However, he does not reject it completely. See his "Remarques sur le sacrifice taurobolique."

134. See the documentation (and critical hesitations) in Thomas, "Magna Mater and Attis," 1525.

135. Firmicus Maternus, *De errore profanorum religionum* 28, trans. Clarence A. Forbes in *Firmicus Maternus: The Error of Pagan Religions* (New York, 1970), 170, slightly modified.

136. On the *taurobolium*, see the anonymous poem *Contra paganos* 57, in which the chariot and procession are also described: *Poetae Latini Minores*, ed. Baehrens (Leipzig, 1881), 3: 286–92 (cf. Hepding, *Attis*, 61). Ch. Morel, *Revue archéologique* 1 (1868): 451 et seq., and Th. Mommsen, *Hermes* 4 (1870): 350 et seq., date the poem to 394 C.E. and interpret it as a missive addressed to Virius Nicomachus Flavianus, who after Praetextatus embodied the pagan reaction against Christianity. Cf. Pierre de Labriolle, *La Réaction païenne: Etude sur la polémique antichrétienne du Ier au VIe siècle* (Paris, 1948), 352–53. G. Manganaro, "La reazione pagana a Roma nel 408–409 e il poemetto anonimo *Contra paganos*," *Giornale italiano di filologia* 13 (1960): 210–24, argues, based on a reference to Claudius, that the poem dates from 409 and was addressed to the urban prefect Gabinius Barbarius Pompeianus at the time of the first siege of Rome by Alaric. Bloch, "Pagan Revival in the West," 1963, addendum to p. 200, p. 217, believes that the reference to Claudius does not imply a later dating and adheres to the traditional interpretation, as does A. Chastagnol, "La Restauration du temple d'Isis," in *Hommages à Marcel Renard* (Brussels, 1969), 2: 143–44. Prudentius's account, in any case, derives from *Contra paganos* and borrows many themes from it: cf. J. M. Poinsotte, "La Présence de poèmes anti-païens anonymes dans l'oeuvre de Prudence," *Revue des études augustiniennes* 28 (1982): 35–58. I am grateful to Pierre-Yves Fux, author of *Les Sept Passions de Prudence: Peristephanon 2.5.9.11–14* (Fribourg, Switzerland, 2003), who called my attention to these other publications.

SEVEN: From Mother of the Gods to Mother of God

1. On the cult of the Mater Magna in Carthage, see J. B. Rives, *Religion and Authority in Roman Carthage from Augustus to Constantine* (Oxford, 1995), 72–76.

2. Augustine, *Civ. Dei* 2.4, trans. Marcus Dods, *Saint Augustine: City of God*, Great Books, vol. 16, *Encyclopaedia Britannica* (Chicago, 1990), 189. The following two quotations, from ibid., 2.5 and 7.26 respectively, are from the same translation, pp. 190, 305.

3. See Anon., *Carmen contra paganos* (cited Chapter 6, n. 136), Prudentius, *Contre Symmachus*, cited by Hepding, *Attis*, 64; Fulgentius, *Mitologiarum* 3.5 (ed. Helm = Hepding, 74–75): "*Fabula Berecintiae et Attis.*" Strabo 10.12 identifies a mountain in Asia Minor, where Rhea, the Mother of the gods, was particularly honored among a Phrygian population, as the origin of the name Berecynthia, and Virgil applies the poetic epithet "berecynthian" to the Mother of the gods.

4. *Acta Sanctorum*, ed. J. Pinius and G. Cuperus, *Augusti*, vol. 4 (Rome, 1867), 494 ("Sancti Acta"). Hepding, *Attis*, 72, cites only two passages, the first from the *Acta primorum martyrum sincera et selecta*, ed. Ruinard² (1713), 79 et seq., and the second (see next note) from a later addition.

5. A medieval commentator attributes words to the text (*Acta Sanctorum*, ed. Ruinard, 497, n. 1, reproduced in the second passage from the Passion of Saint Symphorian by Hepding, *Attis*, 72) that attest to how much this was etched in Christian memory, despite how long ago and distant its occurrence was: "At nunc non in idoli huius cultu porten-

tosam attende superstitionem uestram, quod tu ad opprobrium et exitium tuum ueneraris: in cuius sacris excisas corporum uires castrati adolescentes infaustae imagini exultantes illidunt, et exsecrandum facinus pro grandi sacrificio ducitis, sacrilegi sacerdotes, ut quod immane scelus est, religionis praetextu ueletur, ubi perstrepentes buxos et tibias, fanatici furoris inflati insania, ubi cymbala pulsate corybantes."

6. The model of this substitution of a Christian matron for the Mother of the gods is traceable at least to ca. 389 C.E., when Serena, the wife of Stilicho, a Christian noble-woman, is said to have entered the Mother's sanctuary on the Palatine Hill in Rome and ripped the necklace from the statue of the goddess, which she then put around her own neck. See Zosimus 5.38.3, with François Paschoud's commentary in the Collection des universités de France edition (3, 1: 263–66).

7. See "Symphorien (saint)," by H. Leclercq, in *Dictionnaire d'archéologie chrétienne et de liturgie* (Paris, 1953), 15: cols. 1812–17.

8. Gregory of Tours, *Liber de Gloria Confessorum* 77 (= *PL*71, col. 884).

9. Tertullian, *Apolog.* 22; Minucius Felix, *Octav.* 7; Lactantius, *Div. inst.* 2.7.12; Augustine, *Civ. Dei* 10.16; Jerome, *Adv. Iovin.* 1.25.

10. The Fathers of the Church alluded to her relationship with Attis and called her a "whore" (*meretrix*). St. Jerome, in his *Commentarii in Osee Prophetam* 1.14, *Corpus Christianorum, series Latina* 76 (1969), 44–46, explains why he chose to translate the Hebrew *cadesoth* differently from Aquila ("transvestites," *enēllagmenōn*), Symmachus ("prostitutes," *hetāridōn*), from the Septuagint ("initiates," *tetelesmenōn*), and from Theodotion ("rejects," *kechōrismenōn*): "We have called them "effeminates" [*effeminatos*] to adapt [lit., to open up] the meaning of the word to the ears of our contemporaries. It is a matter of those who, today in Rome, serve the Mother not of the gods but of the demons. We call them "Gauls" [Galli] because it is from among that nation that the Romans chose priests truncated in libido [*truncatos libidine*] in honor of Atys. A prostitute goddess made this Atys into a eunuch [*quem eunuchum dea meretrix fecerat*]. This is why the Gauls, these men who took the city of Rome, are also effeminate, stricken by such ignominy. In Israel, there was a similar kind of idolatry, adhered to most of all by women adoring Beelphegor because of the size of his sexual organ. We would call him Priapus."

11. In St. Augustine's *In Iohannis Evangelium Tractatus* 7.6, we find the priest of a divinity wearing a *pilleus*, or Phrygian cap ("illius Pilleati sacerdotem"), proclaiming that his god is also a Christian ("et ipse Pilleatus christianus est"), but the pilleus could just as well indicate Mithra, or even Castor and Pollux.

12. See Enrico Norelli, "Avant le canonique et l'apocryphe: Aux origines des récits de la naissance de Jésus," *Revue de théologie et de philosophie* 126 (1994): 305–24; id., *L'Ascensione di Isaia: Studi su un apocrifo al crocevia dei cristianesimi* (Bologna, 1994); a critical annotated edition has been published by Paolo Bettolo, Enrico Norelli, et al., in the *Corpus Christianorum, series Apocryphorum*, vols. 7 and 8 (Turnhout, Belgium, 1994). Contrary to the opinion of the former commentators, it is very much a question of a Christian text, possibly written in Antioch. The only complete version of it that we have is of Ethiopian origin. Coptic and Latin versions are attested to as having circulated very early on. R. H. Charles, *The Ascension of Isaiah* (London, 1900), 76, followed by Mario Erbetta, *Gli Apocrifi del Nuovo Testamento* (Casale Monteferrato, 1981), 3: 202–3 (translation of the passage of interest), have already postulated the unity of the text and therefore a very remote date for the episode describing the incarnation and ascent of Christ (11.1–22).

13. See Erbetta, *Gli Apocrifi* 3: 202, note at 11.7.

14. See E. de Strycker, *La Forme la plus ancienne du Protévangile de Jacques* (Brussels, 1961); see too Erbetta, *Gli Apocrifi*, 1, pt. 2: 7–43, translation and accompanying ample commentary.

15. See Averil Cameron, *Christianity and the Rhetoric of Empire: The Development of Christian Discourse* (Berkeley, Calif., 1991), 100.

16. Although this is not mentioned in the text, it is perhaps supposed. Cf. Leviticus 15.19 et seq.

17. The six other virgins wove gold, amianthus, linen, silk, bright purple, and scarlet red.

18. A bit further on in the text, this is explained as being the luminous shadow that covers the grotto in Bethlehem.

19. It is strange to see Joseph go along with the ordeal of the bitter waters, normally a trial reserved for women suspected of adultery. The rite consists of a sermon or oath followed by going to the Temple of Jerusalem to drink pure water mixed with dirt from the floor of the Temple as the "name" of God is written in soluble ink on a parchment. See Adriana Destro and Mauro Pesce, "Conflits et rites dans le Temple de Jérusalem d'après la Mishna," in *Le Temple lieu de conflit* (Louvain, 1994), 132–35.

20. See François Bovon, *Révélations et Ecritures. Nouveau Testament et littérature apocryphe chrétienne* (Geneva, 1993), 253–70 ("La suspension du temps dans le *Protévangile de Jacques*).

21. See Cameron, *Christianity and the Rhetoric of Empire*, 167.

22. With the Naasenians; see Chapter 6 above.

23. See Sarah Iles Johnston, *Hekate Soteira: A Study of Hekate's Role in the Chaldean Oracles and Related Literature* (Atlanta, Ga., 1990), esp. 49–70.

24. This was not necessarily the case in the art of the catacombs: see Ioli Kalavrezou, "Images of the Mother: When the Virgin Mary Became Méter Theou," *Dumbarton Oaks Papers* 44 (1990): 165–72, who underscores this contrast between the theological discourse and the sensibility of the believers, citing the representation of a nativity in the catacombs of St. Priscilla, in the first half of the third century: A. Grabar, *Early Christian Art* (New York, 1968), 99, fig. 95.

25. On Santa Maria Maggiore, see G. A. Wellen, *Theotokos* (Utrecht, 1961), 93–138. Although it was destroyed toward the end of the thirteenth century, this mosaic can be described from ancient accounts. See also C. Ceccheli, *I Mosaici della basilica di S. Santa Maggiore* (Turin, 1956), 51–82.

26. These were qualities that corresponded to the definitions given at the Council of Ephesus. Cyril of Alexandria (*PG* 77, 44–49) was an excellent witness of this, since he specifies that Logos becoming flesh should be understood as participating in flesh and blood in the same way that we do. He therefore came into the world as a man out of a woman, but without abandoning His divinity. This is why the name "Theotokos" was given to the Virgin Mary at the Council of Ephesus. This did not mean that the nature of Logos or His divinity originated with the Virgin Mary, but rather it meant that She gave birth to the holy body animated with a rational spirit. On this hieratic aspect of a Mary who was not yet truly maternal, but who would, from the sixth century on, become more intimate and more human, see Kalavrezou, "Images of the Mother." I thank Gabriel Herman who drew my attention to this article at a time when I did not expect to delve into the labyrinth of late antiquity.

27. See Cameron, *Christianity and the Rhetoric of Empire*, 175.

28. Commentary based on that of Eric Junod and Jean-Daniel Kaestli in *Acta Iohannis, Corpus Christianorum, series Apocryphorum*, 1, 139–40, 143–45.

29. In Tertullian, *De anima* 41.4, the baptism is likened to the wedding of the soul and the Holy Spirit. It seems to be with Origen that Christ becomes the spouse of the soul.

30. Mygdonia's story is set in India, but her name evokes a region of Anatolia confused with Phrygia. Attis too is a Mygdonian. See *RE*, s.v. "Mygdon": Mygdon = Phryx.

31. The most obvious manifestation of this attitude, of course, is that of the sacred virgin who became Christ's bride. See Suzanna Elm, *Virgins of God: The Making of Asceticism in Late Antiquity* (Oxford, 1994).

32. Schol. Lucian, *Juppiter tragoedus* 8: "Some say that he was the authentic son [*gnēsion huion*] of the goddess." The hymn transmitted at the beginning of the third century by Hippolytus is the most ancient evidence. See also the Greek inscription "Mēteros athanatōn phrygion thalos aglaōn" in Roman-era Lydia cited by Sfameni Gasparro, *Soteriology and Mystic Aspects in the Cult of Cybele and Attis*.

33. In Ephesus, Nestorius would have preferred, contra Cyril of Alexandria, that Mary be designated *Christotokos* rather than *Theotokos*, "for fear that people would make the Virgin into a goddess" (*monon mē poieito tēn parthenon thean*): *Acta conciliorum oecumenicorum*, 1.1.6, ed. E. Schwartz (Berlin, 1928), 5, ll. 33–34; see commentary in *Acta Philippi, Corpus Christianorum, series Apocryphorum*, 11, ed. Fran Bovon et al. (Turnhout, Belgium, 1999).

34. Epiphanios, *Adversus haereses (Panarion)* 79 = *PG* 42, 740–41. See also Vasiliki Limberis, *Divine Heiress: The Virgin Mary and the Creation of Christian Constantinople* (New York, 1994), 118–20; Stephen Benko, *The Virgin Goddess, Studies in the Pagan and Christian Roots of Mariology* (Leiden, 1993), 170–95.

35. Qur'an, sura 5.116. See *Encyclopaedia of Islam*, new ed. (Leiden, 1991), 6: 629, s.v. "Maryam."

36. See Limberis, *Divine Heiress*, 89–97. The Greek text can be found in *PG* 92, 1335–48. Limberis gives an English version of it, 149–58. The anthem referred to in P. F. Mercier, "L'Antienne mariale la plus ancienne," *Museon* 52 (1939): 229–33, seems to be the *sub tuum praesidium*, known in both the Byzantine and Roman liturgies. The Greek text of this appears on a papyrus in Egypt from the third or fourth century; see *Catalogue of the Greek and Latin Papyri in the John Rylands Library*, ed. C. H. Roberts and E. G. Turner (Manchester, 1938), 46.

37. John of Damascus in his *Homilies on the Dormition of the Virgin, PG* 96, 741.

38. As Limberis, *Divine Heiress*, esp. 14–21, shows. See Averil Cameron, "The Theotokos in Sixth-Century Constantinople: A City Finds Its Symbol," *Journal of Theological Studies* 29 (1978): 79–108.

39. François Paschoud, in his edition of Zosimus in the Collection des universités de France, commentary at 2.31 (p. 228, n. 42).

40. Iohannes Malalas, *Chronographia* 13.13.

41. See Hesychius, *Patria*, no. 390 Jacoby, para. 15 (to which François Paschoud's commentary and V. Limberis's analysis each in its own way refers).

42. Zosimus 2.31.1–3.

Index of Ancient Authors

General Index